I Have Come to Tell the World that
God Exists

The Best of "The Spirit of Medjugorje" Volume III

2005-2009

Compiled by

June Klins

authorHOUSE®

AuthorHouse™
1663 Liberty Drive
Bloomington, IN 47403
www.authorhouse.com
Phone: 1-800-839-8640

First published by AuthorHouse   11/19/2011

ISBN: 978-1-4670-6857-4 (sc)
ISBN: 978-1-4670-6856-7 (hc)
ISBN: 978-1-4670-6855-0 (ebk)

Library of Congress Control Number: 2011918794

Printed in the United States of America

Editor's declaration:

About the Title

Recently I heard a youth minister say that when he led a retreat at a Catholic parish a few years ago, only six of the 60 teens admitted that they believed in God. This was a very chilling statistic. My heart was filled with pity for them. I was working on this book at the time, and knew right then that I had to name the book by the words Our Lady told the visionaries in the first days of the apparitions in Medjugorje: "*I have come to tell the world that God exists.*" (The entire quote of Our Lady was too long for the title: "*I have come to tell the world that God exists. He is the fullness of life, and to enjoy this fullness and peace, you must return to God.*")

About the Cover

The picture in the center of the cover was not my first choice. It was, in fact, not my choice at all. I had the cover design done – or so I thought – until one night in Adoration, I felt in my heart that the Lord was asking me to use the photo of the Second Luminous Mystery Monument (The Wedding Feast of Cana) behind St. James Church in Medjugorje. That *never* would have been my choice for the center picture, but God's ways are not our ways. And how perfect this picture is for this book!

The picture depicts the Wedding Feast of Cana, where Jesus performed His first public miracle. In John 2:11, we read, "Jesus did this as the beginning of His signs in Cana in Galilee and so revealed His glory, and His disciples began to believe in Him."

His disciples began to believe in Him. So now, almost 2000 years later, He sends His mother to the little village of Medjugorje, and His glory is revealed once again, and His disciples begin to believe in Him!

The last words Our Lady speaks in Scripture are at the Wedding Feast of Cana. She says, "Do whatever He tells you." Those words of Our Lady are in the fifth verse of the second chapter of John, usually written John **2:5**. Is it just an interesting "God-incidence" that Our Lady gives a public message to the world on the **25th** of the month? Is She not, in these messages, telling us to do what He tells us?

Surrounding the center picture are depictions of the "five stones" – which you will read about throughout this book: Prayer with the heart, Eucharist, Confession, Bible reading, and fasting. All the photos were taken in Medjugorje, except for the photo representing **Bible reading**, which was taken in a Franciscan convent in the neighboring village of Miletina. The crucifix above the Bible was broken during the war, and it was decided not to repair the crucifix in order to show that *we* are to be the arms and legs of Jesus.

The photo below that represents **Confession**. Although there are many confessionals in Medjugorje, sometimes the crowds are so immense that priests will hear confessions on the lawn near the church.

Going clockwise, the next photo of bread and water depicts **fasting**. Our Lady asks us to fast on Wednesdays and Fridays, preferably on bread and water. The bread in Medjugorje is so tasty that it does not even seem like fasting!

The next photo represents **prayer with the heart**. The photo was taken at the Blue Cross on Apparition Hill. This is where the visionaries used to have their apparitions, when hiding from the Communists. Mirjana has her second of the month apparitions there now.

On the very top, is a photo depicting the Holy Sacrifice of the Mass. Our Lady asks us to make the **Eucharist** the center of our lives. That is why it is in the center and at the top. The Eucharist should be our top priority!

This book is dedicated to Our Lady, Queen of Peace, and to Her faithful son, Msgr. James Peterson, who has been the spiritual adviser of "The Spirit of Medjugorje" for many years.

ACKNOWLEDGMENTS

I am very grateful to the Holy Spirit for the inspiration to compile this book, to Our Lady, for Her loving guidance through this project, and to all the people who prayed for this book to become a reality.

I am thankful to Joan Wieszczyk for her sixteen years of loving service as editor of "The Spirit of Medjugorje," and for her blessing and support in the publishing of this book. I am very grateful to Louise Lotze, Chris Maxwell, and most especially to Ruth Burick for their help with the arduous job of proofreading. I would like to thank Mike Golovich, Wendy Ripple, Louise Lotze, Carolanne Kilichowski, Dennis Todaro, Diana Stillwell, Bernard Gallagher, Gloria Marinelli, Johannes Dittrich, and Brian Klins for the use of their photographs. And, last but not least, I would like to thank all of those who consented to the re-publishing of their works in this book.

Contents

Introduction

In the Introduction to Volume II of *The Best of "The Spirit of Medjugorje,"* I had written, "There may not be a Volume III, since all but three of the issues after December, 2004, can be read on the Internet. I do realize, however, that not everyone has Internet access, so I will do whatever Our Lady and Her Son direct me to do."

In mid-February, 2011, I began to feel a bit of a prompting to publish a Volume III book. Several people asked me within the same week when I was going to publish Volume III. I said I would pray about it, and I did. Then I said to the Lord on a Friday, "I will publish another volume if someone asks me to this weekend."

It was Sunday evening, about 10:30 at night – an hour and a half to go. My friend, Pat Berrier, and I had just finished proofreading the March issue of "The Spirit of Medjugorje." Pat said something to the effect, "This is a great issue. You have to do another book!" I probably scared Pat to death with my screaming laughter.

Shortly after I began working on this book, the sewer in my basement backed up. Yuck!!! Spiritual warfare for sure. It took me weeks to clean up, and I was diverted from the book. I was busy with other things and decided it would be my summer project since I am off from my "paying" job as a part-time math teacher. By the second week of July, I had finished it – or so I thought. I always take our newsletter to Mass and Adoration every day and something always changes. The same thing happened with this book.

The day after I thought I had finished the book, a subscriber called and asked for a copy of the September, 2006 newsletter, because the person to whom she had lent her copy lost it. She wanted it as a keepsake because she was featured in one of the stories. As I looked for that issue, I noticed that there were some good articles that I had somehow missed when going through all these newsletters. So, it was "back to the drawing board." The result is what you are reading right now. I love how God works!

My Objective

My objective for publishing this book remains the same as the objective of our monthly newsletter – to **instruct** people about Our Lady's messages and to **inspire** them to live and spread the messages. I hope, with the profits, to be able to donate copies of this book to prisons, schools, libraries, etc., and maybe even finance a Volume IV, if it is God's will.

Who Should Read This Book?

This book is for everyone. For those who do not know much about Medjugorje, it serves as an "extended beginner's guide." (We also publish a "beginner's guide" newsletter for those who know little or nothing about Medjugorje.) For those who have followed Medjugorje, it will serve as a "shot in the arm" to stir up that fire again.

How to Read This Book

This book should *not* be read in one sitting, but should be read a little at a time, so to digest all that Our Lady is telling us. This is especially true for Chapter Two on the visionaries. The talks of the visionaries are very similar – as well they should be, as a sign of the authenticity of the apparitions. This is also true for Chapter Four, which focuses on how to live the messages.

The date at the top of each article is the issue in which the article was originally published. The articles are not in chronological order. I prayed to the Holy Spirit to help me compile and order all of the articles. The quotes at the beginning of each chapter are messages of Our Lady of Medjugorje.

My Prayer

I hope and pray that every person who reads this book will be inspired to live and spread the messages of Our Lady – messages of peace, love and joy. I will pray every day of my life for everyone who reads this book. Thank you for responding to Her call.

CHAPTER ONE

All about Medjugorje

"I want to save all souls and present them to God" (8/25/91).

(12/08)
Special Edition—Beginner's Guide

Suppose you were told that you could have a glimpse of Heaven without having a near-death experience?

In the early 1980s, 17 year old Vicka Ivankovic-Mijatovic and 10 year old Jakov Colo, visionaries from the village of Medjugorje in what is now Bosnia-Herzegovina, had such an opportunity. Vicka claimed, "Our bodies disappeared from Jakov's house. Everyone looked for us. It lasted 20 minutes in all." Vicka described the experience:

"One afternoon, I was with Jakov at his home and Our Lady came, telling us that She was going to take us to show us Heaven, hell and Purgatory. Before we left, we were wondering how long the journey was going to take, whether we would go up, or down, or how many days we would be traveling. But Our Lady just took Jakov's left hand and my right hand and we went up. We could see the walls just moving aside, giving us enough space to go through. It took us just a moment, and we found ourselves in Heaven.

"Heaven is one, huge endless space. There is a special kind of light that does not exist on earth at all. We saw people dressed in gray, yellow, and pink gowns. They were walking, praying and singing together. We were able to see small angels circling around. There is a special kind of joy in Heaven. I have never experienced anything like that at any other time. Our Lady told us to see how overjoyed were all the people who were in Heaven.

"Purgatory is also one huge space, but we were not able to see people. We could only see darkness – an ashy color. We were able to feel the physical suffering of the people. They were shivering, and struggling. Our Lady said we need to pray for those people so that they can get out of Purgatory.

"As for hell, there is one huge fire in the middle. First, we were shown people in normal condition before they were caught by that fire. Then as they are being caught by that fire, they become the shape of animals, like they have never been humans before. As they are falling deeper into the fire, they yell against God even more. Our Lady says that, for all those who are in hell, it was their choice, their decision to get there. Our Lady says for all those who are living here on earth who are living against God's commands, even here they are living in a kind of hell so when they are there, they are continuing just the same life as before. Our Lady says that there are so many who live here on the earth who believe that when this life is finished, everything is finished, but Our Lady says, if you think so, you are very wrong, because we are just passers-by on the earth."

So how do we get in the door to Heaven? Jesus told us 2000 years ago, but for those who did not listen to Him, He sent His Mother, as the Queen of Peace to remind us and remind us and remind us . . . .

Since 1981 She has been coming to earth every single day to tell us how to live so that we can enjoy eternal happiness and avoid eternal damnation. When will we begin to listen?

Statue of Our Lady on Apparition Hill overlooking
the village of Medjugorje

In the Beginning

Medjugorje is a small mountain village in Bosnia-Herzegovina, the former Yugoslavia. The following testimony was given by Ivanka Ivankovic-Elez in Buffalo, NY, on November 23, 2008:

Going back in history – on the 24th of June, 1981, my life changed forever. I never thought that something like this would happen, that the Mother of Christ could appear to me, and I never heard about Fatima or Lourdes at that time.

My family and I at that time were living in Mostar, and we came home to Medjugorje on summer vacation. And visionary Mirjana was visiting from Sarajevo. So on the 24th of June, Mirjana and I and some other friends of ours, after Mass, decided to go outside the church and talk about our summer vacation. I don't remember how long we were there walking around, and we couldn't wait any more for the rest of the girls to come, so we decided to go back to the village. On the way back, something was pulling my eyes to the hillside. When I looked on the hillside, I told Mirjana, "Mirjana, look up there! There is Our Lady!" She did not want to even look up there, and she said, "Don't talk nonsense. It could not be."

Mirjana was just remaining quiet and we continued to walk. When we came to the village, Marija's sister, Milka, said she was looking for her sheep. As soon as she saw me, she said, "What happened to you? You look different." I told her, "I just saw Our Lady." Then all three of us walked back to the same place and we all saw Our Lady at that time. Our Lady was on the hillside, standing about 600 meters up on the hill and She was motioning Her hand for us to come closer. But we were just standing still. We were afraid to go up there.

In the meantime, Vicka came to join us, and she said, "What is happening to you?" We said, "Hurry up! We see Our Lady!" When she heard that, she simply took her shoes off and started running back to the village, and on the way to the village she met two Ivans – Ivan who is the visionary, and his friend also called Ivan. She told them what was happening and then all three of them came to join us. Even though there were more of us now, we were still afraid to go up the hillside. We were still very excited and very confused at what was happening. Some of us went to the closest home and we went inside and told the people in the household what we saw. We just told them, "We saw Our Lady," but the people said, "Don't play [joke] and don't tell that to anyone." Then they chased us out of the yard.

When I came to my home, my grandmother was there and I told her what I saw, and she told me, "It's probably someone tending their sheep." I was only 15 years old at that time, and that night was never longer in my lifetime as that. Whenever we told any of the other people what we saw, they did not interfere. But the next morning, even though Medjugorje had only one phone in the whole village, the news went around to other villages what was happening in Medjugorje. So the next day more people gathered. My grandmother then raised her hand and said, "Whatever is happening, no matter who is up on the hillside, you are not leaving my sight."

When we reached the place where we were standing before, we saw flashes of light on the hillside, three times, and something was pulling us forward to come closer. So six of us were pulled so quickly other people could not keep up with us. When we came close to Our Lady, we saw the beauty that no words can describe. My eyes never saw anything more beautiful than that. Our Lady has a gray gown, white veil, a crown around Her head with stars. She has blue eyes and dark hair, and She's standing on a cloud. At that very moment, we all knelt in front of Our Lady.

Two months before that began, my mother had died; she passed away because she was very ill. That day when we knelt in front of Our Lady, I asked Our Lady, "Where is my mother?" Our Lady just smiled and said, "Your mother is with me," and Our Lady said, "Do not be afraid of anything. I will always be with you. I will come tomorrow."

In the meantime, some other people who started to walk with us reached the base of the hillside and they saw something unusual happening to us, and they suggested that the next day when we come, we should bring holy water and sprinkle the apparition. So when Our Lady appeared on the third day, Vicka took holy water and she said, "If you are of God, stay with us; if you are not, go away." Then She smiled and She said, "I am the Queen of Peace," and the first message of Our Lady was **peace**. Later on, She added **conversion, prayer, fasting** and **penance**. So those are the main ones, the most important messages from the first days.

From 1981 to 1985 I had daily apparitions. Through all those years Our Lady was talking to me at each meeting about the future of the world, and the future of the Church and also Our Lady's life story. I know everything in those notebooks, and so when Our Lady tells me that it is closer, She will tell me the time and I will give the notebooks.

The 7th of May, 1985, was my last daily apparition, and Our Lady stayed with me a whole hour, and She gave me the tenth secret. Our Lady told me that She was not going to meet with me every day, only once a year, on the 25th of June. So from 1985 until now I have only one apparition a year. On the day when I was talking to Our Lady, She gave me a beautiful gift that I'll never forget. Every person is asking himself whether there is life after this. I am a living witness that there is life after this because Our Lady showed me my mother. My mother talked to me and she said, "My daughter, I am so proud of you."

It's already been 27 years that Our Lady has come to visit us, giving us the words of wisdom in every message, showing us how to live our life. It is only up to us to accept these words.

Each one of us visionaries has our own mission. Some of us have the mission to pray for sick people or for the priests or the Church. I was chosen to pray for families. Our Lady is inviting us to pray for families, together to renew the family there in our homes. In the beginning, Our Lady requested that we pray seven Our Father's, Hail Mary's, and Glory Be's a day, then later the whole Rosary. Our Lady wants us to display the Bible, Holy Scriptures, in our homes and to read it often, every day if possible, and then the Bible can be our life; and to go to Holy Mass often, especially on Sunday; and to go to Confession once a month.

I pray for families every single day, for all families, not only in my village, but around the world. I'm asking all of you to pray for my family and the families of the visionaries. Thank you.

Editor's note: On the second day when Ivanka, Mirjana, Vicka and Ivan returned to the hill, Milka's sister Marija and 10 year-old Jakov Colo joined them. These are the six visionaries. Ivanka, Mirjana and Jakov have all been given 10 secrets. As of this writing (7/8/11), Ivan, Marija and Vicka have nine secrets and continue to receive daily apparitions.

The "Secrets"

The following excerpt is from a reflection written by Fr. Petar Ljubicic, who is the priest chosen by visionary Mirjana to reveal the secrets to the world:

Concerning the secrets, Mirjana herself states that she thinks the day of their fulfillment is nearing. And lately, Our Lady calls her to a specific program of how she should pray and live. At the same time, through Mirjana, She calls all people of good will to join with Her in prayer.

God has announced to us that He will send signs of preliminary warning. He wishes to show clearly that He is forever "Master of the world." God will send us some early signs and then He will give us a permanent sign. Mirjana says that when the signs appear, many people will be converted, many who doubted until now and who deliberated about whether the event in Medjugorje came from God or from some other source. It will be clear to everyone who is open to the Spirit of God that God is indeed here and dwells among us.

Concerning us, specifically, of course we'd like to know when all of this will take place. I believe that curiosity can best be satisfied by fasting and prayer, and people who do so don't need to be afraid. Everything will turn out right. I don't know what misfortunes and catastrophes will come; and naturally, I don't know what will happen to us. I know only this: Without God's wisdom, nothing will happen to us. Everyone can receive what he needs to fulfill God's plan in his life. I believe that from this, we can conclude that God loves us today, too. I see positive proof of this in the fact that God is sending His Mother to us, and that He has already given us many signs. There are many witnesses who have meditated about this and have been converted. They are the people who began to fast and pray. I believe these are signs and that they are more significant than physical signs. Material signs can be momentarily impressive, but the joy and happiness which one experiences in the soul remains and is not easily forgotten. That's the treasure we carry in our hearts.

Shortly after Mirjana's visions ceased, I was informed by the other visionaries that she had chosen me as the priest of her confidence. At that time I thought I was too far away from Medjugorje. I was a priest in another community and there was no indication that I would be moved to Medjugorje. Mirjana, who moved in the meantime, to Sarajevo to continue her studies, told me that God will put everything in its place. Mirjana asked Our Lady whether she had acted correctly, and Our Lady told her that everything would happen at the proper time. And indeed, since the fall of 1985, I've been in Medjugorje for more than a year.

Mirjana told me that Our Lady comes more often lately and that she hears Her voice at a predetermined time. She said Our Lady is preparing her for the fulfillment of the secrets. Our Lady wants everything to develop in order. She gave Mirjana something similar to paper, which contains information about the individual secrets. Ten days before, she'll know what will happen. Three days before a secret is revealed, it will be announced to the people so they'll know exactly what, where, how, what time, and for how long it will take place.

The first two secrets will come as advance warnings and as proof that Our Lady was here in Medjugorje. The third secret will be a visible sign. This secret is the same for all the visionaries. No one knows how many secrets are the same for all of them. As far as the visible sign is concerned, the exact information will be received three days in advance. All of us have to prepare for this with prayer and fasting.

The Visionaries

Vicka Ivankovic-Mijatovic – Vicka is the oldest of the visionaries. She was born September 3, 1964, in Bijakovici, and comes from a family of eight children. Her prayer mission given by Our Lady is to pray for the sick. Vicka, her husband Mario, and young daughter and son live in the small village of Gruda, a few kilometers north of Medjugorje. In January of 1983, Our Lady began to tell Her life story to Vicka. The information Our Lady dictated to Vicka over these two years will be published when Our Lady tells Vicka it is time. Vicka: "The only way to peace and love is prayer and fasting."

Mirjana Dragicevic-Soldo – Mirjana was born March 18th, 1965 in Sarajevo. Her prayer mission from Our Lady is to pray for all unbelievers. Mirjana graduated from the University of Sarajevo where her family lived. Mirjana, her husband Marco, and their two daughters live in Medjugorje. On August 2, 1987, Our Lady started appearing to Mirjana on the 2nd day of each month to pray with Mirjana for all unbelievers. Mirjana tells us that Our Lady defines "unbelievers" as those who have not yet felt God's love. She tells us that if we only once saw the tears in Our Lady's eyes for all unbelievers, that we would all begin praying intensely for this intention. Mirjana: "The Mass, the Rosary, and fasting, especially on bread and water only, can stop war, can change the natural law, particularly if they are done with great faith and great trust and great love."

Marija Pavlovic-Lunetti – Marija was born on April 1, 1965, in Bijakovici. Her prayer mission given by Our Lady is to pray for priests and consecrated people. She also prays for the souls in Purgatory. She has three brothers and two sisters. When the apparitions started, she was studying in Mostar, about eighteen miles away. She is the visionary to whom Our Lady gives the public message to the world on the 25th of each month. Marija, her husband Paulo and their four children live in Italy. She visits Medjugorje a number of times each year. Marija: "Fear comes from Satan. Those who trust the Lord do not experience fear."

Ivanka Ivankovic-Elez – Ivanka was born on July 21, 1966, in Bijakovici. Ivanka's prayer mission from Our Lady is to pray for families. Ivanka has one brother and one sister. Her Mother Jagoda, died in May, 1981. When the apparitions first began, Ivanka asked the Blessed Mother about her mother. God has allowed Ivanka to see and speak to her mother, who is in Heaven, five times over the years. Ivanka and her husband Raico and their three children live in Medjugorje. Ivanka: "People know whether they are living in God's will or not by how much peace they have. If they don't feel peace in their hearts, they know they are not doing the right thing. Those who are doing God's will have peace."

Ivan Dragicevic – Ivan was born on May 25th, 1965 in Bijakovici. His prayer mission given by Our Lady is to pray for priests and the youth of the world. There are three younger children in his family and although Ivan and Mirjana share the same last name, they are not related. Ivan, his wife Laureen and their four children reside half the year in Medjugorje, and half the year in Boston, MA. Ivan: "All prayer is pleasing to God. It is Satan who always tells us our prayer is not good enough, that we are not good enough. The least prayer is very much."

Jakov Colo – Jakov is the youngest of the seers. He was born on March 6, 1971, in Sarajevo, and was only 10 years old when the apparitions started. His prayer mission given by Our Lady is to pray for the sick. Jakov, his wife Annalisa and three children live in Medjugorje. In the early years, the presence of the young fidgety boy among the group of seers is significant in terms of the authenticity of the apparitions. It was highly improbable that he would come to church for two to three hours of prayer every single day, in winter as well as in summer, year after year, simply to make believe that he is seeing the Blessed Virgin. Jakov: "We need to learn how to thank God because He gave us too much, and we do not understand that. We are constantly asking for more."

Editor's note: Pictures of the visionaries can be found in Chapter 2.

The Locutionists

Besides the six visionaries in Medjugorje, there are two locutionists (people to whom God speaks "with the heart," an experience which is known in the history of the Church as "locutio cordis" or inner locution). In December, 1982, Jelena Vasilj, nine years old, began to hear Our Lady speak to her. In March of 1983, Marijana Vasilj (no relation), age eleven, began to also have inner locutions of Our Lady. The messages to these girls were similar to the visionaries. In March of 1983, Our Lady established and led a prayer group through Jelena. Our Lady dictated to Jelena consecration prayers and a prayer for the sick and recommended the reading of Matthew 6:24-34 every Thursday.

The Official Position of the Church Regarding Medjugorje

On March 17, 2010, it was announced that an International Commission had been established to investigate the phenomenon of Medjugorje. The Commission consists of cardinals, bishops and experts, under the chairmanship of Cardinal Camillo Ruini. The investigation could take years to complete.

Editor's note: Chapter 5 has an extensive explanation about the position of the Church.

Little Known Fact about Medjugorje

In 1986 the U.S. State Department became very interested in what they were hearing about Medjugorje. The U.S. Ambassador to Yugoslavia at that time, David Anderson, was told to send political officers to investigate the rumors of apparitions. Reporting back to Anderson the two political officers stated, "You're not going to believe this, but there is something going on there."

Editor's note: The above information is excerpted from a book called **Medjugorje Investigated** *by Michael Kenneth Jones. For more information visit Michael's website, www.medjugorjeusa.org.*

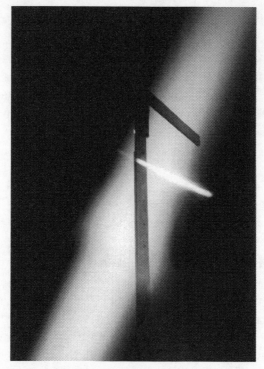

Mysterious lights that appeared in a photo taken in
daylight of the cross on Apparition Hill

Signs and Wonders
By June Klins

On my first trip to Medjugorje I was very excited because it was anniversary time and I expected to see a lot of miracles. I had heard that the sun spins like it did in Fatima and that some people see "gold dust," or the cross on Mt. Krizevac light up or disappear mysteriously. Well, after four trips there, I have never seen any phenomena like this, even while people standing right beside me were witnessing these things. Many people have miracle photos they took in Medjugorje. These signs and wonders are gifts that are given to certain people for a reason only God knows.

On my first pilgrimage, I randomly picked up five stones on Apparition Hill. I later discovered that four of the stones had images on them. One has the face of Jesus with a fetus above His head, and the other three have Our Lady with Baby Jesus. I wondered why I got these stones. I certainly did not need them to believe. I carry these stones, which seem to have a pro-life message, in my purse and show them to people at any opportunity. The scriptures tell us that the gifts we receive should be shared with others.

What is the purpose of these signs and wonders? To get our attention! Jesus performed miracles from the very beginning of His ministry on earth. The miracles were a means to an end. Once Jesus got their attention, He could work the real miracles of changing hearts. The same is true in Medjugorje. The "miracle of the sun" is to show that God exists and then to point us to the real "miracle of the Son" – Jesus in the Holy Eucharist. Those who go to Medjugorje must be on guard not to focus too much attention on the signs and wonders, at the risk of ignoring the abundant graces available in Medjugorje through a conversion of heart, the real sign and wonder at Medjugorje.

The Five Stones

Father Jozo Zovko, who was the pastor of St. James when the apparitions began, speaks often about what he calls "the weapons" or the "the five stones" against Goliath. They are: prayer with the heart, especially the Rosary; Eucharist; Holy Bible; monthly Confession; and fasting.

It is important to approach each of these slowly, so not to get discouraged. When Our Lady first appeared to the children, She asked them to pray the "Peace Rosary," which is the Creed and seven Our Father's, seven Hail Mary's, and seven Glory Be's. Later She had them pray the five-decade Rosary, and then worked up to the 15-decade Rosary.

Our Lady asks for frequent attendance at Holy Mass. It might be good to first start by going a day or two during the week, then work up to every day if possible. Our Lady always says that when given the choice of going to Mass or to one of Her apparitions, one should always choose Holy Mass.

To read the Bible, one need not read a whole book or even a whole chapter daily. Even a sentence or two in the morning and in the evening is beneficial. We need to be constantly fed with the Word of God to fight the good fight.

As for monthly Confession, Our Lady told the visionaries that there is not a person on earth who does not need to confess monthly.

Fasting is the most difficult of the five. Fasting means that we give up something that we like and offer that sacrifice to God. Our Lady asks that we fast weekly on Wednesdays and Fridays. One can give up sweets, coffee, cigarettes, alcohol, television, etc. But, Our Lady stresses that the best and most powerful fast is on bread and water. Great graces come from fasting and it can help with situations in your life that seem hopeless. Because it is so hard to fast, one should always pray for the grace to be able to do it. Again, one should work up to it, starting perhaps by giving up eating between meals, then one day of bread and water, and finally two days of bread and water.

The Fruits of Medjugorje

"You will know them by their fruits. Grapes are not gathered from thorn bushes nor figs from thistles, are they? So every good tree bears good fruit, but the bad tree bears bad fruit" (Matthew 7:16-17).

There have been many physical healings through Our Lady of Medjugorje since 1981. The parish office reports that as of 2001, there were 445 documented reports about miraculous physical healings. David Parkes, Rita Klaus, Char Vance, Artie Boyle, and Tom Rutkoski are just a few of the people who have received a physical healing that defied medical science. Each of these people, in recorded testimony, also had spiritual healings as well, and do not hesitate to emphasize that, given the choice of a physical healing or a spiritual healing, they would take the spiritual healing.

It would take hundreds of books to contain the testimonies of the spiritual healings and conversions that have taken place through Our Lady of Medjugorje in the last 24 years. More than a few members of the clergy have also had healings as well, including a priest who had left the priesthood and returned 17 years later through Our Lady of Medjugorje. (His story is in our June, 2003 issue.)

Organizations which reach out to the homeless, poor and orphans have been created by people upon returning from Medjugorje. *Gospa*

Missions in Evans City, PA, *Mission of Mercy* in Buffalo, NY, *St. David's Relief* in Mesquite, TX, *His Work in Progress* in Yardley, PA, *Mother's Hope Foundation* in Pittsburgh, PA, and *Gospa Florida* in Palm Coast, FL are just a few of the many fruits of Medjugorje.

Many priestly and religious vocations have been fostered through Medjugorje. Fr. Donald Calloway (whose story is in our April, 2004 issue), Fr. Ed Murphy (April, 2005 issue), Frs. Ljubo Kurtovic and Miro Sego (September, 2004 issue), are just a few of the many religious vocations which have been fostered through Medjugorje. "A good tree cannot produce bad fruit, nor can a bad tree produce good fruit" (Mt 7:18).

A Medjugorje Pilgrimage
By June Klins

Before June of 1998, Medjugorje was never in my travel plans. I was afraid that it was dangerous, that I would not like the food or the experience of staying in someone's home, and that I would be bored.

Nothing could be farther from the truth in every case. I will be eternally grateful to the travel agent who booked me on the plane to Medjugorje without my having agreed to it! I never experienced such peace in my life, the food was wonderful, the people were so hospitable and joyful that I did not want to leave, and I was never bored for even a second. There is much to do, including climbing two mountains – Apparition Hill and also Cross Mountain, where a large cross was built in 1933. Ana Shawl, who takes pilgrims to Medjugorje, testifies: "No matter how many times people come to Medjugorje, it's the same as when you go to visit your mother. There's always something more, there's always more conversations with her, and no two conversations with our mothers are the same. That's the way I feel about being there. I know we have our Mother in Heaven wherever we are and She is always close to us, but I think there is something so special about coming to Her little Medjugorje – two mountains, rocks, vineyards and a church. To make the trip is difficult, but once there, most everyone has difficulty coming home. Like during the Transfiguration with the apostles, they wanted to pitch tents to stay there; they never wanted that vision to end."

The Cross on Mt. Krizevac

(9/06)
Cross Mountain

By Darlyne Mary Fujimoto

I am a lightweight history buff. In my informal research of Krizevac – forever a significant place on earth for my husband and me, as that is where we felt closest to Mother Mary and where She touched us to our core – I came across a most intriguing article on the mountain. Seems as early as 1932, God began preparing Medjugorje for its future role:

The first strange incident took place in 1932, involving Pope Pius XI. This pope, born Achille Ratti, in Milano, was an enthusiastic mountain climber. One night in February 1932, Pope Pius XI was asleep in his Vatican bedroom and dreamed that he was climbing a mountain – a mountain he had never seen before. He knew he wasn't in Italy – he had scaled nearly every peak in the Alps. When he reached the summit, he found Miriam (Mary) waiting patiently for him there. She was wearing a light gray dress with a long white veil. "Achille," She told him, "I want you to build a cross on this site because this place will become very important in the future." Looking around in bewilderment, he mumbled, "Where am I?" "Yugoslavia." And smiling gently, She added, "Remember this mountain, Achille." And the Pope suddenly woke up. That was a weird dream, he thought.

A few months later, Pope Pius XI received a petition from the Archbishop of Mostar in Yugoslavia (now Bosnia-Herzegovina). The diocese wanted to erect a concrete cross on Mount Sipovac commemorating the 1,900th anniversary of the crucifixion of Jesus Christ. When the Pope saw a photograph of the proposed site, he gasped out loud. It was the mountaintop he had seen in his dream. He signed the construction order immediately.

Editor's note: Darlyne is from Cerritos, CA. Mount Sipovac later became better known as Mt. Krizevac, meaning "Cross Mountain."

(7/08)
Medjugorje

By Msgr. James Peterson

I have made several trips to Medjugorje. On the second one, a young ex-convict was traveling with me. We left from Cleveland late one rainy night. Early in the morning he came and awakened me. He said, "Father, come and see this. I think I am seeing things."

He had a window seat; I looked out. The clouds below us were splendidly gold. Right below us was a perfectly circular double rainbow of brilliant colors. In the center of the circle was a silhouette of our plane going with us. When I told him what I saw, he knew he was not seeing things.

On this trip and on others, I saw many signs in the sky, in changes from other colors to gold rosaries and medals. To me they were all secondary to the messages and to the sacraments.

On my first trip there, the "confessionals" were, in each place, two milking stools roped together. On the side of St. James Church were signs of the language the priest could handle – German, Slovak, Spanish. I took a sign saying "English," put it down next to the milking stool I was seated on.

Almost immediately, people started to come. And that is what spoke to me most of the presence of God there. Tourists who had come to see this phenomena and stayed because of a heart-felt conversion. Religious, priests who were almost burnt out, who found the help to begin again with trust and hope.

Some of them talked to me later. We both knew the power of the Spirit working there, and left with the certain sense of mission to carry Mary's plan for peace and to share in spreading the urgency and joy of Her message.

(7/07)
Something Special is Happening Here

By Msgr. Matthew George Malnar

I have visited many of the shrines of Our Lady in the world, but Medjugorje is somehow different. The experience of faith is so powerful here. For me, Medjugorje is a place of prayer, a place of reconciliation. As a priest, I also need to be renewed in faith and that is what I experience each time I come here. Medjugorje falls into a category of open questions; it is neither confirmed nor condemned. So I always say to people: **Do not be holier than the Church. If the Church says that you can go there, you cannot say the opposite**. You can come here. I have come and will come again, because I believe that something very special, something very important is happening here.

I brought a group of pilgrims to Medjugorje and told them many times to be open to the Holy Spirit and to the inspirations that Our Lady is giving in order to experience stronger faith. "If you do not pray the Rosary daily," I told them, "maybe you will begin. If you have neglected Confession, maybe you will discover the beauty of the sacrament of Confession and Penance. If you do not read the Holy Scriptures, if you do not fast, maybe you will feel the need. Therefore, when you come to Medjugorje, be open." I always emphasize, "Put away all that you have heard about Medjugorje – good or bad – and let Our Lady lead you.

That is the only way to come to Medjugorje." I think that Medjugorje has a meaningful message for every person, but we need to open our hearts to hear it.

Editor's note: Msgr. Malnar is from the Diocese of Amarillo, TX.
MIR Peace Letter, July 2003

Painting from 1974 © Bernard Gallagher

(10/09)
Prophetic Painting

Viewing the artwork above, one might suppose that it was painted to illustrate Our Lady's appearances at Medjugorje – yet the painting was done in 1974, seven years before Our Lady first appeared in Medjugorje! The simple painting is the work of Vlado Falak from the hamlet of Šurmanci, which is part of the Medjugorje parish. It used to be displayed in the choir loft of St James Church.

The Medjugorje Message, UK

CHAPTER TWO

The Visionaries

"These days you have felt great joy because of all the people who have come and to whom you could tell your experiences with love. Now I invite you to continue in humility and with an open heart speak to all who are coming" (6/25/85).

Marija

(8/05—9/05)
Testimony of Marija Pavlovic-Lunnetti

This talk was given on March 24, 2004, at Corpus Christi Basilica, Manchester, England. The talk, spoken in Italian, was translated into English by Marija's husband, Paolo, and was recorded and transcribed by Phil Townend.

It is a great joy for me tonight to be here with you and give you my testimony. We thought that we would start at six because thinking of the time of the apparition in Medjugorje, that is at quarter to seven. But we made a mistake because we forgot that we are an hour ahead here in England. Our Lady had foreseen everything. And I think She wanted to say to all of us, "Welcome!" And also through my testimony tonight I want to make each and every one of you fall in love with Our Lady.

When Our Lady first appeared to us, none of us could imagine that this could happen. We started this wonderful adventure on the Apparition Hill, this adventure that touched the heart of so many of you. We were amazed by this grace when it first happened that Our Lady appeared, and we thought: "Why did She choose us, why just us?"

We had many questions in our hearts, but we also started following all that Our Lady was asking of us. I remember the first days when we started praying with Our Lady, the Our Father's, Hail Mary's, and Glory Be's, and She would keep silent in the moment we prayed the Hail Mary, and She would start again with the Glory Be. We were wondering why Our Lady was not praying the Hail Mary. Then we realized that Our Lady couldn't pray to Herself. So we started praying, and we recommended to many people who had begun to come. And we started praying together with Our Lady.

Our Lady said She had come as the Queen of Peace. She said because today what we miss is peace. So She has invited us to pray because true peace comes only through prayer. She has invited us to pray for peace in our hearts and in our families, saying that when we get peace in our hearts and in our families, then we can also pray for peace in the whole world.

She has started asking us to be instruments in Her hands – instruments of Her peace – peace that comes through Our Lady from God. And we began feeling important, and we began to pray with more devotion. And Our Lady said pray the Rosary, which is my most preferred prayer. So we started, and it was a bit difficult for us, not being used to praying a long prayer, but we got used to that, because we started falling in love with Our Lady. And every time we said, "Hail Mary," it was saying to Our Lady "We love You." In the same moment we were also thanking Our Lady for Her presence among us. And many times we remained without words thinking how Our Lady had chosen us.

Then Our Lady asked us to put the Holy Bible in a visible place in our houses and to read it every day. She invited us to create prayer groups in our parishes. I remember once when Our Lady said to us, the members of the prayer group, that we should pray three hours every day. We protested and we said, "Isn't this a bit too much?" Because we are young and there are so many pilgrims coming to our houses, and we were almost every day speaking all day long about Our Lady and about God. Our Lady made a wonderful smile, and She said: "When a dear friend of yours comes to your house, you don't think of how much time you spend with him, and you are happy that he can stay with you as long as possible. So Jesus must become your best friend." So we started praying and increasing prayer and prayer became joy for us.

Also today in Medjugorje we pray after Mass the Creed, and the seven Our Father's, Hail Mary's and Glory Be's, as a thanksgiving to Our Lady, and this was the first prayer we started with Her. Every time we kneel down, we pray this prayer with great joy.

We also learned with Our Lady to fast because She said through prayer and fasting we can even keep wars far from us. These wars are not only in the world, and between the people, but also in our hearts and in our families; if we don't have prayer, we don't have God with us. So Our Lady began inviting us to fast. She said that the best way of fasting is on bread and water. For those who cannot fast if they are sick, they can offer their sickness, with love. Even a child can make his little renounces to candies or to TV, and the same we can do to things we [are] attached to like cigarettes or TV or alcohol.

Now we are in Lent, and this is a special moment when we can start fasting. Our Lady said you cannot speak about fasting if you haven't tried yourself to fast. Today in the Church fasting has been forgotten, and Our Lady wants to help us to waken up again this practice. We know from the Bible, it's written that there are certain evil spirits that can be kept apart from us only through prayer and fasting. Considering all the bad things we receive and we absorb by television, or by many things that modern life can offer us, I think that really we need to fast. Many times we need to fast with our eyes because our eyes can see a lot of impurity.

And Our Lady invites us to Confession. I remember the first time Our Lady spoke to us about Confession. It was a day that Our Lady said to us She would appear to us a second time in the evening. We prayed the Rosary and Our Lady appeared. The moment She appeared She said we could all get close to Her and touch Her. We said, "How is it possible, only the six of us can see you and nobody else can?" Our Lady said, "Take their hands and get them close to me." And so we did. And Our Lady allowed that everybody touched Her. Everybody felt something when they touched Our Lady. Some cold, or warm, or perfume of roses, or like an electric shock, and they all believed that Our Lady was really present. That moment we could see that Our Lady's dress was becoming more and more dirty while people were touching Her. We asked Our Lady, "Why is your dress so dirty?" Our Lady said, "These are your sins," and invited us to go to Confession; to choose a priest as our own spiritual advisor who can make us understand more clearly what is sin and what is not sin. From that moment, in my opinion, Medjugorje has become the most important place in the world for Confession – where people make a real encounter with God. So also through this experience, by touching Her, Our Lady showed us how important Confession is.

Many people have started living conversion as Our Lady is asking. They live in holiness in their own life. Our Lady has invited to holiness – first of all the parish through Her messages on every Thursday, and through the messages given on the 25th of each month. She also wants to help us learn how to read the Holy Scriptures. She wants us to give time to prayer, in the simplicity of our everyday life. She wants little by little that all our life can become prayer, also our work and our meeting people. She wants us to change our mentality. She has started to invite us to live in a very practical and concrete way, holiness – particularly living Holy Mass at the center of our life.

She invites us to create prayer groups, and groups for Adoration of the Blessed Sacrament. I remember the times when we used to pray in front of the Blessed Sacrament during the night, and we used to fall asleep at the time. We had no experience, but great good will. We used to say that we started deep meditation, because we actually fell asleep and we started snoring. But then we learned how to do, for example, by reading the Bible, by reading and singing songs from 3 to 4 A.M. when it is the hardest moment in the night, when you more easily fall asleep. And in the morning, when the priest celebrated Holy Mass, we lived the most beautiful moment of our life. We had a lot of joy. This joy arrived from deciding freely to spend the whole night together with Jesus. Many young people decide to spend their nights in discotheques, on their Saturday nights for example, but we decided to spend this time with Jesus. And we think we received much more joy than they do. And if I could go back in time and again have to decide which of the two, in going to the discotheque or going to be with Jesus for the whole night, I would choose again to be with Jesus.

Our Lady once said that we could celebrate Her birthday, and as a prayer group we ordered a big cake, and we brought it on top of Krizevac, the Mountain of the Cross, at half-past-eleven at night, when Our Lady said She would appear. You can imagine us carrying this cake, climbing the hill for this long forty-five minutes walk. But we did it with great joy. And in the moment of the apparition we sang Happy

Birthday to Our Lady. We had created this cake with many roses made of sugar, and even had the idea of taking one of these roses and to offer it to Our Lady. And Our Lady took this rose and She took it with Her. We said that it's impossible that Our Lady is bringing back to Paradise this rose. The following day, early in the morning we climbed the hill to see if we could see the rose anywhere. But the rose wasn't there, and we were full of joy in our hearts. We also ate the cake – it was very big – at the end of the apparition and at the end of all prayers, and I must say, the cake was very, very good, because at that moment we were tired and hungry, and we were joyful.

I remember when the police stopped us from climbing the hill. We asked Our Lady, "What should we do?" She said to us, "Go to church; there you will be protected." And from that moment, Our Lady told us to ask the priest to celebrate the Holy Mass. So now every evening Rosary starts at six, and at seven, Holy Mass. Before that there was no program in the afternoon, but now there is Our Lady's program, as She wanted it.

On the same Mountain of the Cross, where there is the big cement cross, Our Lady said that this was in God's plan. It was built a long time before the apparitions in 1933. Now all the pilgrims, when they go on their pilgrimages, climb this mountain at least once. And so at Medjugorje we can say that we have this frame with the hills, the Apparition Hill and the Hill of the Cross, around the Church, which is the center where all the Liturgy is, the Mass, and the Adoration. So when people go there, they feel they are invited to live this special atmosphere because you can almost feel and perceive the purpose of Our Lady.

We can see that Medjugorje has touched the hearts of people all over the world. Many prayer groups have started. We generally say that Medjugorje is not a 'movement' because people tend to say we belong to this or that movement. Our Lady actually allowed us to fall in love with Her. And we did; we started living all that Our Lady asked us to. And finally, when She saw we had fallen in love with Her, She led us to Jesus, and She said, "I am not important." So we have fallen in love with Jesus, and Our Lady has said that the most important moment is the moment of holiness.

Although every day we were waiting with great joy for the moment of the apparition, we can see that people that go to Medjugorje, go back to their houses renewed and with a wish to renew their family life and their spiritual life. Many parishes, after people belonging to them, have come back from Medjugorje, have experienced becoming more active, because people, when they go back from Medjugorje, witness not to belong to a particular group, but witness their belonging to Jesus Christ. So we feel the need to do more there where we are, because our own personal church is very important. Not only as a building, but also particularly as a community, particularly nowadays when we feel these great threats caused by terrorism. Our Lady says that we can even stop wars with prayer and fasting. We believe so. And when we are all together, there are many of us.

I remember the Bishop of Split, a friend of Medjugorje, when war began in Croatia, he said, "I invited all the people to fast and pray." His city has been protected. They started Perpetual Adoration, 24 hours, in their chapel. Many people were sick, prayed, and were healed. Jesus said that where two or three of you are joined in prayer in My name I am there with them. That is why God sent to us Our Lady, to tell us He loves us.

Once we asked Our Lady, "Why are You so beautiful? You are so beautiful we cannot even try to describe this beauty to other people." Our Lady answered, "I am beautiful because I love." Now I want to leave you with these words I wanted to give to prepare for Holy Mass, remembering that Our Lady said that She wants the Holy Mass to become the center of our life. May God bless you all.

Jakov

(1/07)
Jakov Speaks at the Youth Festival, 2006

Since you are all here in Medjugorje, you came for God, because this is what Our Lady wants, and this is why you were called here. Thank you for having responded to Our Lady's call. You chose to be here to meet your Gospa in a special way, to meet your Jesus in a special way. Through Our Lady we will better know Her Son and what He is like.

People will say, "Why does Our Lady give so many messages, and why so long?" Instead of asking that, we have to say thank you – thank you, God, for so many years that You are sending Our Lady here, and that You let Her come. If we open our hearts towards Them, there will be no more, "Why?" She comes for a reason because She is our Mother, and that She wants to show us the way to peace and to Her Son. Our Lady's messages are the path to know Her Son. We all have to tell Our Lady "yes" and start our new life with God.

Your experience doesn't end here, but you take this home with you. Everywhere we go then, when we return home, for us will become Medjugorje if we desire this.

Our Lady says, "Pray the Holy Rosary," but when you pray, pray with your heart. Feel at peace and let that open your hearts to happiness.

Prayer with the heart is a gift from God; we have to want this gift, and desire it and work towards it. Every day to pray more, then our prayer will be better. Our Lady listens to all of us, not just those who are receiving the visions, but She came and is the same for every single one of us.

"Why is it important to fast?" people ask. It is important because Our Lady asks this of us. "Dear children, with prayer and fasting, we can accomplish all and abolish wars." And this is why fasting is so important.

When we say, "God, where are You? Why do You leave me alone?" we should be asking ourselves, "Where were we? How much did we pray in our lives? How many times did we seek Him?" He is always close to us, but because of our sins, we ourselves are the ones who can push Him away.

Change your hearts, all of you who come here. It is not important to see the visionaries, and we should not come to see signs, because the biggest sign in Medjugorje is conversion and a new life.

You don't have to have a fear of converting, such as, "What are we going to say to our friends? Are they going to make fun of me?" But when we know God and all the peace that He wants to give us, it's not important what others will say about us, because we will have that closeness of God in our hearts.

God will always show us the right way. And when we go back to our homes, it's not as important to say you were in Medjugorje, but let Medjugorje live in your hearts and be the example to others about Medjugorje.

One other message from Our Lady – She says, "Dear children, if you only knew how much I loved you, you would cry with joy." Every day, we need to think of this. And to think of the graces we receive from Her. She says, "If you only knew." When you open your hearts toward God and Our Lady and you give your "yes," then you start being with Our Lady and Jesus.

I will pray for all of you and all of you who have come here, and you please, pray for the visionaries.

(5/06)
Panel Discussion with the Visionaries, Ivanka, Mirjana, Ivan, and Father Petar Ljubicic, 1993

(selected excerpts)

Q: When will we receive the story of Mary's life?

A: Mirjana said at the very beginning of the apparitions, when Our Lady started to appear to them, they were able to ask Her questions. One question they asked Her was that they saw very little written in the Bible about Our Lady's life, and being so important for salvation, they wanted to know about Her life. So Our Lady gave them a story of Her life as Mirjana has written in one notebook; Vicka was writing in three notebooks. It could be the same story, but they do not compare them. Ivanka also said she wrote down what Our Lady told her about Her life. So these stories will be revealed to the world when Our Lady says so, but for now it is still to be kept aside.

Q: Does Mary ever speak about disciplining your children – for example spanking them?

A: Mirjana said that when Our Lady came to them they were children. They were not perfect and they made mistakes. But She gave them an example of a Mother. She always gave an example with a good word and with Her example as a Mother. They did not ask about spanking the children. Ivanka said that all we have to do is be patient with our children and have perseverance as Our Lady is with all of us.

Q: Can Father Petar tell us the mission of Vicka?

A: As for Vicka – through her, Our Lady wants to tell us that the suffering we have in this world – that if we can accept it, then we can receive an abundance of grace. Even the illness itself should be accepted as a gift, as grace. And Jesus is an example in all of this, for all of us. Some of you may know, Vicka suffered for about three and a half years of an incurable illness. Sometimes it was so hard for her that she was unconscious for some time – at times for about 40 minutes or so. Once, even her mother, seeing her suffering so much, asked, "Why wouldn't you ask Our Lady to lessen your suffering?" But she told her that she accepted this suffering herself as a penance. Vicka did not explain for what purpose.

Q: For Ivanka – How does your experience of the Blessed Mother affect your vocation as wife and mother?
A: Ivanka said she is not perfect; she is like everyone else here. When problems arise, every family experiences difficulties in the family one way or another. But with having Our Lady's message in mind and following Her message, it is easier to keep her family in the spirit of Christ, to keep the family in the Christian spirit. It is easier for her, but for those who do not have such experiences, they might find it harder sometimes when the family is in a crisis. But for this reason it is easier to overcome problems.

Q: Do her children listen better because the Blessed Mother is teaching her?
A: Her children are the same as yours!

Editor's note: We thank Queen of Peace Ministries for permission to transcribe the tape of this talk which was given at the National Conference on Medjugorje at Notre Dame University. We also thank Carolanne Kilichowski for transcribing the tape.

Ivanka

(7/05)
Ivanka – Witnessing as Servant of God and a Messenger of Our Lady

By Carlotta Zuback

On my two pilgrimages to Medjugorje, I was blessed to stay with Ivanka, the first visionary to see Our Lady on June 24, 1981. Ivanka has a beautiful home that she opens up to pilgrims who come to Medjugorje. She gives talks with the help of an interpreter both privately and publicly about her visits with Our Lady. She answers all questions, even though she has so many other duties at home, helping her family and the pilgrims. Ivanka has a most infectious smile that brightens up a room. I was so humbled that I could hardly look into her eyes. As the days went by, I saw her as a person whose mission was to serve.

One morning, arriving after Mass, I saw her straightening up rooms, picking up towels from tired pilgrims and always smiling. She didn't speak much English, so we talked with our eyes and hearts. I can also attest to her fine cooking by the weight I gained on the pilgrimages staying in her home! Every meal she made was perfected with native seasoning.

Someone asked Ivanka if she thought she should have been a nun. Ivanka asked Our Lady about this, and Our Lady told her to take it to prayer and do what she thought best. She chose marriage to Raico, and they have a daughter and two younger sons. Raico has a tennis court that he created for his family and the whole community comes to take lessons from him daily. He also helps Ivanka with many of the everyday chores in the home. As I would pass one particular door, I got chills knowing that Ivanka received her visits with Blessed Mother in that room of the house.

The apparitions with Our Lady started shortly after the death of Ivanka's mother. Ivanka asked Our Lady where her mother was in her first meeting with Her, and Our Lady said, "She is with me." Ivanka has seen her mother many times since then, and has spoken with her mother on several occasions. During one visit with Blessed Mother, Ivanka was given the choice to see Heaven, hell and Purgatory. She asked if she could only see Heaven and Purgatory. Ivanka describes Heaven as a place of joy and peace like nothing one can experience on earth. Purgatory was dimly lit with sounds of suffering and many saying prayers.

Our Blessed Mother was dressed in the most beautiful gown on May 7, 1985, when she told Ivanka this was to be her last daily visit. Our Blessed Mother remained with Ivanka for a full hour and gave her the tenth secret. Our Lady asked Ivanka what her heart desired the most, and she replied, "To see my earthly mother." Her mother appeared and gave Ivanka a hug, and said how proud she was of her, and then she disappeared. Ivanka asked Our Blessed Mother if she could kiss Her and She nodded. Before She left, She said, "Go in peace with God," and She slowly went away followed by two angels. Ivanka said she withdrew for awhile because she greatly missed Blessed Mother's visits. Our Lady has promised Ivanka that she would see Her on the Anniversary of the Apparitions, June 25, and these visits will continue for the rest of her life. She told us that each visionary has a prayer vocation and her special mission is to pray for families.

In April of 2004, Ivanka had given a talk in the newly created grotto for Blessed Mother in the dining room of her home. My husband, Tony, lightheartedly asked Ivanka what Our Lady thought of Mel Gibson's "The Passion." She smiled back at him and said, "She was there and already knew the story."

On my second visit to Medjugorje, Ivanka was five months pregnant, but lost the baby the next month in May. I cried for her, as I knew she was so happy with the baby coming, but then I thought of her visit with Our Lady in June. That gave me great comfort for Ivanka.

Her younger sister, who has two small children, lost her husband in an automobile accident a few weeks before our visit. I can remember seeing Ivanka's sister crying when our group took some gifts and toys for the children. We tend to think that just because one sees Our Lady that everything in life will be a rainbow. Even visionaries have crosses, often much bigger than the crosses we tend to complain about, doing our daily routine. If we give up all our suffering to God, He will use it for the greater good. They seemed to have no idea who this beautiful girl was, serving them food and beverage. I asked our tour guide if they knew who she was, and her response was "No." She served with a smile, humility and love, that I thought of Our Lord at the Last Supper with the Apostles.

The last day we all hugged Ivanka and her family goodbye. By the grace of God, we will return to this village filled with peace, a peace that only God can give. We all witnessed a true servant of God who shared her love and peace with us, which we, in turn, bring back home to our friends and families.

Editor's note: Carlotta is from Venetia, PA.

(7/06)
Question and Answer Session with Ivanka

The following questions were asked by a group of pilgrims visiting Ivanka on August 6, 2001. We thank Mark DiCarlo of Michigan for videotaping this session with Ivanka.

Q: Is Ivanka tired of all of us coming here?
A: I am not tired. Just imagine, for 20 years Our Lady has been repeating to pray, to fast, to live the Christian life, so that I am not tired. I don't have permission to be tired!

Q: A lot of people who come to Medjugorje expect to see visions, to see Mary, and they feel disappointed if they don't. What would you say to them?
A: You do not look for miracles outside yourself. The only thing you must do is to clean your heart, and when you do that, you will be able to see and find miracles in your life. The one who looks around doesn't pray.

Q: Is there any message Our Lady gave to the people of the United States or to the Church?
A: For Our Lady there is no Herzegovinans, no Americans, no Croats. We are all the same Church. And because She is a mother, She loves all Her children the same.

Q: Are we getting close to the time when the secrets will be revealed?
A: Every day we are getting closer and closer.

Q: In one of the apparitions was Our Lady holding the Child Jesus?
A: The first day, and also for Christmas, 1983 and 1984 Our Lady came with the Baby. [1984 was the last time Ivanka saw Our Lady on Christmas.]

Q: Can you describe?
A: It's a spiritual feeling. For eyes it is gorgeous, so beautiful, but also it is more beautiful the feelings you get in your heart.

Q: What color eyes does Our Lady have?
A: Blue

Q: Is Our Lady ever upset about the way people come to Medjugorje, irreverent?
A: Medjugorje is open to all people. I met so many people who came here who did not have any respect for themselves, nor the Church, nor other people, and they came here maybe out of curiosity, but they went home changed. So Medjugorje is open to all people.

Q: Can Ivanka remember every single message?
A: Everything that needs to be written is written down, so the main messages I write everything down.

Q: How long will Ivanka have her annual apparitions?
A: Till the end of my life I will have the annual apparitions. At the beginning they asked us to ask how long She would appear to us, and She asked us if we were already tired of Her. That was the only time we dared to ask. We never asked again.

Q: How do you explain to people that without the priesthood there would be no sacraments?
A: We must pray to God for priests. We see where the young people are going today, and we need to pray to have first a lot of peace in our hearts. Pray, pray, and pray, is all Our Lady says. And everything is going to be fine if we stay together with God, and the only way to stay is with prayer. We, all people, are the same – when everything goes well in our life then we forget about God. When we get a little cross, then we start to pray. God is always close to us, but we have to open our hearts.

Mirjana

(3/09)
Mirjana's Talk at the Medjugorje Peace Conference in Irvine, CA

By Mary Kemper

I was able to hear Mirjana Soldo speak at the Medjugorje Peace Conference in Irvine, CA the last weekend of October. I transcribed part of her talk, because I found it interesting. There is certainly no shortage of gloomy news, but Mirjana presented hopeful thoughts when she spoke about the Triumph of the Immaculate Heart.

On October 24, 2008, Mirjana Soldo said through her interpreter, Miki Musa: ". . . We are all the same before Our Heavenly Mother. But if there is anybody . . . if we could still speak about the privileged ones . . . then we would speak about the priests. Our Lady has never said what they should do, but She always says what we should do for them. She says they do not need you to judge and criticize them. They need your prayers and your love because God will judge them the way they were as priests, but God will judge you, the way you treated your priests. Our Lady says if you lose respect for your priests, after that, you will lose respect for the Church, and in the end with dear God, as well.

"During the apparitions on the second of every month, Our Lady always emphasizes the importance of the priests. For example, during the apparition, when She gives us Her blessing, She always says, 'I am giving you my motherly blessing, but the greatest blessing that you can receive on earth is the blessing coming from your priests, because when they bless you, it is my Son Himself blessing you.' Our Lady puts a priestly blessing above Her own blessing. Then She says, 'Do not forget to pray for your Shepherds, their priestly hands are blessed by my Son.'

"Lately, all of you have been following Our Lady's messages on every second of the month . . . they are going in a direction that Our Lady has been preparing us for something. I can tell you something the way I understand it. We live in this time that we live in, it is the way it is . . . we are waiting for the Triumph of Mother's Heart. From the time we live in right now, until the moment of Her Triumph, there is a bridge . . . and the way I understood that bridge are priests. Our Lady desires that we pray for them a lot, so that this bridge can be firm and strong, so that we all could cross that bridge in order to reach the Triumph of Our Mother's Heart. She says that we should not judge. In this time that we live in, there is so much judgment and so little of love, but Our Lady desires that we are recognized through and by love. Only dear God is supposed to be the Judge, but His judgment is completely different from ours because He does it through love. Every one of us knows how we judge. In Medjugorje, where we come from, thanks be to God, we still have respect for our priests. If a priest enters into the home, every member of the family will stand up and nobody will start to talk before he does, because we know that through this priest, we have Jesus entering our home. It is not our assignment or task to judge whether he truly represents Jesus or not. Dear God will do it. But if you look around a little, everybody is complaining about that we have a lack of vocations. Imagine who would decide to become a priest when you hear that people only judge and criticize priests! That is the reason why we have responsibility. That is the reason why Our Lady says, 'Do not judge and do not criticize. Pray for them, love them because that is the way to help them' and I am saying that today to you as well."

Someone questioned Mirjana about the ten secrets she was given by Our Lady. Here is Mirjana's response: "Everything I was allowed to say about the secrets, I've already said. But Our Lady doesn't want us to be fearful, to be afraid, because the true faith does not come from fear. The true faith comes from the heart. But I never said to anybody whether the secrets are good or bad. If Our Lady says Her heart will triumph, then what should we be afraid of?"

The next day Mirjana said, "I am not touching upon the secrets, but what I'm allowed to tell you is, be not afraid. Do not trust those . . . do not believe those people who want to frighten you, who talk about the darkness in the future . . . that is not true. That is not what Our Lady desires for us. She doesn't want us to have fear in our hearts. No mother wants her child to fear. The true faith is not the faith that comes out of fear. The true faith is the faith that comes out of love. Our Lady said, 'What I started at Fatima, I will finish, accomplish in Medjugorje. My Heart will triumph.' So if Our Heavenly Mother's Heart will triumph and win at the end, what should we fear?"

Editor's note: Mary is from Temecula, CA. She is the author of **Flowers for the Triumph: Flower Miracles in the Life of the Catholic Church.**

(6/09)
Questions and Answers with Mirjana

The following questions are excerpted from the Question and Answer Session with Mirjana at the Totally Yours Conference in St. Charles, IL, 4/26/09. Mirjana was very joyful and joked a lot. She said Our Lady wants us to be joyful.

Q: Can we put butter on our bread [when fasting]?
A: I would like to say one thing, in fact. God is Love and He truly loves His children, and even if you put butter on your bread, He will still love you. But do you love yourself? That is the question. I cannot be the one to decide about that. I can only repeat what Our Lady says, and how you shall do that further is going to be your choice. God gave you freedom. He is just telling you through His Mother what is good for you. But it doesn't mean that you have to do it right away. Go slowly, step by step.

A friend of mine named Joyce, when she comes to Medjugorje, she always says, "For Friday I will fast on bread and water," and she doesn't know that they tell me she was eating cheese as well. [laughter]

Q: Why does Our Lady ask for Wednesday and Friday to fast?
A: When the things through Medjugorje are supposed to happen, then you will be able to understand why Wednesday and Friday – or why every 2nd of the month and every 18th of March. Every day and every date has a meaning.

Q: Can we drink tea or coffee with our bread?
A: Guy (the MC) complains of this, and I know him so well. In Medjugorje he eats nothing but bread, and I'm sure he's asking because of some other people, and the answer is the same. [laughter] [By "the same," we think she means the same thing she said in her talk the day before, when she said that you can drink coffee on fast day "as long as you get up before Our Lady."]

Q: How much bread can we eat and how much water can we drink?
A: Our Lady didn't talk about the amount of bread or about water, but believe me, I tried. I ate so much bread, I thought it would satisfy my hunger, but I just got a big stomach [ache] and I was still hungry.

Q: I was told that if I fall asleep praying my Rosary, my guardian angel will finish it. Is this true?
A: And why wouldn't it happen that when you want to put butter on your bread, you decide, "I will give this butter to my guardian angel and then I will eat only bread?" [roaring laughter]

Q: We went on a pilgrimage and we were blessed to stay at your house once, and we noticed the Pope's shoes are in a little display at your house. Can you tell us how Pope John Paul II's shoes arrived there?
A: I am the only one of six visionaries who was lucky enough, had the honor, to encounter Pope John Paul II. You can imagine how the other five are jealous of me. [laughter] Jakov always says, "Oh, yea, you have been with Pope."

I was in the Vatican, St. Peter's Basilica, with an Italian priest. Holy Father was walking by and he was blessing us. When he approached me, he blessed me and he just continued to walk. However, this Italian priest loudly said to him, "Holy Father, this is Mirjana from Medjugorje." He came back and blessed me again and he set out. And I said to the priest, "He just thinks I need a double blessing." But then after, he received a note, an invitation to Castle Gandolfo, close to Rome, in order to encounter the Pope. I couldn't sleep all night because I really loved him and I respected him and I could really feel his love for Our Lady.

So the next day when he and I met alone, I was just crying. I couldn't say a word out of excitement. He noticed that I was excited. I think he tried to talk to me in Polish because he thought in the Slavic languages there are things in common. I didn't understand a word! But I finally had enough strength and courage. I asked him, "What are you trying to tell me?" Then we talked. Among other things he said to me, "I know everything about Medjugorje. I've been following Medjugorje. Ask pilgrims to pray for my intentions, to keep, to take good care of Medjugorje, because Medjugorje is hope for the entire world. And if I were not Pope, I would have been in Medjugorje a long time ago."

So recently on the Mount of Apparitions, I saw a pair of shoes of the Pope in front of me, and after the apparition, this gentleman who brought these shoes (he didn't introduce himself), he said, "It was the Pope's desire for a long time to come to Medjugorje. I said, 'If you do not go, I will take your shoes.' And that is how I brought his shoes, so they may be present during the apparition."

Now I have a pair of his shoes in my home. But what is funniest in this, a man who made the shoes for the Pope, an Italian from Rome, he heard that I have a pair of the Pope's shoes, and imagine, he wouldn't believe it. He made two pairs of Pope's shoes for me. My number's 38 [in the USA, size 7].

Ivan

(2/07)
Ivan's Visit

By Jason Smith

In November [2006], I attended Ivan's visit in Methuen, MA. I've heard Ivan speak several times, and it's always nice to see that he never gets tired of his goal. He is totally committed from his heart to travel and share Our Lady's messages with sincere devotion and love. A couple of things he said really became serious to me, and I want to share them with all of you. Ivan mentioned that Our Lady wants us to absolutely choose God each day over all sin and evil, to start praying with our families from the heart because there is too much infidelity, immorality and division, and that through prayer, especially family prayer, we'll begin to know peace again and have peace. Ivan seemed very concerned for the health of our souls and explained there is no healing in our lives unless we have spiritual healing first. He defended Our Lady's Messages with love and seriousness.

I saw Ivan as a son defending his Mother which helped me finally realize how real this all is, and that She is our Mother, and we are all Her children. He also describes his visits with Mary as truly heavenly, and that coming back to reality here can be difficult. This really caught my attention, because since I went to Medjugorje that's how I've felt about coming back home – things that used to matter don't matter so much anymore, and I've learned to realize we are just here temporarily. I'm embarrassed to say this, but it's the truth – I've been in self pity a lot of times, and I realize hungering for God is great and that I'm not always happy here on earth, yet I've got to make the best of it and start praying more and taking the focus off of myself and put my trust in God. Then there will be faith, happiness, trust, peace, love and so on.

Ivan mentioned Our Lady appeared that night with tears of love in Her eyes and She was joyful. This made me so happy because in my heart I felt Her Love and how happy She was to see us, and I could really feel the joy Our Lady has about Christmas in Her Heart, Her Son, Our Savior's birth and the indescribable joy She must be so filled with.

This evening I felt peace, love, yet a serious urgency to start praying more. Ivan mentioned that we find time to do all the things that we want to do, yet prayer becomes neglected. Life is full of mountains and valleys, yet we've got to stay on the ship. I pray that all of us will continue to pray for one another and have hope. God is with us, and He keeps all His promises. I know that everything we struggle with, pray for, day in and day out, will all be answered someday, and that the life we have here is just a glimpse, and the indescribable love and joy we're going to experience eternally someday. It's what we have to look forward to.

Editor's note: Jason is from Goffstown, New Hampshire.

(2/08)
Ivan's Talk in Brunswick, Ohio

The following is an excerpt from Ivan's talk in Brunswick, Ohio, April 24, 2007.

She [Our Lady] calls us to monthly Confession and Adoration of the Holy Sacrament. And She wants us to pray the Rosary within our families, and She wants us to read the Bible in our families. And She says: "Let the Bible be in your family in a visible place. Read the Holy Bible and by reading, Jesus will be renewed and reborn in your lives. Forgive others, love others." And She is carrying all of us in Her heart.

And She says very clearly in one of Her messages: "Dear children, if you knew how much I love you, you would be crying for joy." So great is the Motherly Love. One of the most important messages that Our Lady calls upon is the prayer from the heart. So many times She has repeated Herself saying: "Pray, pray, pray, dear children – not from the mouth, not from the mind, but from the heart." How is She teaching us to pray from the heart? What does it mean to pray from the heart? Pray from the heart means to pray with love and out of love, to pray with your whole being, so that our prayers will be a meeting with Jesus, a conversation with Jesus and it is rectifying with Jesus. So by praying you can be full of peace and joy. And we can say: "How is this possible?" "How can you concentrate on prayer all the time?" Our Lady knows that we are not perfect; however, She desires that we go to the school of prayer – that we pray every day. She wants us to pray three hours daily. That is Her wish. She doesn't say that we need to pray for three hours just the Rosary. There is Holy Mass, the Holy Rosary, reading the Holy Bible and doing good deeds.

One of the pilgrims came to Medjugorje, and she came to me and asked me: "I cannot believe Our Lady wants us to pray three hours; how can She ask for that?" I told her, "That is Her wish." The next year when the same person came to Medjugorje, she came to me again, and she put the same question to me. "Is She still asking us to pray for three hours?" I said: "No! She is not asking for three hours; She is asking for twenty-four hours." And do you know what she said then? "Then I will pray for three hours!"

She is not asking much of us. She only asks of us that which we can accomplish. Dear children, if you want to go to the School of Prayer you must know that there is no weekend in the School of Prayer. You go to the School of Prayer every day. If you wish to pray better, then you need to pray more. And to pray more is your personal decision. And to pray better is grace, and it is a grace to give to those who pray more. Many times today we say that we don't have time to pray, that we are tired, we work a lot, and that the family is not together at the same time. The kids go to school and time is always of essence. But Our Lady says very simply, "Dear children, time is not of essence. That is not the problem! The problem is Love. When you love something then you always make time for it, but if you don't like something then you will never find time for it."

That is why She is asking us so much to be involved in prayer, and that prayer will return peace to the world. Peace will return within the families and peace will return among young people and in the whole world. And She wants to wake us up from this spiritual dying of us. She wants to wake us up from this spiritual coma and She wants to make us stronger in holiness and in our prayer.

Editor's note: Our thanks to Mary Jane Muslera for transcribing this talk.

Vicka

(9/08)
Vicka Speaks about Family Life

By Sr. Emmanuel

Visiting Vicka recently, I was ushered into her house and mixed in with a small group of Italians who were listening intently to Vicka's words. She answered their questions and spoke to them from the heart, which gave me an opportunity to again witness her incredible wisdom. After all, that is her trademark (ask anyone from the village): wisdom grounded in solid common sense! When I came, she was speaking to several Italian families who were deeply suffering in their family life. Naturally Vicka responded to their distress by expressing a few observations on family life today:

"My father (Petar Ivankovic who died a year ago) spent 35 years of his life working on construction sites in Germany to be able to feed us. In our village it was necessary for many men to go abroad, to find work, to help their families. My father never thought of himself. He never thought about the sadness of not living with us, the solitude in his exile, or the hardship of his work. (He was one among many men whose living quarters, 'algecos', were by the roadside, bitterly cold in winter and torrid in the summer). No, he saw all these things as his necessary responsibility to ensure the survival of his family! He loved us and he was courageous. He sacrificed everything for us.

"Today, it's not like that. Families go through crisis because people think first of themselves before their families. Everything becomes more important than the family. They no longer take time to pray together because they think they have more important things to do. This is a big mistake! They no longer want to give of themselves or to freely give time to their family. Each person lives for himself, without taking the time to be together, talking, being interested in each other. Or, they watch television and there is no conversation, no dialogue. Then, with this selfishness come jealousy, hatred, and misunderstanding.

"Satan is at work, he wants to divide and destroy the family. Each person is concerned with material things, trying to get the most advantage out of his situation. Material wellbeing becomes the most important thing. It's a disease! Hearts and souls do not receive any nourishment and become starved. The incessant quest for material wellbeing wears the family out and closes the members to each other. Each one suffers alone and, without prayer, it often gets to be unbearable. God does not hold the first place; the young ones do not receive enough love; sadness grows as well as discontent and anger; and families break up. They don't even see why they are breaking up and they say to God, 'Why did You let my family break up?'

"But no! We should not behave this way! We are responsible! The most important thing is to protect family life and family unity! Unity of hearts comes with prayer, when God is given the first place and we give ourselves for our family. I am not saying that material things do not matter. They do, of course, but they can be very simple. For example, today many people want to buy designer clothes. The result is that people become as rigid as statues and cannot move, as they would like. They're worried that their designer's label won't be noticed! They are slaves of other peoples' look and they lose their freedom. Spending too much money to buy designers' clothes brings comparisons and conflicts. That's the illness; wanting more and more!

"For 26 years the Gospa has been asking us to take the time to pray as a family every day. She knows why! She wants to protect us from disaster! But many do not listen to Her and then they cry in front of Her saying, 'Save us!' We have to make the right decisions now! We only need to decide, and God, Who is good, will help us. But we should begin today and say, 'Now, I am going to do what You say, I will do everything I can, and You, please, do the rest!'"

Children of Medjugorje, www.childrenofmedjugorje.com (March, 2008)

(9/06)
Questions and Answers with Jakov, 6/21/06

Q: Does Our Lady say anything about abortion?
A: Our Lady has never said anything to me about abortion. But I think it means that She does not have to say anything to us. We all know what abortion is. God gives life and we cannot destroy that life.

As if to answer that question, here is Mirjana's message 11 days later, on July 2, 2006:

> *"Dear children, God created you with free will to comprehend and to choose: Life or Death. I as a Mother, with motherly love, desire to help you to comprehend and to choose life. My children, do not deceive yourselves with false peace and false joy. Permit me, my children, to show you the true way, the way that leads to life – my Son. Thank you!"*

(9/07)
Mirjana Answers Questions of Pilgrims

The following questions were asked of Mirjana outside her home after her talk on June 19, 2006.

Q: What can we do to bring back the teenagers who stop practicing the Catholic faith they were brought up in?
A: When the children are adults and they leave our home, I would like to give you some advice – to pray for them and to pray that She [Our Lady] can do with them what She considers correct. We should never judge, criticize, or push them, but to show them with our own lives the love of God. This is the best way.

Q: My prayers are gravitating towards the whole world more than for my family and friends. Has the Blessed Mother said anything about that?
A: I do not consider that as wrong. I do the same. I would say, when I pray, say, "Dear God, you know what we need because I do not know what we need. I will pray, and You, dear God, You lead my family." But it is not wrong, at the same time, to pray for your family and friends. But somehow I feel closer to God praying like you just said.

(5/07)
Questions and Answers with Jakov, 6/21/06

Q: What about the influence of television in our lives?
A: Are we forced to watch television? (The crowd shouts, "No!") You see, nobody is forced to watch TV, so we should not allow television to bring up, raise our children. *We* raise our children. *We* educate our children. You see, we are the ones who place televisions in our homes, and when we look at our homes, do you know where the television is placed? It is always in the center of our living rooms. Is that right? (Heads shake in agreement as the crowd says, "Yes.") And let's try to imagine – let's place a cross instead of a television. You see, it's not wrong to watch television. That's not wrong, but we are those who choose what we are going to watch on television.

I am sure all Europeans watch the soccer World Cup. And I'm sure all of you are going to cheer for Croatia! (laughter)

Q: Can you tell us how Our Lady picked Medjugorje for Her apparitions?
A: Can't you see – Medjugorje is so beautiful?! (Crowd claps in agreement.) We asked Our Lady at the beginning of the apparitions why She chose Medjugorje, and Our Lady said only once, "I have found a strong faith, that people are faithful to God in this parish." And we can explain it – you see, we used to live in a Communist country, and in a certain way it was forbidden to attend Holy Mass and to be Catholic, but in spite of all these problems we used to have people stay faithful to God, and we prayed and we always believed in Him. And I think this is a great gift from God to all of us, for entire Medjugorje, but also this is a gift for the entire world.

Q: What were your feelings when Our Lady gave you the tenth secret and Our Lady said She would not appear on a daily basis any more?
A. You have to understand, I was having apparitions on a daily basis for 17 years, and I grew up with Our Lady. And you see, I knew only about this life, and this is my life. And of course, it is normal when I was given the tenth secret, and when Our Lady told me that She would not appear to me on a daily basis any more, I cannot describe the pain I felt in my heart. And I can tell you that this was the most difficult moment in my

life. You see, you ask yourself then many questions. How will I be able to continue my life? How is it possible that I do not see Our Lady any more? And what am I going to do in that hour when I was meeting Her? But also Our Lady says, "Pray and you are going to get all answers." And I really understand and, you see, I had this gift from God – I was able to see Our Lady, and I'm thankful to God every moment of my life for this gift He gave to me. And now when I'm not able to see Our Lady on a daily basis any more, I know that She is with me all the time. It is more important to have Our Lady in our hearts and She wants to be in every single heart. But also, I can't wait for Christmas to come! (*Our Lady told Jakov that She would appear to him every Christmas Day for the rest of his life.*)

(4/08)
Questions and Answers with Mirjana

The following questions were asked of Mirjana following her talk in front of her house in Medjugorje 6/23/06:

Q: How can I convince my children to come to Mass with me?
A: With your example – so that the children can see God and God's love within yourself. I would like to recommend you to put your children into Our Lady's arms, pray for them, fast for them, and give them your own example. Don't criticize, judge, or force them to do things, because they will just do the contrary. Love is the answer to everything.

Q: How much daily prayer do you have?
A: If you think I'm measuring the time, no, I don't. I say the Rosary. Our Lady also was asking us to pray seven Our Father's, Hail Mary's and Glory Be's on our knees. And I have my mission to pray for unbelievers, and I pray for that intention.

Q: Are we supposed to correct the wrong things we see?
A: I didn't say we should keep quiet and never say a word, but I would always say, before anything you say, before any conversation, we should pray, because if we do pray, then Jesus will be talking through us. But if we do not pray and we just talk, we will just do the contrary, because

then our words will be empty. That's why we should pray, so that prayer can lead us in conversation with other people, so that we can in a right way correct those who are doing wrong, to do it with love.

Q: What does Our Lady say about other apparitions?
A: What I can say is that here in Medjugorje Our Lady mentioned only Fatima. Our Lady said, "What I started in Fatima I will finish, accomplish in Medjugorje." As for other apparitions, for people who claim they have apparitions or inner locutions, Our Lady says you will recognize them by their fruits, and we know that from our own, that the true apparition will be recognized by its gifts. For a few times we asked Our Lady about apparitions in the world, the only answer She gave us was, "Pray for them." That was all.

Q: Can we be present for an apparition (on June 25) and how should we dress?
A: It is the visionary Marija who will have an apparition and I do believe she will have the apparition in her home, and Ivanka also in her home. And in talking about the way people are dressed, I would like to emphasize one thing that I noticed when you're in Medjugorje in the church. You will not see the local people to go into the church with sleeveless T-shirts and very short shorts and short skirts. That is something that we just cannot imagine because during Holy Mass, Jesus is with us and we should be aware of that.

(7/07)
Conversation with Ivanka Ivankovic Elez

Q: Is it hard for you to wait the whole year to see Our Lady again?
A: Every day I am preparing myself for this moment, and now I could cry and laugh at the same time.

Q: What do you see when Our Lady comes?
A: Before Our Lady appears, I see the light three times. Then I see the most beautiful image of Our Lady and everything else disappears.

Q: Was anyone able to paint what you see?
A: None of the paintings come even close to the beauty and radiance of Our Lady.

Q: Can you tell us anything about the secrets? Many people are afraid.
A: I can only say about the sign that will appear here in Medjugorje when the time comes. This sign will be for those who do not believe. Those who live according to the commandments of God have no reason to fear.

Q: There are so many people here for this anniversary; does it bother you and others?
A: Our Lady is so glad when more people gather here to pray with Her and with us. The more prayers, the less evil in the world. This should make us all feel good.

Q: What would you like to say to people in the USA?
A: Parents should teach their children about God and pray with them.

MIR Peace Letter, June, 2000

(11/07)
Vicka : "We Live What We Have Chosen"

By Sr. Emmanuel

Visiting the cemeteries of Medjugorje on All Saints Day at night is really moving since the multitude of vibrant, colored candles give them almost a fairy tale aspect. It is lovely to think that each candle represents a relative or friend who has come to the aid of a dearly departed soul, helping them cross the threshold of Heaven.

However, it would be a pity to wait for someone to die before helping him with our prayers, since the choices we make on Earth hold immense consequences. We don't always realize this.

Taking advantage of All Saints Day, I asked Vicka what would be the best way to transmit this message during my missions. She replied, "As the Gospa has told us, it is already here on earth that we each make the choice of going either to Heaven, or to Purgatory, or to hell. After death we then continue to live what we have chosen on earth. Each one knows how they are living on earth. As for me, I try my best to do all I can to go to Heaven with all of my heart. I have a great desire to go to Paradise since I am a Christian (here Vicka speaks as a person who has suffered under atheistic Communism). On earth some people choose Purgatory, that is to say, they have not completely decided for God; they deliberately pick and choose with the Gospel. Other people here on earth choose to do everything against God and against the will of God. In doing so, they choose to live in hell. They start a hell in their heart and after death it is the same hell that continues for them. What we become after death depends on us, since God has given free will to everyone. It is we who choose our future in all freedom.

"After death, life continues, our life on earth is a short journey, a kind of a walk! The Gospa has said to us, 'Many live only for this world. They believe that after death everything stops, that it's all over, that there is nothing more.' 'No!' She said, 'this is a big mistake! Life continues and after death there is eternity!'"

May these words become little candles for us that twinkle to remind us how unique and precious every hour of our existence is here on earth.

Dearest Gospa, we definitely choose Heaven, please help us persevere in our decision!

Children of Medjugorje, www.childrenofmedjugorje.com

(8/07)
Mirjana Answers Questions of Pilgrims

The following questions were asked of Mirjana outside her home after her talk on June 19, 2006.

Q: The weeping Jesus (behind St. James Church), has Our Lady said anything about the knee?
A: No

Q: Do you feel the weight of the secrets?
A: What would you say, looking at me? (laughter) This is what Our Lady said: "Do not think about the secrets. Pray, because the one who feels me as a Mother and God as a Father, that person has no fear of anything." Our Lady says that only those who have not yet come to know the love of God have fear. But we, as human beings, always talk about the future – what, when, where will happen. But who among us present here can say for sure that we will be alive tomorrow? Our Lady has been teaching us that we should be ready this very moment to come before God. And in the future, God's Will will be done, and our task is to be ready for that. And I would really like to tell you not to bother yourself with the secrets, but you should worry about your soul, because Our Lady does not want our faith out of fear. She wants our faith out of our heart. And that is why . . . pray in order to get to know the love of God, and then you will not be afraid of anything.

Q: What does Mirjana believe Our Lady means when She talks about the "signs of the times" in the April 2 (2006) and March 18 (2006) messages? [also June 2, 2007]
A: I'm so happy and glad you asked that question, because those messages are telling me a lot. Our Lady is addressing every single person individually. And now I'd really like to recommend you to take those messages from your guide in English and go to a quiet place where you will be alone to pray, and to try to understand through prayer what God is telling you through those words – because your "signs of the times" could be completely different from mine. That is why I am not authorized or have the right to tell you the way I understand. You have to understand that through your own prayer on your own. It is definitely important because Our Lady mentioned it on March 18 and April 2 as well.

Note: In her talk before the questions were asked, Mirjana said, "When Our Lady gives me a message Our Lady does not explain that message to me. Same as everybody else, I have to pray so that through this prayer I can realize what God wants to tell me."

(8/06)
Questions and Answers with Jakov, 6/21/06

Q: What are we supposed to do when we have a problem with prayer?
A: People ask this question very often. When you pray, and when your thoughts are lost somewhere, for instance – you pray and you think what am I going to cook for lunch – it is important that we do one thing – we have to stop and we have to ask the help from God. We have to talk to God with our own words. "I want to pray. I want to be united with You in prayer. Help me." And just try to remember how many times Our Lady has said, "Wherever good is, there is also another side which wants to, to desire to, destroy everything." And, you see, if we do not stay persistent in our prayer – we give up – something else will happen, and this way we will lose the prayer. And also it is important one more thing when we pray – the time and the place.

Q: There is so much war and terrorism in the world. Can Jakov tell us anything about that?
A: Everything that I've said before, and that is: "Dear children, with fasting and prayer you can stop all the wars." And if Our Lady says so, and She does, what can we do? Open our hearts and start living this message. And, you see, we always ask what we are to do, we always ask these questions. Let's start living the messages of Our Lady.

(8/08)
Witness of Marija Pavlovic-Lunetti

This witness was given May 10, 2008, at St. Mary & St. Michael Church, London. It was transcribed by Judy Pellatt.

I want to greet all of you with my heart, and through this witness of mine may you come closer to Our Lady and Her messages.

In 1981 Our Lady started coming to us. We were believers and come from families that pray, but through this presence of Our Lady, Queen of Peace, we saw a great change in our lives, in our families and in our parish. Our Lady worked in the hearts of many people, particularly those who were open to receive Her messages. When we first saw Our Lady, we were scared and ran away; we could not imagine that Our Lady would appear to us – but She actually chose us. She once said to us, "God allowed me to choose and I chose you." But She also chose many other people who are open to Her messages. Many vocations have taken place through Our Lady's presence, and now many parishes have a pastor through Our Lady of Medjugorje.

One grandmother told me that she kept asking her grandson to go to Medjugorje and light a candle for her. He used to work in a hospital, but he was a drug addict and an alcoholic. One rainy day he went to Medjugorje to light this candle for his grandmother. Someone told him he could not come to Medjugorje and not climb the two hills. When he climbed Krizevac he felt the need to kneel down. He was healed, and he also felt in his heart a vocation to the priesthood. He became a priest and worked with a cardinal who was a friend of John Paul II. This cardinal was in a wheelchair and Josefano used to push the wheelchair when they went to lunch with John Paul II. Many times after lunch the Pope would ask Josefano to witness how he received his vocation. He did this so many times that sometimes he would try to make his witness shorter, but the Pope would say, "Josefano, you forgot something!"

Every one of us can speak of our own experiences of Our Lady. Our Lady is asking us to pray, and She told us to have prayer groups – but the first one has to be in our family. In this month of May, in a special way we should pray the Rosary. Our Lady is asking each one of us to be Her outstretched hands.

Many times we ask ourselves, "Who do we belong to – a parish, a certain group?" Many times we forget we belong to Jesus, who has suffered and died on the cross for us, but above all, the one who was resurrected. St. Paul says that our faith is in vain if there is no Resurrection. Unfortunately, many times we act as if we believe Christ died but didn't rise. We witness our faith with sadness. Our Lady says that our faith has to be joyful and that we should give example with our lives. She calls us to witness and to be Her extended hands. This is why Our Lady has been appearing for so long, why Jesus sends Our Lady for so long.

Through my witness I want to help you, to show that we are normal, not crazy. Many times journalists think that our apparitions are hallucinations, but we have certificates to say that we are normal! Through this simple witness we can really touch the hearts of many. Our Lady chose us not because we are better than others. Once we asked Our Lady why She chose us and She replied, "God let me choose, and I chose you." God, even today, walks among us and works in us.

There was a couple who had no children for many years. I told them that Our Lady says to pray, go to Confession and adore the Most Holy Sacrament of the Altar. Then I saw the miracle of a baby coming to this family when doctors had said it was impossible. They also can now witness.

There was a sick lady sent home from the hospital when the doctors had said they could do no more. She started praying, "Lord have mercy," and for her children, too. She couldn't lie down because of the tumor she had, and one night she fell asleep crying with a picture of Our Lady on her chest. She awoke in the morning and began to feel better. She could breathe and had no more problems.

There are many stories like this, but most important of all is when the hearts of people change. We visionaries are just simple people and we are not important. We didn't know how to meet people, but Our Lady said, "Open your houses," and then we opened our hearts. People were coming all of the time. We would share bread, tell stories and pray with these people. We started climbing the hills at night. Vicka's grandmother told us to take holy water and throw it on the apparition. Our Lady smiled and said, "I am the Mother of God and I come here as the Queen of Peace." Through prayer and fasting we can even stop wars. In the Bible we are told that certain evil spirits can be cast out only by prayer and fasting – so we started to fast and pray more.

Teenage boys are able to go to discos all night, so we thought we could pray all night. We asked our parish priest for all-night Adoration, and so we started this way of prayer, which has not been easy. We would sing and pray, but around 3:00 A.M., we became very sleepy. Some of us even started to snore, so we called that "deep meditation!" We tried to keep each other awake and during the critical hours we would sing and read the Psalms as it was easy to fall asleep during the Rosary. Some of us got engaged and then married and we went to pray the Rosary with the newlyweds. Sometimes they fell asleep, and when they got a dig in the ribs they would wake with the words, "Hail Mary . . ."

I am inviting you to be witnesses with your lives. We don't need to go to Africa to be missionaries, we can witness in our own families. Tonight I prayed for you in a special way at the moment when Our Lady appeared. I asked Our Lady to bless you, and She did, and She prayed over us. I am sure She has seen into our hearts. I am sure that tonight She also said to you, "Thank you for responding to my call."

I want to end this witness with a prayer for you, for all our needs and all that is within our hearts. We pray at all of these gatherings, that Our Lady will bring us to Paradise. I remember when Our Lady said She would take Jakov and Vicka to Paradise; Jakov asked Our Lady to just take Vicka as he was an only child! So many times we are afraid of going to Paradise. Our Lady says, "Don't be afraid, because God made us in His image." Our life is like a flower, quickly over. In the same way, Our Lady wants us to witness in this world with joy and to be grateful to God, and then we will be able to witness for all generations.

The Medjugorje Message, UK

(11/06)
Questions and Answers with Jakov, 6/21/06

Q: Could Jakov describe to all of us what he saw in Purgatory, hell, and Heaven?
A: When we had this apparition, I was only 11, and try to imagine a child of 11 years old – a child of that age really does not think about death. And, you see, that is one ugly word we are all afraid of. And we all think that you die and you are gone – nothing happens. So just try to imagine how I felt. Imagine how I felt when Our Lady said, "Now you are coming with me." But, you see, I did not want to die, so I said to Our Lady, "Why don't you take only Vicka? She has eight children in her family, but I'm the only child my mother has." So, you see, I was a gentleman and let Vicka go. But Our Lady said, "Do not be afraid. I am with you."

So the first thing Our Lady showed to us was Heaven. And Heaven is endless space. And we saw this special light, and we saw many people who were praying together, who were talking to each other, and all of them were wearing like garments, and we did not see any age differences. So this is what I can describe with words. And, you see, I told you really nothing, but you see what Heaven is. Heaven is what we feel in our hearts and the beauty of Heaven is what I felt in my heart. The beauty was in the peace I felt, and this beauty was the joy I felt in my heart. And this is what I was able to feel of those people that I know in Heaven, and I'm sure of one thing – if we accept God here on earth, and we place God first in our lives, we already have Heaven in our hearts. This is a question I have always been asked, and this is a normal thing. But I always tell to all the people the same thing. We should ask ourselves one more important question: Are we ready to go to Heaven? Are we doing everything so we can get into Heaven? If God invites me today at this moment, am I ready to go to Him? So these are the most important questions we should ask ourselves.

Our Lady showed us Purgatory as well. But we saw the darkness in Purgatory. We were not able to see any people in Purgatory. But we felt the movement from this darkness, and Our Lady said, "Dear children, pray for the souls in Purgatory, because they are in great need of your prayers." And how important it is to pray for the souls in Purgatory! We can see through the mission which Our Lady gave to Marija, visionary, so Marija prays for the souls in Purgatory, and this is what we are to do – all of us – to pray for the souls in Purgatory.

And I never talk about hell. I always talk about more beautiful things. And I always talk about Jesus and God. But also we have to understand that there is another side. But also we have to be thankful to God because He gives us a chance so that we can get into Heaven. And let each new day in our lives become a thanksgiving to God. We have to thank Him because He gives us another chance that we become better people.

(2/06)
Question and Answer Session with Ivan

Ivan Dragicevic spoke in Seattle, Washington, on October 29, 1997. Ivan's entire presentation was tape recorded and transcribed by Linda Rogers and printed in the November, 1997 "Children of Mary Center for Peace" newsletter. Below is an excerpt. The session in its entirety can be viewed at www.medjugorje.org.

Q: When you receive all 10 secrets or when Our Lady stops appearing, will the school of prayer be finished?
A: No. Do you know when the school of prayer will end? It is when we die. Our conversion ends when we die. We are in the process our whole lifetime of converting and learning how to pray and these are gifts that we must pray for.

Q: What do you know about the sign that everyone will see throughout the world? Does just Vicka know that or do you? Do you know when or does Vicka?
A: Yes. Everybody will be able to see. Yes. I know when, and I know what.

Q: Should we be afraid?
A: I'm not afraid. Don't fear. Don't fear. This past 15 years Our Lady has been guiding us to the year 2000, to the millennium. I would suggest that together with Her, we prepare ourselves, and that is why She is guiding us. We need to pray together with Her about this plan that will happen that She knows, and we need to pray with Her for that to become reality.

Q: How do you respond to people who are preoccupied with the three days of darkness?
A: As I said already at the beginning, that is not coming from Our Lady to us and so I don't know where it is coming from, but as I also said, if we believe that Our Lady is with us, what would we fear? Why would we fear?

Q: Is there any reason given for the secrets and is mention made of any timetable?
A: I believe so – that there is reason why She gave it to us. The secrets Our Lady gave are tied with the world, with the Church and one day will be revealed, and it's also other things involved in those secrets.

Q: If She never mentioned about three days of darkness, does She mention about any chastisements or WWIII or anything like that?
A: No. I know you must probably have another thousand questions, but I will change these questions with something much better. Let us decide to pray more and I guarantee that if you pray more, you will have no questions.

CHAPTER THREE

Testimonies

"I have come to tell the world that God exists. He is the fullness of life, and to enjoy this fullness and peace, you must return to God" (June, 1981).

(6/06)
My Medjugorje Journey

By Mladen Martinovic

Reading through the stories and experiences of conversions, it is not hard to see God's love for each of us. For me everything started on June 24, 1981. It was St. John the Baptist's feast day, and there was a celebration in my home in Miljkovici, the first village just on top of the hill when you drive from Mostar to Medjugorje. I was thirteen years old at that time. We had a lot of guests in our home. One of the guests was my cousin Danijel Setka, a four year old boy who was in wheelchair. He was born with some kind of a muscle sickness so that his muscles did not grow and were paralyzed. He didn't even talk, nor was he able to express himself in any way. His father Ivan was working in Germany at that time and visited every doctor who could possibly help him, but all the doctors were clueless.

The next day rumors started to spread, since we were only 20 kilometers from Medjugorje. At that time Yugoslavia was a Communist country and everything religious had to be expressed in church only. So people kept it to themselves.

On the sixth day, Ivan and his family came to Medjugorje and asked the visionaries to ask Gospa (Our Lady in Croatian) to heal Danijel. She replied that Ivan had to have faith. So nothing happened at that moment and they started to go home. Because they were tired and hungry from being outside all day, they stopped in a restaurant to eat. Still under the impression of the happenings, Ivan was calm. When the waitress was leaving, after taking the orders, Ivan stood up and hit the table with his hand and then ordered free drinks for everybody in the restaurant. His son Danijel stood up from wheelchair, hit the table with his hand and started to talk for the first time: "Give drinks for everybody."

Today Danijel is taller than I am, and is working in his father's construction company. This was, I believe, the first miracle in Medjugorje, and after that one, many more followed. I would need a lot of time to write down all of them.

The Communist police started to prosecute and harass pilgrims. I was taken into the police for interrogations. They followed me and harassed me up till 1990. Yugoslavia started to fall apart. My mother demanded that I go to live in Germany with my aunt. At first I didn't follow my mother's advice, but after the war started in the Croatian and Slovenian parts of Yugoslavia, I filled out an application for a passport, and to my surprise, I received it in two weeks on Friday. It just so happened that Ivan was on vacation and was heading back to Frankfurt where he was living at that time. So I left my home on Sunday morning with Ivan and was in Frankfurt that night. Monday morning the military police came to my home to arrest me.

I feel that Gospa, like my mother did for me, is doing the same for us. The devil is working hard to get our souls and She knows that, and with loving "nagging" is trying to save us from the perils of hell. With us, and through us, She is trying to reach for many more.

Don't get discouraged that other people are not responding, because they are responding, like many of us did in the beginning. We hear testimony from somebody else, put it aside and then later we get it, and Medjugorje becomes a part of our life. With God's blessing and united in prayer we are making changes in our lives and lives of people around us.

God bless you all and Kraljice Mira Moli za nas (Queen of Peace, pray for us).

Editor's note: Mladen and his wife and children are now living in Colorado.

(12/09)
"I Took You to Bethlehem . . ."

By Thomas Rutkoski

At the age of 16, I walked away from my Catholic faith. As a non-practicing Catholic for over twenty-five years, I lived life for myself. My life was very materialistic and laced with enough sin to guarantee me a place in hell, if I continued that course. This story, in short, tells of how Jesus and Mary brought me to conversion.

I am a professional photo-journalist. In September of 1982, I left with a crew from KDKA TV NEWS for Beirut, Lebanon, to follow the tour of Senator Arlen Specter. Our mission was twofold; first to do a story on war-torn Beirut, then to obtain an interview with Manachem

Begin in Jerusalem. I, with my colleagues, persevered, and we were successful on both counts.

The night of the Beirut interview, we all went out and celebrated, before heading back to the United States. A strange thing occurred. I was sitting at the dinner table, and about halfway through my meal, a man came up to me on my left. He said, "Excuse me, how have you liked Jerusalem?" Being a little reluctant about speaking to strangers, I simply replied, "Fine." I went back to eating. The man persisted. "Is there anything you would have liked to have seen that you have not seen?" Offhandedly I responded, "Yeah, Bethlehem, Christmas and all that." "I have a car outside. Come, I will take you there," he replied.

Why I left with that man, I don't know, but I did. He took me to Bethlehem. We drove through a gate, he stopped the car and I got out. I was only in Bethlehem for a moment. A strong emotion immediately overwhelmed me. My eyes swelled, and I started to cry. He got out of the car and asked me if everything was all right. I said yes. He told me to get in and he would take me back to the hotel. He dropped me off, and the next day I left for home.

In October of 1985, my Uncle Stanley, a very good friend of mine, and I, decided to take a trip to Europe that included traveling through France. What was not on the itinerary was a stop we made at a shrine to the Blessed Mother called Lourdes. Again, a strange set of circumstances led us there. Although at the time, I didn't connect it with Bethlehem, the same phenomena occurred. For no apparent reason, tears started rolling down my face, and I got a very powerful feeling in my flesh. This feeling came as I was making fun of Lourdes and its miraculous water and cures. Did this change my life? No, unfortunately it did not.

In 1986, the thirst for overseas travel struck again. Two of my friends joined my wife and me for our vacation through several European countries. After two weeks, our friends returned home. My wife and I continued to Madrid, Spain, and up into France. While traveling to Lisbon, Portugal, for our departure to the U.S., another strange set of circumstances caused a deviation in our planned route. This time, we happened upon a shrine to the Blessed Mother called Fatima. The same scenario occurred as at Lourdes. While looking at a statue of the Blessed Mother, I said, "Hi there. It's me again." Immediately, tears started to roll down my face. I got the same feeling as I did in Lourdes and Bethlehem, but I was, for the third time, to leave a very holy place unchanged.

In August of 1987, my Uncle Stanley visited my home with a small newspaper that reported the apparitions of the Blessed Mother to six children in Medjugorje, Yugoslavia. The non-religious atmosphere in which I lived, led me to poke fun at the article, but the story did give me a bizarre idea. If I could convince my employer, KDKA TV, to buy into the story about Medjugorje, I would get a trip overseas. Their response was negative. Being persistent, I initiated an effort to find a connection linking Pittsburgh to Medjugorje. I wanted to generate some interest at KDKA. In my search, I found a man by the name of Pat Geinzer. Pat was quitting his job as a radiologist at Mercy Hospital and going into the priesthood. [He has since been ordained as a member of the Passionists.] I contacted Pat. After listening to his amazing story, I left with a book he gave me called, *The Queen of Peace Visits Medjugorje.*

Not being much of a reader, because one of my many physical problems is dyslexia, I carried the book around for quite a while, not reading it. While sitting on my boat at the Fox Chapel Yacht Club, one of my favorite former pastimes, I found myself very much alone, and there was the book, lying on the seat beside me. I picked the book up, and my usual problems with reading didn't bother me. I soon found myself immersed in reading about Mary's apparitions in Medjugorje. It was in the third chapter of this book that the course was charted for the remaining years of my life. A voice spoke to me and said, *"Thomas, I took you to Bethlehem; I took you to Lourdes; I took you to Fatima. Can't you understand that this is real?"*

There was no need for further communication from the Lord; I knew it was Jesus. That profound revelation took me from my boat to the closest Catholic church in a matter of moments. I found the pastor and made my first confession in twenty-five years.

Between that visit to the priest and my first trip to Medjugorje in September of 1987, I truly came to believe that the Blessed Virgin Mary was appearing there. I would learn just how real Her presence was on that first trip. I experienced many miracles on my first pilgrimage. The miracle of the sun was amazing, but it paled in comparison to my apparition of the Blessed Mother. I was praying the Rosary behind St. James Church when I glanced at the cross [on Mt. Krizevac]. I was moved to tears again. One would think that would be as good as it gets, but the grand finale occurred Thursday of that week. My traveling companion, Uncle Stanley, badgered me into going to St. James Church for a healing service. Although I rejected the idea of the healing service itself, I went, and I was cured of rheumatoid arthritis. One minute the pain of the disease was destroying me, and the next, it was gone! [Also, my dyslexia was taken away; a wart on my right hand disappeared, and my hemorrhoids disappeared!]

The impact of all this led me to return home and find a local travel agent to book a pilgrimage space for Medjugorje. It was my intent to fulfill a promise I made to the Lord: "I will bring a hundred people here just to say thank you for what You're doing for me." I returned to Medjugorje the following year with 101 pilgrims that the Lord put in my care. I said to the Lord, "If You want someone to lead people here from the heart, rather than the pocketbook, I might consider it." When you give your life to Christ and live the messages of Medjugorje, you have to be careful what you say to the Lord, because He might take you seriously . . . and He did.

In 1990, I founded a Catholic, nonprofit foundation dedicated to evangelization and humanitarian efforts, called Gospa Missions. Although I had decided that I was not going to tell one person that God spoke to me, it was the Lord who drew it from me. He placed me in a situation that forced the words from my mouth. This caused much religious activity in my life, and I began speaking in churches all over the country and in Canada. In April of 1991, I quit my job at KDKA TV to devote my life to Jesus and Mary.

The Lord spoke to me in August of 1987, and has never stopped speaking to me since. He transformed me from a very self-centered, materialistic individual to one who daily attends Mass and prays fifteen decades of the Rosary. I also fast twice a week as Mary asks. I deliver to the world the same message that my Mother in Medjugorje is delivering: **"I have come to tell the world that God exists."** How could I have been such a fool for twenty-five years is beyond my comprehension. Now I am trying to do all that I can to convince everyone I meet that prayer works, if you pray out of love from your heart.

Editor's note: The above story was taken with permission from the Fall, 1995 issue of "The Queen of Peace" newspaper. Tom passed away on June 7, 2011. His mission continues. You can visit the website at www.gospa.org.

(8/07)
A Baby Cannot Lie

The following witness was given by pilgrimage leader Bernadette Burke of Pittsburgh, PA on April 27, 2007, at the Marian Prayer Group meeting in Ambridge, PA. Bernadette had just returned from a pilgrimage to Medjugorje.

We were in Marija's chapel. Her sister Ruzka takes care of the grounds when Marija is not there, and this is the first time we ever heard this witness.

Ruzka told us about the first days of the apparitions. She lived about 25 miles from Medjugorje at that time. She worked at a factory, and people were coming to her and saying, "Your sister is seeing the Blessed Mother back in Medjugorje. You better find out about that." She said, "What are you talking about?" They said, "We heard about your sister – she's sees the Blessed Mother every day." She said, "I haven't seen my sister. I don't know what's going on. I don't have a phone." (They didn't have phones in 1981 to call back and forth.) So this went on for three days and she couldn't take it any longer. She said usually she's an outgoing, friendly person, but this got to her, all these people talking about her, about her sister, like her sister was a little "cuckoo." And so she said that was it. She went home and said to her husband, "We have to go to Medjugorje to see my sister Marija. Something's going on there. Everybody's saying she's seeing the Blessed Mother. Now I don't know if my sister is crazy or what. I have to get there."

So when Ruzka arrived she saw her sister and her sister looked fine, and she said, "Marija, are you seeing the Blessed Mother every day?" Marija said, "Yes, She'll be here pretty soon. The visionaries will all be in the other room and we'll be praying. Come with us." Ruzka had four little children, the youngest was around 15-18 months, and so Ruzka had to hold the child. But naturally, at that age, they aren't going to stay with you – they want to wander. The little one went to the visionaries, in front of the visionaries, and started putting her hands up. What was she touching? Ruzka could not understand; she thought she was disturbing the apparition, so she was trying to get the little girl to come back. Then she figured she was making more commotion than the baby, so she let her go. Later Ruzka found out from Marija what was going on. Marija said that the baby wanted the Blessed Mother to pick her up, and the Blessed Mother smiled and put Her hand on the baby! (Usually the visionaries see nothing but Our Lady. Marija was given this grace to see the baby for the benefit of Ruzka and all those who will read this story.)

Ruzka was so happy because she said, "Marija, now I know you're not crazy. Why would my little one do that if there wasn't someone there?" And so she was crying with tears. She knew her sister wasn't crazy.

Then Ruzka and her husband went that evening to Mass, and while they were gone, this little one, she took Grandmom and Grandpap into the next room. She went in and looked at the place where she saw the Blessed Mother. She went back in and was playing with her things and minutes later back into the room. She said, "No." She kept going in that room all night, and finally when Ruzka and her husband came home, the grandparents said, "I'm so glad you're home. All we did all night was take that baby in and out of that room. Then she'd go in there and say, 'No.'" They said, "I don't know what she's looking for."

"She's looking for the Lady."

Editor's note: Sister Emmanuel recounted this story also and adds that a priest from Split observed the encounter during the apparition. He had come to Medjugorje to prove that the apparitions were a fake, but at that moment became, not only a believer, but a great defender of Medjugorje. In tears he kept saying, "A child cannot lie."

St. James Church in Medjugorje

(10/05)
Cancer and the Four Answered Prayers

By Walter Senoski

In July of 2004, I was diagnosed with a fatal cancer of the esophagus. The doctors gave me only three or four months to live, as it was quickly metastasizing.

I prayed to the Holy Trinity, and to Our Lady for a healing in Medjugorje. A few days later, I received a call from Father Michael telling me that he would offer daily Mass for me. I shared with him my prayer, and he said he was scheduled to go to Medjugorje, but had to change his plans. I received another phone call, telling me that I was given a complimentary ticket to Medjugorje, from March 31 to April 8, 2005. It was the same trip Father Michael planned on.

My second prayer was to play the "Ave Maria" on my harmonica in St. James Church for the Blessed Mother. This became a reality on our last day there at the 10 A.M. English Mass.

My third prayer was that I asked the Blessed Mother to make Her presence felt in the hearts of every person in that church. As I started to play my harmonica, many people began to hum and sing as softly as a room full of angels. The sound of their voices caused my eyes to tear, as it touched my heart. After Mass, a lady dressed in dark clothes, including a head scarf, tapped my hand twice and said, "Thank you!" For three weeks, I kept thinking of this lady with the warm smile, and then it hit me all at once that she was not an old lady at all, but a beautiful young woman! I knew in my heart that it was the Blessed Mother.

My fourth prayer was to play the Ave Maria for Pope John Paul II. We were to go to Rome and visit him. Our trip to Rome was cancelled, because he died the day after we arrived in Medjugorje. In May, I was invited to play the Ave Maria at a special tribute Mass for Pope John Paul II, held at the Immaculate Heart of Mary Church, on Polish Hill in Pittsburgh, PA, on June 11, 2005. I knew in my heart that John Paul was there to hear me play for him, as well as the Holy Trinity, the Blessed Mother, and the Angels, and Saints. I played one of my best performances ever.

Before leaving home for the trip, I imagined having my throat blessed in St. Blaise Church in Dubrovnik and being healed. Once in the church, I placed my camcorder facing a statue of Our Mother of Sorrows as I played the Ave Maria. After Communion, I noticed the camcorder had shut off, and the music had stopped. As I finished videotaping the Mass and blessing of throats, I had a sudden change come over my whole body. It started with a very cold sweat on top of my head, blurred vision, shaking hands and legs, a headache, pains in my chest and back. I had to sit down very quickly. Some doctors and nurses tried to help me but without success. Father Bill came out of the sacristy, placed his hands on my head and prayed over me then went away. I slowly began to regain composure and felt a change come over my body. In about an hour I felt like a new person. The next day when we climbed Cross Mountain, I was the first one to reach the top.

On April 19, 2005, I had a doctor's appointment and requested a test for my esophagus, an MRI from the waist up and a bone scan.

When I called the doctor's office they told me the results showed, "no sign of cancer."

I am in the process of writing a third book, *In Thanksgiving*, and again am praying to return to Medjugorje in thanksgiving for my wonderful blessing!

I recently received a call telling me I am being given a return trip to Medjugorje this September 7-23. Do you believe it? I will be celebrating my birthday on the 17th as a happy, thankful pilgrim. We will also visit, among other places in Italy, Rome, including Pope John Paul's tomb and also a papal audience with Pope Benedict XVI. I am so very grateful for God's healing and his blessings upon me. What a special way to celebrate my life.

Editor's note: Walter lives in Meadowlands, PA. His book called **In Thanksgiving** *is now available. You can visit his website at www.waltersenoski.com.*

(9/08)
The Physical and Spiritual Healing of David Parkes

By June Klins

In 1998, Irish singer David Parkes spoke at a retreat sponsored by Gospa Missions of Evans City, PA.

"It's funny how God works through your life. In spite of all we do against Him, in spite of how much we kick Him, He's just waiting for us to come back, standing there with open arms." David Parkes continued, "The story I want to share with you is a very human story. It is one of anger, hurt, guilt, but most all compassion."

David related that his story began in 1977, when he was 27. David was playing soccer professionally in Dublin, Ireland, and he and his wife Ann had two children. The little boy, Ken, was born with cystic fibrosis. In January of 1977, David won a major talent contest and a bright future in show business faced him. But in April of 1977, his whole world came tumbling down when he was diagnosed with Crohn's disease, described by David as "one of the most debilitating illnesses the medical community has to deal with." In the first six weeks after his diagnosis, David went from 220 pounds to 99 pounds. Over the next decade he had eight major surgeries for this illness.

On Christmas Eve of 1988, he had his ninth surgery, and it was unsuccessful, so it had to be repeated two weeks later. After an 11 hour surgery, the surgeon admitted that there was nothing else he could do, and David had about 12 to 14 weeks left to live. Eight weeks after this surgery, his band held a benefit concert for him. The tickets said that the benefit was for David's "funeral expenses."

At this concert a man, who was a travel agent specializing in pilgrimages to Medjugorje, offered a free trip for David and Ann. David knew a little about Medjugorje, because he and Ann had spent their honeymoon in Dubrovnik, and every time Ann would hear things about Medjugorje, she would share it with David. But David was not interested in hearing about anything religious. "I didn't want any part of it," he said, "because in 1982, you see, God and I parted company. There were two main reasons for this. The first one had to do with Ken. I couldn't understand how this loving God could inflict such an illness on a newborn baby." The second reason had to do with himself. As he was getting progressively worse from the Crohn's, he wondered why God was giving him so many crosses. So David decided to put God totally out of his life. He told Ann and the kids not to go to Mass, and not even to pray in the house. He also told Ann to get rid of the statues and crucifixes in the house.

Although a religious pilgrimage did not appeal to him at all, he had always wanted to go back to Yugoslavia, so he accepted the trip as a "holiday," not as a "pilgrimage." In April of 1989, he and Ann set out for Yugoslavia. David had a few rules for Ann on this trip: She was not to mention religion and was not to pray in his company.

As David shuffled to the departure gate, he became very conscious of a man sitting in the front row. The man had a hood up over his head. The travel agent introduced David to the hooded man, Fr. Peter Mary Rookey. As they shook hands, David felt threatened because, in his words, "an aura of love came from Father at me. The last thing you want if you're away from the Church is an aura of love to come at you, especially from a priest." So David insulted Fr. Rookey. It was so bad that the travel agent considered leaving David behind!

David was in terrible pain, and the three hour ride from Dubrovnik was very hard for him. After a rest stop on the way from Dubrovnik, the tour director got on the microphone and announced, "We are approximately one hour from Medjugorje, and I would like us all to recite the Rosary." David went berserk! Ann told him to be quiet as he was making a spectacle of himself. The real surprise, though, came when they arrived in Medjugorje and he found out that there are no hotels there and that you stay in people's homes. The house he was staying in was not even fully built. There was no roof. As he protested that the house did not have a roof, the tour director said, "Oh, it will next year when you come back."

David was so weak at this point that he could not even carry any of the suitcases. As they were led into their room, David thought this was the smallest room he had ever been in, and what was worse was that there were only two bathrooms for the house, and 16 people staying there. "I need a bathroom to myself," David protested. "I've two weeks to live." He was so angry that he told Ann that in the morning he was packing up and going to Dubrovnik.

The next morning, Ann talked David into going to Mass, which was to be celebrated by Fr. Rookey. David ended up giving his seat to some elderly ladies and had to stand in agony for an hour and a half. He said his only interest in Mass was counting the pieces in the stained glass windows. He also counted 16 candles and 14 priests, but Fr. Rookey was not amongst them! He felt he had been conned into going to Mass.

After Mass, Ann told David that Fr. Rookey was having a healing service in the graveyard. David did not want any part of it, but Ann promised him that if he went, then when it was over, she would pack up with him and they would go to Dubrovnik together. So David reluctantly agreed.

As he approached the little graveyard behind St. James, he could see about 600 people on three sides, and Fr. Rookey and three other Irish priests in the middle. David watched as the first person got blessed. Fr. Rookey anointed him with oil, traced the Sign of the Cross on the person's forehead and then placed his hands on the person's head. Immediately that person fell to the ground. The same thing happened with the next person, and the next five people. David wondered what was going on.

He left for a bit, and when he came back he described the area as looking like a battlefield, with bodies lying all over. "Ann, this is hypocrisy," he said. "Those Franciscan priests should not allow this to happen." Ann asked him to have a blessing. He said, "Remember, Ann, I am an atheist. I don't believe in God." But Ann retorted, "It would do you good." David left and came back 20 minutes later and Ann pleaded with him for two hours before he finally submitted to having a blessing.

As Fr. Rookey approached David he said, "David, there's something you want to tell me." David looked him straight in the eyes and said, "Father, I don't wish to speak with you. I'm very ill and the doctors say I've maybe two weeks to live." Fr. Rookey reached into his pocket and pulled out a black crucifix containing seven relics of the seven founders of the Servite order, the Servants of Mary. He placed the crucifix in David's right hand and anointed him with oil on his forehead, and then he placed his hands on David's head and began to pray. The next thing David remembered was that he was lying flat on his back. When he opened his eyes, a famous politician from Dublin was standing over him. Embarrassed to be in that position, David said, "Who hit me?" The man said, "Parkes, the Spirit is with you very strongly. You've been out for 20 minutes."

David felt an intense burning heat from the top of his head to the tip of his toes. "I've never, ever had that sensation before, prior to Medjugorje or since Medjugorje, but from that day, all the pains and aches associated with Crohn's Disease have disappeared."

Two days after returning from Medjugorje, David had an appointment with the surgeon, who got the surprise of his life. The David Parkes walking into his office was not bent over in pain, but now walked upright and was four pounds heavier. The surgeon said, "David, whatever you're doing, keep doing it." The surgeon sent him for a week's worth of intensive testing which confirmed that there was no sign of Crohn's anywhere in David's body.

"I also had an incredible spiritual healing," David declared. "At this time in my life I was very troubled." Ken's disease weighed heavily on his shoulders and caused tension in their marriage. In August of 1987, David left Ann and the kids and got involved with another woman. He went home, but in January of 1988, he left again. He had even contemplated suicide. In June of that year, he went back home.

After the physical healing, the desire to leave Medjugorje was gone. "All of a sudden this little village began to take on something very special," he said. Ann helped him climb Apparition Hill. As he sat there looking at the twin towers of St. James, he had the urge to pray, but he couldn't remember the words of the prayers. He was agitated that he could not remember the words, and Ann sensed something was wrong. They embraced and he began to apologize for all the hurt he caused Ann, their children and their parents. Ann started to cry and then David began to cry. They cried in each others' arms for about 10 minutes. When they stopped, David said, "I had the most incredible peace, an inner peace that seemed to allow me to live with myself, and I honestly feel that if we don't have that inner peace within us, it is impossible to converse with anyone else."

David continued, "The graces that I received in Medjugorje have stayed with me till this very day and you know, if Jesus came in beside me and said, 'I want to put you to the test. I'll put you back in the mental state you were in 1989, and I would inflict a physical ailment on you, and I will offer you one healing, which one is it to be?' – there would be no hesitation. I would jump in and say to Jesus, 'I will have the spiritual healing.' I could accept any form of physical ailment You want to give me, because I would accept it as a form of penance – penance for the wrongs I've done in my life. But I could not be without the love of Jesus. It's given me a whole new meaning to life, a whole new will to love life, but most important of all, a will to live life the way that Jesus would want me to live life, not for David Parkes to live in David Parkes' old form of religion."

"That's my story. From that day on, my whole life changed. In September of 1993, I gave up my secure job with the band, a band I had played with for 14 years . . . I decided I wanted to do the work of the Lord. I am the most surprised person in the world to be standing here before you talking about God, talking about His Mercy, talking about His love."

David is now an international Catholic recording artist. Since his healing, he has traveled extensively telling his story and giving concerts. At the present time, David is working in Medjugorje as Pilgrimage Director for Marian Pilgrimages which is based in Dublin, Ireland. If you are ever in Medjugorje, try to find out which day he is giving a free concert in the yellow building behind St. James. You won't regret it!

(8/05)
The Medjugorje Pamphlet

By Fr. Tony Gargotta

I believe I was called to the priesthood when I was young. I first heard the call in sixth grade, but especially heard it in high school. I put the call off for many reasons, including many selfish ones. I went off to school and work and dating, for 15 years, and every time the call came back, I ignored it. Although I had lived a very prayerful life and a life very close to the Lord, after high school when I decided to not enter seminary, I began to lead a very sinful life.

When both of my grandmothers were sick, and one was dying, I was sleeping at the hospital with them. Although I was living a sinful life, I was also trying to do good in the world, mixed with the evil. I was helping take care of some people in extreme circumstances. One day coming out of church (I still went to Sunday Mass although I was sinning much), I saw a pamphlet on Medjugorje. I took it to read at the hospital and it caught my attention so severely. I was so drawn by it. I saw the five messages and said to myself, this is how I used to live in high school. What happened to me? So I decided to go to weekday Mass for one week, like I had in high school. By the fourth day, I was so "aware" of my sins, I was sick. I went to Confession, and began going to daily Mass. Since then, I have gone to daily Mass everyday with the exception of maybe two or three times a year. I have gone to Mass almost every day since May of 1990.

Well, then I took the information down to my friend in Washington, DC, who I had went to high school with in Pittsburgh, and showed him. He had been far away from church in general. He then called me a few days later and said he reserved a spot for me on this trip to Medjugorje with him and most of his family. I never planned on going to Medjugorje, just living the messages, but with God's Grace, we went. It was awesome. I could never explain it all. While I was there I began to think of the priesthood in a way I had never done before that, although as I said I had thought about it many times. When I returned to Pittsburgh, I decided I would still date my girlfriend and marry her. But she never accepted the messages and the change in my life. As I grew closer to God and my parish, I grew farther away from my girlfriend, until the day I went to a priest I knew and told him I had these thoughts of being a priest. He helped me begin the discernment process, and of course my girlfriend and I broke up. I entered the seminary at the age of 33, and on May 26, 2001, at the age of 38, I was ordained a priest for the Diocese of Pittsburgh, PA. I currently serve as the parochial vicar at St. Bernadette Church in Monroeville, PA.

Editor's note: As of this writing, Fr. Tony is now the pastor at St. Bernadette Catholic Church in Monroeville, PA.

(12/05)
Do Not Worry About Tomorrow . . .

By Carolanne Kilichowski

Our Lady has called all Her children to read a certain Bible reading, every single Thursday. It is Matthew 6:24-34. There is one person I know who reads this passage every single day! She is Amy Betros from Buffalo, New York. If you read the passage, Our Lord tells us not to worry – to trust that He will provide for our needs. So why does Amy read this every day? Amy has ownership of an old church in the heart of Buffalo, St. Luke's. It is now known as, "Mission of Mercy." I will backtrack a bit and tell you a little about Amy's conversion before I really answer that question.

In 1989, Amy owned a restaurant called, "Amy's Place." Her cousin, Anna Lahood, upon returning from Medjugorje, gave Amy a Medjugorje chaplet and Wayne Weible's paper. Amy said that she cried for a week after reading the paper, learning all about Our Lady's visits to Medjugorje and asking Her children to convert their hearts. She felt a healing come over her as she read with all of her heart the words on that paper. Then it was on New Years Eve of that year, that she saw a movie on the Arts and Entertainment channel called, "The Lasting Sign," by Martin Sheen. This movie and the Wayne Weible paper changed Amy's whole life. Father Svet's words, "Search for God in your own way and be a visionary yourself," also made a lasting impression.

A month later, a lady came into the restaurant and told her that if she went to Medjugorje it would totally change her life. But how could she go? She had a business to run, she could not afford to go, she was working 80 hours a week to quench her desire to retire at 40 years old. Besides, she only had one week off a year! What would be the chance of being able to go? Her cousin Anna was planning a trip and asked her, since Amy said she would not go without her. They looked into a local trip and the date was the exact week she had off, May 29th. Amy's mother even said she would pay for the trip!

So off Amy went to Medjugorje with an open heart and a strong desire for God. Amy says it was a miracle that she climbed the hills, as she says that she has bad knees. She actually climbed Apparition Hill three times! The climb up Cross Mountain changed her life after seeing tongues of fire the night before at the Cross. At the 12th Station of the Cross, the priest kept repeating, "Jesus died just for you . . . JUST FOR YOU . . ." Amy wept as her heart was being transformed anew filling with God's love. Amy says that conversion comes when we know that God loves us, and that we all have a responsibility to share that love. We are "apostles of the last days."

When Amy returned from Medjugorje, she met Norm Paolini on a trip to Fatima, and together they formed a team to purchase St. Luke's in order to do acts of mercy and live the message of Divine Mercy and of Medjugorje. When Amy walked into the church, the image of the Divine Mercy was painted on the side altar and she knew she had to have this church to do God's work. God was calling her to a new life of sacrifice and love. They purchased this church on trust – trust that if God wanted this to happen, He would provide the means to purchase it. Amy was no longer owner of, "Amy's Place," but a real live Catholic Church!

St. Luke's Mission of Mercy is all about showing people that God loves them. Amy evangelizes to the poor, the hungry, the alcoholic, the prostitute, the homeless, and anyone in need of God's word. She provides them food, clothing and shelter and a place to pray and sleep until they can get on their own feet. At St. Luke's they learn all about the mercy and love of God.

So why does Amy read that particular Matthew passage on trust? Many times at St. Luke's there is no food, no way to pay the gas bill or any other bill that comes. She is doing God's work – "a present-day Mother Theresa." God watches over her as she trusts with all of her heart . . . as someone suddenly appears at her door with a check in just the amount she needed that day to feed the people at the Mission of Mercy. I am confident that Amy could fill a book with stories of how she received exact amounts of money for her needs. People roll up their sleeves and answer the call to help Amy and Norm in the capacity that they are called. Some give old clothes; some their time to work at the church or with comforting the people in need; some who are able, give generous donations as they can afford. There are even Associates that commit to giving of their time and energy for a full year at St. Luke's. There is also a musical group with wonderful voices, along with Norm Paolini. They sing like angels raising their voices high to the heavens!

Amy is an example of what we all should be. She radiates her love to all that she meets. Her life is fulfilling others' needs and in loving God. Amy's group of missionaries even go out to parishes and give retreats to talk about trust and mercy and love. What better way to follow the way of Saint Faustina, than to live and teach acts of mercy on a daily basis.

"Dear children! I am inviting you to a complete surrender to God. Pray, little children, that Satan may not carry you about like the branches in the wind. Be strong in God. I desire that through you the whole world may get to know the God of joy. By your life bear witness for God's joy. Do not be anxious nor worried. God himself will help you and show you the way. I desire that you love all men with my love. Only in that way can love reign over the world" (Our Lady, 5/25/88).

Editor's note: Carolanne lives in Hamburg, NY, and is a Felician Franciscan Associate. To learn more about St. Luke's Mission of Mercy, you can visit their website at www.stlukesmissionofmercy.org.

Apparition Hill

(11/06)
In Front of Mary's Statue

By Sr. Emmanuel

A medical doctor, Bernard, came to Medjugorje for the first time this week. Even though he was baptized, Bernard violently rejected God and his faith at the age of 12. In 1998, thanks to some Catholic friends, a move toward conversion took root in his heart, but his spiritual life remained cloudy.

A couple of days ago, he went by himself to Apparition Hill. Seeing some trash thrown around here and there, he decided to clean up the area. He began by picking up the rubbish and putting it in a bag. All at once, he was overwhelmed by the feeling that Our Lady was calling him to pray in front of Her statue. But he ignored the call and continued cleaning up. A thought then came clear and loud in his mind: "It is fine to pick up trash, but I'd better take care of the 'trash' in my own heart and put it at the foot of Mary." The call became so strong and irrepressible that finally Bernard fell to his knees in front of the statue.

As soon as he began to pray, horrible scenes from his past, that he had forgotten a long time ago, came back to him! The name of a woman came very clearly to his mind and wouldn't leave him. It was the name of a patient, one among the thousands he had encountered during his medical career. This name in particular was from 35 years ago! As he prayed, he could see himself that night as a young medical student working in the hospital. He was placed in the ward for terminally ill patients. Without consulting the patient or asking anyone else for permission – something that was against the rules – he injected her with a high dose of morphine. He was well aware of the enormous risk for the patient, but because of the hardness of his heart and his selfish desire to try a new experiment, he did not hesitate one second. The next morning the woman was dead.

In front of Mary's statue, Bernard saw himself the way he was long ago, stuffed with pride and committing the most heinous sins. Each sin came up from the depths of his heart and was shown to him very clearly. Bernard was indeed cleaning up his own garbage; he was even mystified by the experience! He never thought he was holding within him such a pile of garbage! However, under the loving and non-judgmental gaze of Mary, in this most anointed encounter with his Heavenly Mother, Bernard did not lose hope. On the contrary, filled with a sincere repentance, he decided to throw all of those horrors into the Heart of Jesus so that He could burn them forever. Bernard ran to Confession and received the gift of a very profound interior peace, a peace he had been searching for and that had been eluding him for so long! This is the gift that Mary, Mother of Peace, had in store for this very dear son of Hers, here in Medjugorje!

This example shows us very clearly how the Mother of God works: She attracts to Her the sheep damaged by evil; She casts a light of grace onto them with gentleness and tremendous power; and, through Her beautiful, merciful gaze She gives them the desire to purify themselves; and then She brings them to Her sons – our priests!

A sinner who throws himself into the hands of Mary does not remain stuck to his sins for very long! Furthermore, a priest who works with Mary is a happy priest and never jobless in the confessional: he collects the lost sheep from the hands of Mary and brings them to Jesus!

Dearest Gospa, we place ourselves under your maternal gaze. Please help us purify and change our lives! Rescue us from the oppression of sin, so we may have life!

Children of Medjugorje, www.childrenofmedjugorje.com

(10/09)
"Receive My Mercy and Forgiveness Now!"

By Barbara Kleaveland

It was May of 1986. I was a single mother of a young son, and engaged to be married in August. My gynecologist told me that I was probably not pregnant, but as a precaution, he had a procedure that would take care of the problem. He assured me it was not an abortion and that it was too early to tell if I was pregnant. My fiancé informed me that there would be no wedding if I did not have this procedure. He reminded me that I had already conceived a child out of wedlock. What would people think, if it happened again? I was sitting on the examining table when the doctor walked in. "I have some bad news," he said. "You were pregnant, and my staff have all quit. They told me if I performed one more abortion they would leave." I left his office feeling shame and remorse. This abortion became my deep, dark secret. The marriage took place, and we soon had a baby boy, but it all ended a few years later. Relationships usually fall apart after abortion takes place. In the years to follow, I had two more abortions.

Coming home from the third abortion, I felt a presence in the car. I knew at once that it was my child, and she was a girl. I begged her to forgive me. With tears pouring down my face, I realized that abortion was murder. I was never the same again.

A few months later, I started having panic attacks. I had several while driving my car home from work, and soon I became paralyzed with fear. I never went anywhere, unless someone could drive me. For seven years I did not drive my car into town. My past played over and over in my mind. I was sure that I could never be forgiven for what I had done. My oldest brother called me one day and said, "I don't know what is wrong with you, but I want to tell you that the Blessed Mother is appearing to six children in Medjugorje, Yugoslavia. She is asking us to put God first in our lives and to pray for peace. Barb, you need peace more than anyone I know." When I was growing up, I had a deep love for Our Lady, and the excitement of Her apparitions sparked a new faith in me. A few days later, I received a rosary and a Scriptural Rosary book as a birthday gift from him. I started praying the Rosary, and Our Lady went to work.

The anxiety was getting worse, so I went to see a psychologist, and he happened to be Catholic. For the first time, I was able to tell someone about my abortions. He insisted that I go to the sacrament of Confession. This scared me to no end, but I was given a special grace to go. I will never forget the relief I felt when I was able to unburden myself of my sins. The priest, standing in for Jesus, made me feel loved and accepted. When I walked out of the confessional, I was totally forgiven of all my sins, but it would take time for me to forgive myself. That was OK, because the spiritual doors of my soul were now open for grace to come flooding in.

During my years of anxiety, I tried to relax by doing yoga and meditation. This led me to a new age book written by a well-known actress. Since I had gone to Confession, I started to feel uneasy about this book, and so I asked the Lord to show me if it was evil. The next day, at a family reunion, my sister-in-law, out of the clear blue, mentioned this book by name, and said it was evil. She then said, "We are so blessed to be Catholic. We have the Sacraments and that is all we need."

My cousins from Pittsburgh were there, and they had just come back from Medjugorje. Once again I was stirred spiritually by their stories. They had also been to a retreat in Malvern, PA, and had copies of the talks on tape, which were given to me. I started the first tape, and heard a woman say, "I want to show you how to fall madly in love with the Lord Jesus Christ, through the Sacraments of the Catholic Church." The third tape was on the Holy Eucharist. The woman told about her Protestant friend who was a cripple. She did not believe that Jesus was truly present – Body, Blood, Soul and Divinity, in the Host. If she did, she would fall on her hands and knees to receive Him. At that moment, my entire body was burning up. I knew in my head that the Eucharist was Jesus, but now I knew it in my heart. I decided that I had to receive Him often, and I would be healed. To do this, I would have to overcome a phobia of driving.

One day, I decided that if I professed to love Jesus, I had to trust. I sprinkled holy water over my car, grabbed Our Lady's weapon, the rosary, and asked the Holy Family to come with me. It was one of the hardest things I have ever done. When I knelt down before Mass, I looked up at a life-size crucifix over the altar and said, "Jesus, I am here, but I'm never going to make it home." I then heard these words, "If you come, I will always get you home." I went from going to Mass periodically to becoming a daily communicant.

My brother counsels post-abortive women for Project Rachel. He explained to our family the steps he uses to heal post-abortive women, and I was all ears. "First," he said, "she has to remember her abortion. It is very painful and sometimes blocked from her memory. I then ask her to imagine Jesus coming with her baby. Jesus hands her the child, and I ask her if it is a boy or a girl. She seems to know instinctively. She then names her baby, asks her child to forgive her, and symbolically baptizes the baby. Finally, Jesus takes the baby back to Heaven."

I decided that I was going to try this on my own. Through many tears, I was able to name my children: William, Mary, and Jeanne. My children really took on an identity after this, and I decided to write a song for them. It had to remain a secret though, just like they were. I could not afford to let anyone find out about my abortions, for fear of what they would think of me.

A church in town put on a Life in the Spirit Seminar, and I attended. The last night I noticed people being prayed over. This kind of scared me, but a friend insisted I go up. A woman surrounded by five people laid hands on me. After a few seconds I was resting in the spirit. All of a sudden she pulled me up and said, "What is wrong with you?" Not wanting to bring up the abortions, I said the problem was my husband. When she asked what my husband did to me, I knew I had to confess. I answered in trepidation, "He convinced me to have an abortion." Well, they all started praying and then I heard these words: "Come on, tell them you had three." So I blurted out, "I've had three abortions." A man groaned in pain, and then I heard a stern voice say, "Receive My mercy and forgiveness now!" I knew that I was not accepting God's forgiveness. I then heard it again, "Receive My mercy and forgiveness now." When I heard it the third time it scared me. I felt as though it was now or never, and I let it all go. Peace flooded into my heart. They say the truth shall set you free, and so it did. That evening, I sang the song that I had written in secret for my children.

The next day, I went early to Mass and felt as though everyone in the church knew that I had three abortions. I looked up at the St. Joseph Statue and asked him to help me. I heard these words in my heart, "Jesus has forgiven you, so what do you care?" That really eased my mind.

After Mass, I decided it was time to tell my parents. As we sat around the table, with all the courage I could muster, I explained to them the reason I had been so filled with anxiety. For seven years, they had driven me wherever I needed to go. Before I could even finish, they jumped up and wrapped their arms around me. They assured me that they would always love me, no matter what I had done. With tears in my eyes, I sang the song written for their grandchildren, William, Mary and Jeanne. On the way home, I decided to tell my two sons. I had to apologize to them, because I put them through a lot over the years. After singing to them, my youngest son said, "Mom, can I say something?" I replied, "Yes, what is it?" He then said something that I will never forget, "I'm glad it wasn't me." I replied, "I am, too."

I wanted to tell my oldest brother, since he was so instrumental in helping me, but I just could not find a way to do it. Finally I sent him a letter.

In 1995, I was invited to go to Ireland with three friends. I told them that it was impossible, with my phobia of flying and the lack of funds, but I said I would pray. A few weeks later my mother came into some money quite unexpectedly, and offered to pay my way. I went down to the beach and, while praying the Rosary, I felt joy – something I had not experienced in a long time. All of a sudden, I smelled roses, and I knew that Our Lady was calling me to Ireland.

On the way to the airport I was so fearful; I wondered how I would be able to fly without fainting. All of a sudden, I heard a man's voice say, "When will you trust Me?" I instinctively knew it was Jesus. He then said, "Do you know how happy I would be if you would just trust Me?" I wanted to make Jesus happy, and so in my heart I just said, "OK, Jesus, I will trust You." At that very moment my fear completely vanished. I yelled out, "Alleluia, my fear is gone!" I boarded our airplane without a hitch.

Our first night in Ireland, we went to Maynooth. We visited a priest who told us about the Inter-generational Healing Masses that he was saying. He then said, "If a woman has had an abortion, we say prayers for the baby, too." I began to cry, because he did not know about my abortions or that I had been praying to have a Mass like this said for me. I am Irish, and what better place to pray for my ancestors than Ireland. Father agreed to offer the Mass for me the day before we were to leave for the States. During the Mass, Father prayed for the release of mental illness in my family. All at once, a gush of wind came from my chest and blew up through my head with such a force it threw me backwards. I couldn't help but think of the demons Jesus cast from Mary Magdalene. After the Mass I was given some wonderful advice: visit the Blessed Sacrament often, attend daily Mass, go to weekly Confession, and pray the Rosary daily. This would bring about a total healing.

In 1996, my dream came true. I was able to go to Medjugorje with the help of some good friends who were also going. Most of the people that attended daily Mass went, and that made it even more special. The war was ending, and we were able to bring supplies to an orphanage and a refugee camp. We saw the sun spin, the moon dance, and the cross light up at night, but the most wonderful thing of all was the peace that enveloped us. There is nothing else like it on earth.

The following year, I went back to Ireland. When we arrived in Maynooth, I was asked to give my first witness talk to a prayer group that was meeting that evening. All the readings that night were on fear, and it was pretty comical because I was scared to death. When I got up to speak, the Holy Spirit took over and the fear left. My son had come on the trip with me, and when I took my seat next to him, he said, "Oh Mom, I am so proud of you." After telling about my past, I wondered if the Irish people would think poorly of me, but my fears were relieved when, one by one, they came up and hugged me.

After my return, the long awaited letter from my brother finally arrived. I choked back the tears, as I read these words: "Praised be Jesus and Mary. The cloud is lifted. Your children now are in Heaven. Pray to them, as they are your greatest advocates."

Editor's note: Barbara is from N. Muskegon, MI. She now helps with Rachel's Vineyard retreats and her testimony and song to her children can be seen on YouTube.

(8/06)
Arm in Arm with My Guardian Angel

By Virginia Hogue

My heart was pounding with joy, for the day had finally arrived. I would begin my journey to Medjugorje. It turned out to be a journey I couldn't have anticipated in my wildest dreams.

When I arrived at the airport I learned my plane was going to be late. I feared a domino effect would cause me to miss my connecting flights and end my trip before it started. Luckily, my Lady, Mary, was with me, and I made it to my first destination, New York City, on time.

While I had made it to New York, neither of my suitcases had. I spent several hours in pursuit of my bags. With less than an hour to go before I left the security of the United States, one of my suitcases was finally found.

My heart was still racing with excitement; I would be leaving New York, then on to Vienna, and finally Sarajevo after nine short hours. In route, somewhere over the Atlantic, I was waiting in line for the restroom, when a young woman came up behind me. I could tell right away that she was not feeling well. I quickly grabbed an air sickness bag, opened it and held it at the ready for her. Even with my assistance, she managed to miss the bag completely and hit the next thing in her line of fire – me! While I felt sorry for the girl, my spirits still weren't dampened.

When I arrived in Sarajevo, my now lone suitcase was once again missing in action. The airport personnel there told me, "We will find it and deliver it to you in Medjugorje." Despite possessing but one vomit-stained outfit, my excitement still grew. I was now but a short two hour bus ride from Medjugorje.

Halfway between Sarajevo and Medjugorje the bus developed mechanical difficulties. It took hours to fix. For me, this was the final straw. All the excitement I had been feeling for weeks just drained out of me. I was hot, dirty, exhausted, and literally, had only the clothes on my back. I was almost ready to convert to Buddhism!

When, at last, I arrived in Medjugorje, my first sight was that of St. James Church. For me, this was a dream come true. I began to feel the joy return. It was short-lived though, when I found that there was no room for me to stay at the home of the visionary Ivanka, where I had been told I would stay.

A sense of calm returned, however, when Ivanka compassionately patted me on the leg as she drove me to find housing. A spot was found for me in a home close to town, near St. James Church. Not only could I actually see it from the balcony of my room, but I could also hear the sounds of the church broadcast over loudspeakers.

My first night in Medjugorje I began what would turn out to be a daily ritual. I washed out my one outfit in a basin the size of a medium mixing bowl. Then I would carefully hang it on my balcony to dry so that it would be ready to wear the next day. This system worked fairly well, except for my blue jeans which I put on damp each morning.

I am a very proud person. I am very attentive to my personal appearance, clothes and hair. In the past, I have prayed to Mary to make me like Her, more humble. She answered my prayers. It was very humbling to have none of my regular grooming products, and to wear the same outfit for seven days. I guess you should be careful what you pray for!

The next day I went to get a closer look at St. James Church. On the way back, I somehow made a wrong turn and found myself lost in a strange country with people who did not speak my language. Due to the last minute changes of accommodations, I didn't know the address or name of the people at whose home I was staying. To make matters worse, the temperature, which was supposed to be in the mid-eighties, had soared into the triple digits. It would reach as high as 112. (They said this was an event unprecedented in over 400 years.) I didn't know what to do, and I was beginning to feel the effects of the heat. I noticed a young Croatian girl in her front yard. She didn't speak any English, but, nonetheless, I told her, "I need help. I am lost and I am sick." She took me into her home, gave me a glass of water, and left to find someone who spoke English. About 15 minutes later she returned with a woman who spoke broken English. With Mary's help they got me back to the house where I was staying. In the heat, my feet, ankles and legs had swelled to three times their size. My roommate said they looked like barrels. That night, and every night after that, was spent sleeping on the balcony because the house had no air conditioning.

By this time I had been in Medjugorje less than two days and I was ready to go home. I was battling with Satan and he seemed to be winning. I stayed up all night praying the Rosary. I asked Mary to change my attitude, and not let Satan beat me. By morning my prayers had been heard. My mood had improved, and once again I fell in love with Medjugorje.

One of my dreams was to climb Apparition Hill. However, it is so rocky and dangerous I knew I would never make it on my own. A young man named Anthony, who was staying in the same house with me, generously offered to help me make the climb. Another woman, Mildred, asked if she could join us.

Without Anthony's help I would have fallen many times. As we climbed higher, I became concerned for Mildred. No one was helping her. About halfway to the top, I decided to stop and let Anthony help Mildred the rest of the way. I remained alone, and due to the terrain, I couldn't go up, down or sideways, and it was starting to get dark. I began praying the Rosary. As I prayed, I looked over at Cross Mountain. A little later I looked again, and noticed the cross had turned, and behind it was a soft, pink glow. I continued to watch the cross as it kept turning and intermittently glowing.

After about 30 minutes, several more people came along. I told them to look at the cross, and they too saw it turning. I was hoping Anthony and Mildred would return soon so they too could see it. Anthony got there in time to see it burst into color.

As we prepared to start back down, Anthony said, "I don't know how I can get you both back down." The three of us were standing there alone, when from nowhere there appeared a young Croatian girl. Without a word, she took me by the arm, and we made it down the mountain with such speed and agility, it was as if we were flying.

When we reached the bottom, she released my arm. I turned to thank her, and she had simply disappeared! My two companions didn't reach me for at least another 30 minutes. It was at that moment I realized I had Divine help. A priest and many others have told me they believe it was the Blessed Mother. I believe it was my guardian angel.

The next day was the 25th anniversary of the first apparition. I was at Ivanka's home as she prepared for her apparition. We were preparing to say the Rosary. I was happy, talking and full of anticipation. About two minutes before we were to begin the Rosary, I inexplicably fell asleep in my chair. Never before had I fallen asleep in that manner. I felt as if I had been drugged. I had to be taken to a room where I could lie down. I immediately fell asleep and didn't awaken until just after the apparition had ended. Brokenhearted, I had missed Mary's visit. But the strangest thing happened as I descended the staircase – some Italian women ran up and lovingly embraced me, repeatedly saying, "Madonna loves you."

On my seventh day in Medjugorje, my suitcase finally arrived! In my bag was a cross my son Jerry had made to place on Apparition Hill. Our family name was engraved on one side of it. Anthony offered to take the cross to the top for me and place it near the statue of the Blessed Mother. Anthony told me that due to the rocky terrain he was unable to actually stick the cross into the ground, so he laid it on a rock. He then turned to walk away, and when he turned back around, the cross had become planted between two large rocks. He said he could not explain how the cross came to be wedged between those rocks, but that it was there to stay. He said it was wedged so tightly it could not be moved!

Thankfully I had an uneventful trip home. All in all, it was a good trip. I attended Mass and other services at St. James, and saw five of the six visionaries. I saw the spinning cross, and walked arm in arm with my guardian angel. I pray that Jesus and Mary will overlook the bad attitude I had for a few days, and continue to shower the Medjugorje blessings on this humble servant and her family. (Virginia, Bobby, Jerry, Angela, Taylor, Rachael, Robert and Cheyenne.) Actually, They already have, as my second suitcase finally arrived a week after my return.

Before my pilgrimage I had prayed to have a heart like Mary. I didn't understand the adversities that happened to me on my journey until I was home about a week. And then my eyes became opened to the suffering of Jesus and Mary, and I realized mine was a drop in the bucket compared to Theirs. I needed to be purified, stripped of my pride.

I plan to return to Medjugorje in the future.

"Dear children! This is a time of great graces, but also a time of great trials for all those who desire to follow the way of peace. Because of that, little children, again I call you to pray, pray, pray, not with words but with the heart. Live my messages and be converted" (Our Lady, 12/25/02).

Editor's note: Virginia is from Edmond, OK. She is the founder of the Medjugorje prayer group at St. Monica's Catholic Church in Edmond.

(8/07)
Ransomed From Darkness

By June Klins

"Ignorance is bliss," the saying goes. One person who will tell you that is not true is Moira Noonan, a former Religious Science minister, psychic counselor and therapist, who was ransomed from darkness to the true Light of Jesus Christ through His Mother.

Moira Noonan spoke at the Medjugorje Conference at Notre Dame on May27, 2007. She began her talk with the St. Michael prayer, a prayer she says frequently. She witnessed her conversion story and warned of the dangers of the New Age movement. According to www.beliefnet.com, New Age is "an umbrella term for a wide range of personal and individual beliefs and practices influenced primarily by Eastern religions, paganism, and spiritism." Moira Noonan describes New Age as "a display of power rather than a call to love. People are motivated by the prospect of having their wishes fulfilled, rather than by a sense of surrender to God's Will." Several times in her talk, she referred to the "holy trinity" of New Age as "me, myself and I." God is seen as an impersonal life force rather than a personal God with whom we have a relationship.

Moira was brought up in California as a Catholic, but abandoned her faith at age 15. When she went away to boarding school, a teacher there introduced her to Eastern religions, reincarnation and transcendental meditation. Years later she would be lured into the world of spiritism after a car accident left her in chronic pain. Her insurance company sent her to a pain clinic where they took away all pain killers and gave her a series of messages that were anti-Christian. The messages condemned any acceptance of suffering as redemptive. She called it "professional brainwashing." She says, "My insurance company paid for me to get into the occult." The pain clinic encouraged the patients to join "New Thought" churches such as such as Unity and Religious Science, Christian Science and Unitarian. Moira fell prey to all their ideas and, after four years of "seminary," became a minister in the church of Religious Science. She became certified in hypnotherapy, and developed expertise in past-life regression, astrology, the Course in Miracles, Reiki, channeling, crystals, clairvoyance and other occult practices. Moira did not realize at the time that "through this kind of thinking, demon spirits inflate the ego, sometimes to the point that we believe we are creator gods." This kind of thinking breaks the First Commandment, and soon all the others. She also did not realize that spirit guides, demon spirits can give you signs, wonders and miracles, but these signs are an encouragement for PRIDE. Although she did not elaborate in her talk about the darkness she wrestled with during these years, she did write about it in her book, Ransomed From Darkness. .

One day Moira was reading a magazine called "New Age Journal" and there was an article in there by a leader in the New Age movement who went to Medjugorje. She said that Our Lady was a "goddess" and that She was coming to earth to see the "earth goddess." As soon as Moira read that, she knew this was wrong. (She credited the nuns from second grade with the shred of Catholicism she had left.) She prayed a simple prayer, "Mother Mary, I know You're not a goddess. I know this article is not true, but if You are coming to earth in any way, shape or form, I'd really like to meet You."

Little by little, Our Lady answered that prayer. One evening at a table tipping session (where they would call on spirits to move objects around) Moira felt a presence of something beautiful and angelic. She wondered about it, and an interior voice answered, "I am the Queen of Peace."

In July, 1991, "Life" Magazine wrote about the miracles of Medjugorje. Soon after Moira read the magazine, she turned on the TV and it just happened that Joan Rivers was interviewing two priests and author Michael Brown about Medjugorje. Joan Rivers was holding a rosary that had turned gold.

By this point Moira was really intrigued and wanted to know more. Her babysitter's mother, who was Catholic, led her to a Catholic bookstore, where she and another spiritism minister walked in on a talk about Medjugorje. After the talk, a Bible class began, but Moira and her friend thought they knew everything about the Bible, so they left and went to the beach. Her friend pulled out her crystal pendulum, which is something New Agers carry to channel spirit guides for spiritual direction. Although Moira did not know at the time, she now proclaims, "Of course, it's demonic – false locutions, counterfeit gifts, not from the Holy Spirit." Her friend could not get the pendulum to work, so she asked Moira to do it. As Moira went to reach for it, there was an invisible wall between her hand and the pendulum, and she could not touch it. And at the same moment she could see a beautiful white rosary over her hand, and she heard a very sweet interior voice say, "Pray the Rosary for your prayers to be answered." She told her friend, "I'm not allowed to touch that pendulum or any pendulum ever again." They wondered about where to get a rosary, so they went back to the Catholic bookstore. A lady at the bookstore gave Moira a copy of the "Pieta" prayer book, where there is an explanation of how to pray the Rosary. This same lady told Moira about a priest in Scottsdale, Arizona who took groups of pilgrims to Medjugorje.

Before long, Moira enticed a vanload of people to go to Sedona, Arizona to the site of the "UFO's" (CNN called this place the "New Age Capital of the World") and planned to stop at the church in Scottsdale in the same trip. Moira arrived as Mass was going on. It was her first Mass in almost 30 years and everything seemed so foreign to her. She stood up, while everyone else was sitting, and prayed, "Lord Jesus, if this priest is from You, give me a sign right now or I'm leaving and I'm never coming back." Immediately, right above the priest's head, she saw the face of Jesus, with His crown of thorns, blood dripping down, similar to how He looked in "The Passion of the Christ." She heard an interior voice speak with authority: "This is My Son. He is My Disciple. Sit down. You are home." At Communion time, as she sat in the pew, all the sins of her past life flashed through her head like a movie. At the same time God's grace came through and she remembered one of the great gifts Jesus gave to the Church – the sacrament of Confession! After Mass she went to look for the priest and found him in the parking lot. She began her first confession in 30 years right there in the parking lot! After 25 minutes, Father asked her to return the next day to finish. The next day he told her to go back to California and get a spiritual director at the Benedictine monastery. The priest she got was from India and knew all about how she had been transformed by the Eastern religions. He took her through three years of healing of memories. Since that time many people have come to the faith or come back to the faith through her, including an Oriental Medicine doctor who practiced Tibetan Buddhism!

Several years later Moira finally made the trip to Medjugorje. She waited six hours in line to go to Confession there, and then spent two more hours in the confessional. The priest told her that he wanted to see her in his office the next day. He told her he was approved by Pope John Paul II as an exorcist and asked her if she would be willing to have an exorcism. She agreed. It took 16 hours for the exorcism. She was finally ransomed completely from darkness!

Moira ended her talk with the Hail Mary "in honor of Our Lady who cries for Her lost children." The spirit of New Age seeks the ruin of souls. Let us pray for people who are involved in these practices. As Moira says, they are actually looking for the gifts and fruits of the Holy Spirit, but are looking in the wrong places. She adds that Christians need to be vigilant. Ignorance is NOT bliss.

*Editor's note: Moira is the author of **Ransomed From Darkness: The New Age, Christian Faith, and the Battle for Souls**. She is available to speak for your group or parish. You can contact her through her website, www.spiritbattleforsouls.org.*

Vineyards in Medjugorje

(7/06)
Angels Over the Vineyards

By Cathy Karem

It was a beautiful fall evening in September, 2005. Father Donald Calloway, the spiritual director for another group from the US, walked into Pansion Nada, where he and his group were staying and where I always stay when coming to Medjugorje. I was sitting at a table having a cup of coffee after awaiting my husband's phone call from the States.

Fr. Calloway looked at me and said, "Excuse me, could you please come outside with me for a minute?" I said, "Sure, Father." I didn't know why or what, but I followed him out the front door to the driveway, which is located right across the street from the vineyards, and to the right of Mount Krizevac. He pointed up into the sky and he said, "What do you see?" I looked and I gasped, "Oh my gosh, Father. There's angels!" They were going around in a circle in the sky. It looked like they were playing chase! All of a sudden a huge bolt of lightning and a big thunder boom struck the sky and everyone who had started gathering for this heavenly spectacle gasped with awe.

The angels kept chasing one another in a circular motion and we then noticed inside the big circle of angels was a smaller circle of baby angels chasing one another. After what seemed about 10 minutes or so, another huge bolt of lightning lit up the sky and a huge boom of thunder clapped. That was number two. We all screamed with excitement again! Priests and pilgrims were running out of their rooms and were gathering to see this beautiful heavenly display. Everyone was "ooohing" and "awing" and saying, "Wow! Look at these angels!!!" These precious little heavenly creatures were having a great time playing "Catch me if you can" over the vineyards.

Now, after what seemed to be another 10 minutes had gone by, the third and biggest bolt of lightning struck. It seemed to cover the entire sky. You could see the whole village of Bijakovici. The thunder bolt was so loud it seemed to shake the earth!

Everyone was so excited! And with that, the angels were gone! The sky went black and everybody was silent. You could have heard a pin drop. It seemed like the heavens opened up and they were called back to the Heavenly Court.

Why? How??? I kept asking myself. I remembered that Ivan had called us to the Blue Cross for a message and apparition of the Blessed Mother this night and I couldn't go on this particular evening because I had to wait for my husband's phone call from the States. As a rule, I would never have missed Her call to the Blue Cross, but I knew, after having missed my husband's call the previous night, that the Blessed Mother would want me to be considerate and be there this time for my husband's phone call. When I go to Medjugorje I usually stay a month, so I knew that in all probability that the Blessed Mother would call us again to the Blue Cross, and I would go then.

Boy, am I glad that I listened to my heart and that I had awaited his phone call!

Our Blessed Mother has called me to come to Medjugorje many times, and I have been very blessed and privileged to have been able to answer Her call. I have seen the Miracle of the Sun many times, my rosaries have turned gold, and many other beautiful miracles have happened, but never in all my days had I seen a visual miracle of heavenly creatures like these angels!

Our Blessed Mother gives us so many blessings and miracles from Her Son Jesus, but they don't always hit us like streaks of lightening and bolts of thunder. But this was definitely a gift and all I can say is that miracles do happen and they come in many shapes and forms, but we must open our hearts to receive them.

This beautiful place called Medjugorje is truly a precious and indescribable gift to the world. How God loves us so much to have sent His Heavenly Queen, our Heavenly Mother all these years to help us through our lives. This place called Medjugorje has truly marked me and millions of other people. Mary's presence is there! And you can feel Her wrap Her loving arms around you.

I must add something very important to this story . . . THANK YOU, Blessed Mother and Jesus, for loving me!

Editor's note: Cathy is from Louisville, Kentucky.

(9/07)
After a Startling Vision of Jesus on the Cross, Comedian Turned into a Catholic

By Michael H. Brown

When life seems to be closing in on us, in a world that so often seems upside-down, there's one way to exit, and that's through humor. A sure cure for our ills is found in laughter! Usually, we should be laughing at ourselves. And one thing that should make us smile is how silly it is to worry when we have God. In the Light of His eternity and angels and watchfulness, there is nothing to fear but lack of prayer. We can even pray for a good sense of humor!

Many of you have heard the experts talk about how laughter can help us recover from serious illnesses. That's because humor is a spiritual release and when we release something on that level, it goes to both our emotions and bodies. A great example of this – of both healing and laughter – is Char Vance, the television producer and comedian from New Orleans who is often out there speaking at conferences and causing people to roll in the aisles. Char had been in the radio business when she suffered a horrendous accident. It was on Halloween night at a farm she owned back in the 1980s. She and a group were riding on a tractor-pulled wagon when suddenly they caught sight of the barn on fire. Char jumped off in hopes of running to the blaze, but got caught underneath, injured so badly it looked like part of her leg would have to be amputated. The ankle was severely damaged, just crushed. No bone support at all. It looked like a lifelong handicap.

At the time, Char Vance was not a Catholic, but a friend got her to go to the apparition site of Medjugorje – much besmirched these days by the devil. And for good reason: this is a place of enormous conversion. Ask Char. Her recounting of her trip and her conversion to the Catholic faith – more importantly, to faith in Jesus – is a hilarious excursion into deep spirituality. Finally, it has been captured on videotape.

At Medjugorje, where Char hobbled in a huge, lumbering cast, the Louisiana woman climbed the holy highland of Mount Krizevac despite those who thought it was crazy, and despite her own skepticism. "I wondered why [after Apparition Hill], they wanted us to go up the mountain," she jokes. "I said, 'Why do you have us climbing two hills, two mountains in one day? It's not like we're going to run out of fun things to do here!'"

Here she was in a place with no TV and no hotels and no pools, drinking beer while everyone else was praying the Rosary in a way she saw as strange and obsessive.

But Char went up the "hill." As she walked a dirt road on the outskirts of the village, something had said to her, "You know, it will be just your luck if something big happens up there and you're gonna miss it." That's what had finally convinced her to go up. She and her companions caught a cab. When they got to the mountain, many others were doing the same.

"I didn't know a lot of prayers," says Char, who was not a Catholic at the time. "I knew 'Now I lay me down to sleep' and the Lord's Prayer, but that's the most wonderful thing you Catholics have: you have prayers for everything," she jokes. "You know, you got department heads. You lost something, you got St. Anthony. You got bad eyes, you got St. Lucy . . ."

Heading up the mountain and praying at the Fourth Station of the Cross, Char propped up her cast on a boulder and here comes a monk – a very unusual monk. "He had on this white robe and the hood up and he's carrying a tripod with nothing on it, no camera. And he's looking directly at me," says Char. "And coming to me, he says, 'You know, when I was in Germany, I had the good fortune of meeting Theresa

Neumann.' To me it was like saying, 'I met John Jones.' He said, 'You know who that is, don't you?' I said, 'No.' And he said, 'Well, she was a stigmatist.'" "Got me again," said Char. "Don't you know what a stigmatist is?" the man asked. "Uh uh," replied Char. He explained what a stigmatic was (someone who had received the wounds of Christ) and, pulling out a rosary, told her that he had put it on her stigmatic wounds and that it had since healed people of many problems, including cancer. "Here I am with this big cast on the rock, and he says, 'I would like your permission to put this on your head!'"

It's hard to convey how Char tells this story. Her inflections, her timing, her side comments are hilarious. The tape shows an audience in constant stitches. But she was telling a serious story. "When something like this happens, you think 'somebody has tapped into your thoughts' – and you better start thinking some holy pious thoughts QUICK!"

The mysterious stranger told Char to say seven Our Father's, Hail Mary's, and Glory Be's, and when she got to the top, the Creed. "When he left he would talk to others," she recounts. "If they were French he would begin talking in French. If you were Spanish he would start speaking Spanish. It was like he knew what you were before he got there."

At the seventh Station, the comedian noticed the "monk" was kind of winded. Char offered him a canteen of water. "He smiled a smile that went all the way through me," she says.

Medjugorje is famous for the reports of mysterious strangers – including monks or nuns in white. When Char got to the top, the seers were ready to have an apparition. Char didn't want to see anything – afraid there would be hysteria and she would fall off the mountain! They were at the large cross there. "All of a sudden it gets quiet, quiet, quiet. All of a sudden, that cross lit up, and it lit up, best I can describe it, like those old strobe lights, quick, and I see Jesus on the cross. I saw Him like I have never seen a person before or since. He looked horrible – horrible – His nose was laying over, and He had this enormous crown, not this little crown like you see. This thing was like a big bird's nest. That quickly it lit up again and I saw it again."

Vance wasn't alone. Others in her group were astonished to witness the same thing. The mountain is known for a wide array of phenomena – although this particular type we had not previously encountered. It is the cross where the Blessed Mother says She prays each day.

A woman next to Char said, "Did you just see Christ on that cross?" Char felt "totally zapped." She now knew without a doubt that God and the Blessed Mother existed. When she got back, she had to go to the doctor for x-rays. She went in the waiting room "and all of a sudden the technician comes out with all these x-rays and he says [in a loud voice], 'Charlene Vance, you've been healed, you've been healed!'"

"You should have seen the people in there with their 'People' magazines!" she jokes. But it was true: the nurse ran in too, and then the doctor arrived – gracing them with his "presence." "When's the last time you saw a doctor come into the waiting room?" she recalls with a roll of her eyes. "The nurse said, 'Did you hear that?'" The doctor said he had to take a look at it. It looked like there was bone growth! He asked Char to slowly try to see if she could move her toes. She could do more than that. She could rotate her whole ankle! She was with her mother. "I started dancing around and saying, 'Ma – Ma, I can walk, praise God I can walk!' He runs out and brings out another doctor and they look at the x-rays and my mother says, 'Doctor, doctor, what is it?' and he says – direct quote – 'There's absolutely no correlation in her x-rays before she went and when she got back. There's total bone growth everywhere.'"

Jesus is the same as He was 2,000 years ago, she tells those who see her. "Miracles do happen. Believe in miracles. Expect a miracle. Miracles do happen," says Char, who now helps produce videos for Focus International, headed by retired Archbishop Phillip Hannan. "The real miracle was when God healed my head with the gift of faith. Miracles do happen, but they happen in God's time and in His way."

Char had some medals from Medjugorje and started walking all around and passing them out to the people in the waiting room. "Have a medal! Have a medal!" She walked out of that office and never needed crutches like they said she would need crutches and never received a day of therapy.

And yes: Charlene Vance became a Catholic six months to the day that she had climbed the mountain.

www.spiritdaily.com

Editor's note: It is interesting to note that Char and Theresa Neumann were both born on April 8, and both born on a Friday. Theresa Neumann was injured trying to put out a fire in a barn. She injured her ankle, which was healed a year later.

(9/06)
Father Robert Thorn, Back in Medjugorje!

By Sr. Emmanuel

Father Robert Thorn (former teacher of Transcendental Meditation) offers us a first hand witness about false peace: "I had a close friend who was so calm and at peace all the time and I asked him how he did it. And he said, 'Well, I do Transcendental Meditation.' I got a little information from him, and decided I wanted to try it. From the moment I started it, I felt so much peace flowing into my body. I really felt an incredible amount of peace. It got me away from drugs, because the TM program didn't allow it. Eventually, I became a teacher of TM.

"Because of the encouragement of my brother, I came to visit Medjugorje but only as a tourist, out of curiosity. One night, up on Apparition Hill, I was kneeling at the foot of the cross doing my Transcendental Meditation and some other pilgrims were praying next to me. One of them began to pray in tongues, and as soon as he started, I had this uncomfortable feeling in my gut. I felt like I had to say something. All of a sudden I began to speak in tongues and he and I began to converse in tongues! This shows that the evil one can also speak in tongues!

"After my experience in Medjugorje, I continued my work and travels, but began reading the Bible and praying the Rosary. I was still doing TM and was experiencing uncontrollable attraction for different women. I was living in sin.

"I returned to Medjugorje (en route to rendezvous with a Turkish woman for a romantic getaway in Istanbul). After a few days, I cancelled the rest of my plans and remained in Medjugorje. I had an experience one evening at the healing service in the church, right after Mass. I was kneeling down, imagining the blood of Christ just flowing over me. I had my eyes closed, and all of a sudden I saw this ugly black creature, kind of a cross between a lobster crab and a beetle, just going across my mind's eye. I said instinctively, 'That is an evil spirit. I need to get rid of it.'

"When a priest heard this in my confession, he said 'Ahh, that is interesting. Tell me, have you been fasting?' I said, 'Yes,' and the priest replied, 'Good, because the power of the Holy Spirit is greater when you have been fasting.'

"This priest was an exorcist and so, through a long intense night of prayer, we renounced and bound, in the name of Jesus Christ, the spirits that were in me. I felt incredible pain in my gut. It would start coming out my throat as burps, one time I actually saw a jet of steam come right out of my mouth! I was flat on my hands and knees on the floor and the priest was sprinkling me with Holy Water, he placed the crucifix against my gut and the pain was incredible.

"At one point during this night, when the priest demanded, 'In the name of Jesus Christ, who are you?' I found myself reciting my mantra from TM. Now it is forbidden to say your mantra out loud because it weakens its power to take you 'within,' so it surprised me that I would be saying it. I later asked the priest if there was anything wrong with TM, and I explained that what I had recited was my TM mantra. He said, 'Well, it responded to the power and authority of Jesus Christ!' Later, both he and I found out the meaning of this mantra, and it was the demon of lust. At another point during the process, the name of one of the demons was that of a master in TM!

"After this, I stopped doing TM 'cold turkey' and started coming frequently to Medjugorje, spending time on Krizevac and praying for discernment. I started a novena and on the third night, while attending Mass, I clearly heard, during the offertory prayer 'I want you to be a priest.'

"I was shocked. I didn't know what to do. I walked out of the church, in a daze, to the restaurant I always went to. I was praying to Mary. I said, 'Mary, if this is really what You want of me, You have to help me with my desire to get married and have children.' She said in response, 'I'll give you more children than you could ever imagine.'"

Sr. Emmanuel: How do you explain the kind of 'peace' you had when you started TM?

"Now, I recognize it as a false peace. In going back and looking at all the teachings of TM, all of a sudden it was all just as clear as day to me that what they are talking about are demons! In TM you will feel that you have all you want fulfilled, because you go into this field and the demons provide for all your needs. And of course the demons are going to provide for your needs because every time you meditate, you are caressing them and stroking them and they want you to come back! This peace that you feel through TM is a false peace, centered on yourself. You are just caressing your own EGO and then you feel good. You don't realize that you are becoming 'Jesus resistant' so to speak! But true peace flows from God to you when you turn to Him. TM instead is total self gratification."

Remember the words of Jesus, "Peace I leave with you, my peace I give unto you. Not as the world gives do I give unto you" (John 14:27).

Dearest Gospa, Queen of Peace, in our hearts and in the world, may Your voice prevail over those which deceive us!

Children of Medjugorje, www.childrenofmedjugorje.com

Stained glass window in St. James with the
Croatian word for peace – MIR

(4/08)
Journey to the Light

By Mary's Child

As I sat in my living room, smoking cigarettes and drinking wine, I realized that my only escape from this incredible sadness my life had become was to end it – as quickly as possible. I was so determined to end my life that all thoughts of my beautiful teen-aged daughter, my family and friends that would have to deal with my violent death didn't matter to me. Nothing mattered but ending the pain. With all of the dark thoughts racing through my mind, I had a moment of clarity. I called my friend Katie. I told her what was about to happen. Within what seemed like minutes, my friend appeared at my door. She talked to me, listened to me, and tucked me into my bed as soon as she had a promise from me not to do anything drastic that night.

I had been very depressed for quite a while. My doctor had prescribed Zoloft for me. And for a time, it worked. But something else was happening to me. I thought that my depression sprang from my mother's death the year before. I was depressed because I couldn't get out of bed. I was depressed because I couldn't work. I was depressed because my father was no longer speaking to me. I was unkempt and not able to function. I stopped the Zoloft.

A few weeks passed. Now, instead of sleeping for days on end, I could hardly sleep at all. I complained to my sister, who had tried very hard to convince me that I was Bi-Polar. I knew that she was wrong! Up until my mother died, I believed that I was one of the happiest people alive. She had to be wrong! Giving up on the argument for the time being, she recommended that I start to say the Rosary when I couldn't sleep. Not long afterward, I took her up on her suggestion. I didn't really know how to pray the Rosary, but I did remember the Our Father on the large beads and the Hail Mary on the small ones.

I started to pray the Rosary, and after about three weeks, while saying this incredible prayer I felt a warmth flood my body. I couldn't move! I felt a strange sensation spreading through my bones and I began to cry. When I could function again I immediately made a call to a parish that I had visited from time to time during my 25 year hiatus from my Catholic faith. Asking the priest for an hour of his time to hear my Confession, he invited me to come in the next day. After making my Confession, I began going to daily Mass. I joined the Legion of Mary at my parish. Within weeks, I went to visit a psychologist on the advice of my physician. I was diagnosed Bi-Polar 2. I began medication for that disease and within a few months' time the right combination of drugs was working! I was a new person! I was becoming truly happy . . . not manic happy, but truly and miraculously happy! Joyful!

Within months I learned that there was an opportunity to go on retreat with Father Jozo near Medjugorje. Having heard about Medjugorje shortly after the apparitions began in the early 80s, I was very excited to go there and made my reservations. A few years earlier I had read a book on Medjugorje and had read about Father Jozo. But I didn't realize what a gift this was nor what a life-altering experience it would become.

My conversion was in full swing. I came back from this experience filled with the Holy Spirit. My desire to drink was miraculously taken away from me. The only drink that I take now is the Precious Blood of Jesus at Mass. I became a Eucharistic Minister. I began to cook for and feed the homeless. Since that time with Father Jozo, I have been to Medjugorje twice more in two years. All three times I have had incredible, miraculous experiences in that holy place. Daily Mass and learning to actually enjoy fasting has become my reality. I have been blessed to begin a hospital ministry with a particular devotion for dying patients and their families, among various other ministries through the Legion. Now, having started, with the blessing of my new parish priest, a Legion of Mary at that parish also, I continue on with my first group and now have successfully begun a second.

Now, the only reason I don't want to work is that working for money interferes with my work for God – work done and accomplished through our Blessed Mother. But I force myself to make a living anyway – although not the type of living that I had once been accustomed to! And happily, I want peace now, not material goods. Happiness and joy is my new life's direction. Our Blessed Mother has made this great gift a reality. Blessed Mother, I love you and thank you with all of my heart for leading me to Jesus. Jesus, I adore You!

Editor's note: The author wishes to remain anonymous. I am including this story as I thought it might help someone.

(6/06)
In the Galaxy of 'Stars' is Loretta Young and Her Account of an Angelic Mystery

By Michael H. Brown

We're not much for celebrity, and even wonder if it's in God's plan. In our culture we seem to use actors, actresses, and other prominent people to fill inner voids. The magic of television and the big screen turns folks into idols, which is not very healthy.

Note the word "magic," and also the word "idol." Often one is led to wonder from whence such charisma comes! But that doesn't mean celebrities are bad people. Some are wonderful (literally: full of wonders). We have reported on former Treasury Secretary William Simon, who wrote about his rosary turning gold at Medjugorje. There is former football coach Don Shula, who also visited the famous apparition site, where his wife saw the miracle of the sun. There is actor Martin Sheen, who narrated a documentary on the place; who knows what he saw!

Now, to the formidable list of diplomats, cardinals, bishops, businessmen, royalty, singers, writers, politicians, actors, and assorted other famous people who have visited, we can add Hollywood legend Loretta Young, a devout Catholic who died in 2000.

Before she passed, Loretta related the account of her pilgrimage for a book by Joan Wester Anderson, who writes all the wonderful angel books.

We weren't aware of it until recently, but in an authorized biography called *Forever Young*, the actress cited several fascinating (and, yes, "alleged") supernatural occurrences at Medjugorje. So powerful were the experiences that afterward Young began to pray the 15-decade Rosary daily as well as to fast on Wednesdays and Fridays! "Medjugorje solidified everything I'd always hoped and prayed for," said the superstar. "I have visited several shrines but no place has affected me quite as much."

While purchasing a statue at the apparition site in 1988, Young suddenly heard a woman shouting to look at the sun. According to the biography, Loretta's eyes had been scorched twice by klieg lights; if she stared at bright objects, her eyes would rather easily burn. "But before

I realized what I was doing, I looked right at the sun, and it started to grow," she recounted.

What the actress saw was a pulsating golden orb grow from avocado size to the size of a watermelon – changing to red, green, and white. "Then the Communion wafer appeared in the center of it," she said.

Young – who in her heyday co-starred with the likes of Clark Gable, Spencer Tracy, Douglas Fairbanks Jr., William Holden, and James Cagney – had her most incredible experience after tripping on a step inside St. James Church and severely twisting her ankle. She was with several companions, including her son. They figured it was a bad sprain. As pain shot through the famed actress, an Indian nun came from out of nowhere, telling them she was a physician and instructing them to bring Loretta outside.

There the physician left for a moment, "then returned, carrying what appeared to be a pot of mud and some bandages," notes Anderson. "She slathered the goop on Loretta's foot, and bound it up with bandages, telling her not to take the bandages off."

Diverted for a moment, neither Loretta nor those around her noticed that the nun had disappeared. They never saw her again. But, miraculously, what she had done caused the pain to disappear. Young was able to finish the pilgrimage.

When she returned, a visit to the doctor revealed that it wasn't a sprain after all. Loretta, as it turns out, had broken six bones in that foot. When they took off the bandages, it suddenly swelled to twice its normal size! Somehow those muddy bandages had kept her foot pain-free throughout the journey.

On a return trip there with her husband, Jean, their tour group stopped to speak with the seer Vicka. Later, when Jean went to take a rosary out of his pocket, everyone gasped.

As in the case of William Simon, the links had turned to gold. The lesson? "Abandonment to His will – isn't it thrilling to watch it work?" asked the legendary actress.

www.spiritdaily.com

(7/07)
Look to the Heavens

By Christina Treadwell

I was a lost soul who left the Church for a time, due to the grumbling of an old priest. Through my mom's pleas and prayers, I slowly, yet reluctantly, returned to the Church. During a car ride to Saint Vincent College for a healing Mass, I asked my mom if she had heard of a place called "Med-ja-something."

A short history lesson later, I learned all about this quaint little village where the Blessed Mother was appearing. I knew nothing of Medjugorje other than what I felt in my heart and knew that I had to get there somehow. To make a long story short, I met Father Bill Kiel after the healing Mass and guess where he was going! There were two seats left and I said, "My mom and I will take them."

Getting there, however, was a different story. First, my mom lost her passport a few weeks before we were to leave. She rushed to get a replacement passport. The new passport came in a week!

Second, our group was supposed to leave only days after September 11th happened. Because of the danger of travel, the trip was postponed until July.

Third, at that time I worked for a professional outdoor soccer team. July was a difficult time to get away because of games and a youth soccer tournament we held at that time. Not knowing what to do, I asked the Blessed Mother to help with the tournament sign-ups. It was the largest tournament turnout during my tenure with the organization. How was that for help?!

When we finally reached Medjugorje, what truly made this trip special, besides sharing it with my mom, were the feelings of hope and love that filled my whole being. This was such an overwhelming feeling and it allowed me to open my heart to God. So many things happened to me in Medjugorje but I rarely share them. Our Heavenly Mother lets me know when and with whom I should share my stories.

When June asked me to write one of my experiences for the newsletter, I really prayed about it. This experience is from my first trip to Medjugorje and it was on the day of the apparition with Ivan Dragicevic. It was nearing dusk when everyone had gathered by the

Blue Cross and began saying the Rosary. I had my head bowed and my eyes closed. We were on the third decade when I heard, "Look to the Heavens." So I did. Nothing. Then something.

I was not sure if I was really seeing them (yes, them) at first, but there they were, fluttering around the sky above us, encircling to prepare the path for Our Lady to come. I really questioned what I was seeing and yet, I was filled with an abundant amount of awe that kept my eyes fixated on the Heavens. They were *eyes with wings*.

Soon after, the Gates of Heaven opened and armies of angels poured forth. The Archangels were dressed in battle attire, ready to protect Our Lady from all evil. They lead the armies of angels to each fluttering eye closing in the circle and creating a pathway for Our Lady. The angels were too numerous to count. All were in different attire and carrying different things. It seemed as though God's mercy kept emerging forward and that there would be no end to it.

And then in the clouds, I saw Our Lady – smiling a comforting smile that a mother gives to her child when they are sad, in trouble, asking for help. "Is this a dream?" I kept asking myself. "Is this a dream? Why show this to me? Why allow such a sinner to see such love come from Heaven arrayed in splendor?"

"Because love came to earth in my Son, as I now come to you. As a mother comes to a child, I come to you to bring you to my Son, for He loves you very much. His love is never ending, my child." With that, I saw nothing but white clouds and blue sky. I once again bowed my head and continued to feel the presence of Our Lady until the end.

Afterwards, I was so excited to share what I had seen with my mom. She, of course, did not believe me, and I was still a little hesitant as to what I had seen. When I told her about the winged eyes, she turned to me and asked if I was sure I saw winged eyes. I said, "Yes," and that no matter how they turned, it seemed that there were many tiny eyes that made up the eye itself.

Stunned, she shared with me a story. My parents had an icon made of the Archangels. It took over two years to make, but it is beautiful. When the gentleman who made the icon delivered it, he said that in all the years that he has been doing icons, he has met many interesting people. He said that some of these individuals had seen the Archangels and no matter who was telling the story, the descriptions were all the same. He found it amazing because each person who told him about the angels had no connection with the previous person. He also talked about the winged eyes that accompanied Archangels which was also something that was always mentioned. He thought that the way people talked about them that they would be considered the Seraphim . . . the ones closest to God.

"In the center and around the throne, there were four living creatures covered with eyes in front and in back . . . The four living creatures, each of them with six wings, were covered with eyes inside and out. Day and night they do not stop exclaiming: 'Holy, holy, holy is the Lord God almighty, who was, and who is, and who is to come.'" (Rev 4:6, 8)

Even now, I sit here with tears in my eyes thankful for hearing Our Mother's call, opening myself up to God the Father, Jesus Christ and the Holy Spirit. I still hear the call to Medjugorje and am thankful that every time I am there to be able to refresh my faith and become closer to Our Mother and Jesus.

Editor's note: Christina is from Clairton, PA.

(4/06)
I Am No Longer the Man I Was

By Michael K. Jones

In 1984 I was in need of a very special blessing, so there I was, an atheist, on his knees praying to the "invisible man." I quickly realized talking to someone I can't see seemed foolish. Somehow I managed to muster up enough courage, talked to the wind and said, "Okay, Jesus, this is Your chance, give me this special blessing, and You will have a friend for life." Much to my surprise and delight, I received the blessing during that prayer. My life completely changed after this! For example, I never prayed, but now I could pray at the drop of a hat. And witness, boy could I witness! I was self employed, and every time I worked for a new customer I would witness about my special blessing and confess my love for Jesus. I was born again! My friends all wondered how a confirmed atheist could make a complete turn-around. The answer was elementary, like Scrooge in Charles Dickens's classic, *A Christmas Carol*, I was no longer the man I was.

From winter of 1984, my nose was constantly inside the Scriptures, and I loved every minute. In spring of '89 my life was about to take a greater step beyond anything I could ever imagine. One day while witnessing to a lady, she handed me an envelope saying that inside were clippings of travel agents going to a place where the Virgin Mary is appearing. I had no interest in pilgrimages or the Virgin Mary for that matter, but I smiled and took the envelope. When I got home that night, I cleaned my pockets and put the envelope on the bottom shelf of my coffee table and thought no more about it. I never looked inside.

While in prayer some days later, I heard a voice that said, "I want you to go to Medjugorje." At first I ignored the voice, but the voice remained insistent. The voice continued over the next few weeks, often times waking me in the middle of the night. Upon waking me, the voice would tell me to look at the clock. I found the numbers on the clock to be of equal value, example: 1:11, 2:22, 3:33, and so on. The voice would say, "I want you to go to Medjugorje." Though this is a strange event, even stranger is the fact I had never heard of Medjugorje, I had no clue what it was.

One evening while talking to my sister, I told her about the voice. I tried to pronounce the word Medjugorje but failed. My sister said, "Medjugorje? I've heard of it." It seems her parish priest, Fr. Kelly, was taking a group of people to this little village in a Socialist country, where they say the Virgin is appearing. This was not my idea of a great vacation, but I asked my sister to get me an appointment with this priest. I called a week later to find out about the appointment, but her husband told me that Father was a busy man and most likely would not have time to see me.

Hanging up, thinking on all this, I noticed the envelope the lady had given me on the bottom shelf of my coffee table. I had the impression the envelope was jumping at me, which is why it caught my attention. Written on the envelope was the word, "Medjugorje." This was the first time I had noticed this, and I knew whatever I was looking for was inside.

I quickly pawed through a dozen or so clippings and one caught my eye that said, "Rome and Medjugorje for $1219.00." I knew instantly I was going on this pilgrimage. As I read on, it said, "Under the direction of Father Arnold E. Kelly, St. Rita's Church, Lowell, MA." This was my sister's parish priest, who lived 100 miles away. Shocked, I called my brother-in-law, insisting I meet with Father. After meeting with this delightful priest, I signed up for the 1989 pilgrimage to Medjugorje.

On the fourth or fifth day of the pilgrimage, I climbed Mt. Krizevac. I was standing by the right side of the cross taking pictures of the miracle of the sun. I turned to a voice that said, "Hello, my name is Agnes." I said hello and told her I was not trying to be rude but I had to take pictures of the sun. Agnes said, "Do not be concerned, God will give you the pictures He wants you to have." She gave me a flower and told me God loves me. She said God wanted me to have the flower. I said thank you. Then she said, "I have to go now." When I looked for her a moment later she was gone.

I met Agnes again when we were an hour away from leaving Medjugorje. My roommate was following me around because I tearfully told everyone I didn't want to go home. My roommate, Bill, walked with me to Saint James Parish one last time. While walking back to the house where we were staying, I was again telling Bill I did not want to leave. The tears were swelling up in my eyes again. All of a sudden, Bill said, "Michael, I think someone is calling you." I turned around and there was Agnes. As I walked closer to her, she must have seen my sadness. She hugged me, and as she was doing so, whispered in my ear saying, "You have to go home now and spread the message." My sadness left me, and Agnes walked away with two nuns dressed in habit.

As I reflect on this, I wonder: How can a woman, who briefly touches my life on top of a mountain in a strange land, be able to recognize me from my back side several days later, and then remembers my name, knows what I am feeling, and tells me that I have to go home to spread the message? What are the chances?

I experienced many miracles before, during, and after my visit to Medjugorje, far more than I can describe in the space available in "The Spirit of Medjugorje."

I returned home realizing I no longer believed in God. I had gone a step beyond, I KNOW God exists. I will never doubt in His existence again – no matter what may happen to me – for the rest of my life, be it good or bad. Knowing God exists is for me one of the greatest miracles of all.

Today I am Catholic, and the Virgin Mary who I had no interest in, I now call "The Rose of my heart." I run a Medjugorje website that has some 500 thousand visitors each month from around the world and I am the founder of The POW (Purgatory Oblation Warrior) Apostolate which has over 2000 members worldwide. Later this year my book, *Medjugorje Investigated* will be available, based on U.S. State Department documents I have requested be declassified. Truly, I am not boasting, but simply stating that there are no more "Bah Humbugs" Scrooges here.

So if you are looking for a best friend, try getting on your knees and praying to the "Invisible Man." It worked for me. Just maybe you too will find your best friend.

*Editor's note: Michael lives in E. Wareham, MA. This was a condensed version of his testimony. To read the entire story you can visit his website at www.medjugorjeusa.org. His book **Medjugorje Investigated** is available at this website.*

Painting of Our Lady that hangs in the
yellow building behind St. James

(2/09)
"She Smiled at Me"

By Sr. Emmanuel

In the town of Newrya, Dominican priest, Father Tony, told me about Ivan's visit to his Priory of St. Catherine's on March 24, 1998. Ivan received his apparition before Holy Mass on that day and 2,000 people attended this event. The next day at school, a little girl of 12 named Elana told her teacher that she had attended Mass twice the day before. "Did you?" asked the teacher with surprise. "Yes," she replied.

Elana is actually a mentally handicapped child and she has the understanding of a five year old. She might have thought that the apparition time was a Holy Mass. Here is how she naively explained it to her teacher, "During the first Mass, Our Lady of Lourdes was talking to a man. I could not hear what She was saying to him, but She smiled at me." The reason why little Elana mentioned Our Lady of Lourdes is because she herself had been to Lourdes. Her father goes every year to Lourdes as a helper for the sick, and she only knows Mary as Our Lady of Lourdes, even if the image is of Our Lady of Knock, Guadalupe or Fatima.

As the teacher shared Elana's words with her parents later, the parents asked the child herself about what had happened. She repeated the same story with exactly the same words, and they asked her what the Blessed Mother looked like. She answered, "Our Lady of Lourdes was wearing a blue-gray dress and a white thing around her head, and I could see Her hair. She was smiling at me. There were colored lights behind Her like the lights of a Christmas tree, and they were very bright and like water running behind Her." Since this Dominican priest knows the family, he was able to speak to the little girl and received from her exactly the same report that she had given her teacher and her parents. There was nothing added, nor taken away. Father Tony thought that these lights she saw could actually be the child's way of describing the stars that crown Our Lady of Medjugorje.

The most beautiful part of this event is that from that day onwards, the little girl changed a lot. She is now radiantly happy. Isn't it wonderful that from among all 2,000 present, the Blessed Mother chose to show Herself to a little handicapped child? As we prepare for Christmas [Easter], hasn't Our Lady given us a beautiful example of caring for and giving value to life, especially that life which the world often despises?!

Children of Medjugorje, www.childrenofmedjugorje.com (12/1/99)

(7/09)
To Follow or to Lead?

By George Ripple

My third day in Medjugorje began at 4:30 A.M., when I awoke with an urgent sense that I needed to start praying. My *Guardian Angel Prayer* was finished even before switching on a light and reaching for a copy of *Pieta*. There is a prayer to St. Joseph I have been using for quite some time; I started reading it aloud, but thoughts of "Jesus loves me, Mary loves me" seemed to overtake the words. I was finally wide awake now and couldn't wait for the morning to get started. I love it here! Our group is to leave the pansion at 7:30 by vans for the short trip to the community of Cenacolo to be present for the apparition to the visionary Mirjana.

The road outside Cenacolo was a mass of pilgrims walking and winding through a maze of buses and vans bringing more pilgrims to the apparition. Once inside the entrance the foremost action was to find a spot which would allow a strategic view. A view of what – I had no idea, but I wanted the spot that would allow me to see whatever was going to happen. The community building was already packed to capacity and the surrounding grounds were rapidly filling with people. Pilgrims were standing, or leaning against trees, stone walls, lining the pathways sitting on chairs, fold out seats or just sitting on the ground. Even with so many, for the most part there was a silence and reverence present.

I was walking with my brother's family, Michael, Wendy and Isaac, our friend Rita, and Wendy's sister's family. We walked a short distance on a stone path winding through trees to an area about 30 yards from the corner of the community building where Mirjana would have her visit from our Blessed Virgin Mary. From this vantage point I could see two closed circuit monitors mounted on the building and a third if I turned around to watch in a tent structure immediately behind. As far as I was concerned, nothing could escape or miss my field of vision, and I was ready.

I sat down on a rock used to line the edge of the pathway and settled in for the wait. The Rosary was being prayed in Croatian, Italian and English and could be heard over loud speakers. Even when responding to the Hail Mary's I couldn't stop thinking, "How special this is – does everyone else feel all jittery inside?" The music being played between the decades added a relaxing aspect which allowed me to sort of catch my breath from the reality of "I'm actually here to witness!" I needed to calm down a little bit; after all, no one else seemed jumpy, so I decided to take some photos of whatever was around.

One of the pictures taken was of the mountainside immediately behind and to the right of the community building. After snapping this photo and still looking at the mountain I had a thought, "What a great place to see Mary walking out of the sparse bushes at the top and winding Her way down and around the rocks. Yes, what a great place for Mary to survey all Her pilgrims who have come to hear Her message before somehow entering the building unseen." My thought of Mary was not of some glorious bright light, but just a woman dressed in brown and blue robes.

The passing seconds and minutes became filled with thoughts of my previous two days and the special consideration Mary and Jesus had already given me. What more could possibly be felt, or in my case be shown, to convince me of the graces received? The day dreaming was abruptly interrupted with people scurrying to move around for a better view. Mirjana was escorted up a path about 15 yards from where I was seated. Quietly and quickly, Mirjana moved inside and the closed circuit televisions allowed us 'unfortunate' pilgrims who couldn't be inside with her to watch and hear. Mirjana was kneeling and praying. All eyes inside and outside were affixed on Mirjana; all were waiting and wanting the apparition to begin.

I was now totally focused on the moment and nothing could distract me from Mirjana. I anxiously awaited, staring more intensely at a monitor, when without provocation I changed my view from Mirjana to the mountainside. Calmly I looked and focused on a flock of sheep and a single shepherd. My heart started racing. Am I seeing things? This is in the exact same spot where I had Mary arriving! I held my breath, re-focused and tried to hide an emerging smile. For the briefest of moments I wanted to keep this all to myself. Glancing at the monitor, Mirjana was still praying. I had time to share.

I leaned across the path to tell my brother, "Look, there is a flock of sheep and a shepherd." My brother saw them immediately even without my pointing out the location. "Yes," he nodded, "I see them." I motioned hurriedly for my nephew, Isaac, sitting just behind me to come up and sit on my knee so I could show him, too. Again, without having to give any sense of direction, Isaac nodded his head, turned, and smiled indicating that he saw the flock of sheep and the shepherd.

There was a gasp in the air, and looking at the monitor, I could see the ecstasy in Mirjana's face. I knew our Blessed Mother had appeared.

My gaze returned to the mountainside and I continued to watch the shepherd and his flock. They were staying in the same area as when I first saw them. As soon as the apparition was over the flock of sheep and the shepherd vanished – not from view, but disappeared on the spot! Both Michael and Isaac looked at me with astonished expressions. All three of us had witnessed the same happening.

We instantly knew this was special, and stood looking at each other wide-eyed and smiling. My wide eyes and smile broke down into tears and quivering lips as I managed to find the words to tell Wendy and Rita what we had just witnessed. Isaac was agreeing with every word, "Yes, yes, I saw them, too!" Rita was disappointed that she hadn't seen them. Wendy smiled. Wendy calmly affirmed that this gift was meant for only George, Michael and Isaac to see.

Just about this time Mary's message was being translated to the pilgrims and the loud speakers carried Her message:

"Dear children, today I call you to a complete union with God. Your body is on earth, but I ask you for your soul to be all the more often in God's nearness. You will achieve this through prayer, prayer with an open heart. In that way you will thank God for the immeasurable goodness which He gives to you through Me and, with a sincere heart, you will receive the obligation to treat the souls whom you meet with equal goodness. Thank you, my dear children."

The interpreter paused, then continued to speak, "Our Lady added: *'With the heart I pray to God to give strength and love to your shepherds to help you in this and to lead you.'*"

Isaac immediately broke into tears, ran to me, hugged me and held on tight. Michael smiled and I became quiet, fighting back my own tears. How privileged to receive a personal confirmation during such an important event meant for all pilgrims! Others with us were now asking, "What happened? Is everything ok? What's going on?"

We were the fortunate pilgrims!

Editor's note: George is from West Newton, PA.

(3/06)
St. Patrick's Intercession Leads Us to Discover Medjugorje

By Darlyne Mary Fujimoto

Two years ago, it never occurred to me to associate St. Patrick with Christ, much less Mother Mary, Medjugorje and the Church. How the Lord works in mysterious ways and how wonderfully He uses His saints to gather up His lost sheep. Here's how St. Patrick interceded and got the Medjugorje ball rolling for me:

I'd been laid low by a bad relapse of the virulent Fujian flu that had already claimed thousands of lives. After feeling like a walking corpse for weeks, I was finally beginning to feel better. Although neither Catholic nor Irish, I thought St. Paddy's Day was a good excuse to celebrate my regained health. After weeks of not having an appetite, the prospect of green beer and a corned beef and cabbage dinner was pretty darn appealing.

But the LA traffic that day was notoriously bad and my husband was late getting home. Not one to waste time, I killed that time by "googling" the words "green beer." What was up with that tradition? My search led me to a St. Patrick's website and I read up on that fourth century saint who was born to British nobility, captured as a youth, and enslaved by a cruel Druid chieftain to escape to become a priest and then eventually Bishop of Ireland, changing history forever.

Little did I know then that St. Paddy was to forever change our histories – my husband's and mine. While on the subject of St. Patrick, I vaguely recalled there was another saint that helped people to sell their houses. No, it wasn't St. Anthony. I just couldn't remember. So, I "googled" the words "saint selling houses." Links to St. Joseph websites instantly popped up.

Still no husband on the horizon, so I started perusing a web article on St. Joseph. There was a list of links at the bottom of the page and one in particular caught my eye – something about Mary visiting earth in present time. It sounded like it might be one of those cheesey tabloid articles. But heck, I had the time. Clicking on it, I learned that She was appearing in a faraway land called Bosnia, in a tiny village in the middle of nowhere with an impossibly long and unpronounceable name starting with "M," and had been doing so for almost 23 years.

I must say, I began reading the article with gigantic skepticism. "I pray to Her Son . . . and how is it that I don't know this?" Still no husband, and so I kept reading. The more I read about this mysterious – and miraculous – place called Medjugorje, the more intrigued I became.

Just then my husband pulled into the driveway and we took off. We celebrated my recovering health with hearty "Cheers!" over a pitcher of green beer and I gave no mind to what I had just learned about St. Joseph and Mother Mary until two days later on St. Joseph's Day.

Via inner promptings, Our Lady soon invited me to go on a pilgrimage. "Come, come quickly. You are my 11th hour convert." A few days later, my husband was extended an invitation as well. Our calls were so clear and powerful, we went at the first opportunity. On a mountain in a distant land called Medjugorje, we were converted. Within a year, in 2005, we received the Sacraments of Baptism, Confirmation and Holy Eucharist, and were sacramentally married in the Catholic Church, perhaps the least likeliest of the churches we would have considered joining.

This month we will once again celebrate St. Patrick's Day, but this time with hearts filled with gratitude. For it was St. Paddy who pointed me in the direction of St. Joseph, who in turn went out of his way that weekend to lead me to Medjugorje and his earthly spouse, Mother Mary, who in turn did the job She was predestined for: leading Her children, especially the wayward sheep, to Her Son.

Editor's note: Darlyne is from Cerritos, CA.

(5/08)
My Pilgrimage Journey

By Cathy Howe

I feel compelled to share what Our Lady told the visionaries in Medjugorje at the onset of the apparitions when they asked Her, "Why us?" Our Lady said, "God does not always look for the best."

My life and my family changed in 1991 when I was diagnosed with a very rare blood disease called mastocytosis, which has no cure, and led to an ever more rare manifestation of malignant non-Hodgkins Lymphoma. The disease seemed to take hold of me 26 years ago when I began to experience great fatigue and chronic infections, but the doctors did not diagnose the disease until biopsies were done in 1991. At that time the disease was truly a death sentence because it took me away from all I loved in life, especially time with my family the way I knew it before.

My spiritual healing did not begin until I went to Medjugorje, and I was in a very long dark night. I look back at this time and know that only God's grace and Our Lady's intercession and constant care of me allowed me not to shut down emotionally, spiritually and physically. Simple tasks like making my bed, taking a shower, or cooking a dinner, became huge mountains for me to climb, each moment of each day. I spent the majority of my time in bed every day. During this time, on January 11, 1994, my mom, my best friend and soul mate passed on. Our immediate family had a long history of serious illness, and just before my mom passed on, I truly was asking Our Lady why there was SO much pain and suffering. I went to a Catholic grade school and an all girl Catholic high school, but the part of my journey that I was about to embark on was not taught to me through my Catholic education or faith-walk, but taught ever so gently and sweetly by the Blessed Virgin Mary whom I loved so very much, and a great spiritual gift given to me, in my spiritual director. It was the Blessed Mother I went to, since I was a young child, to go to God for me because in ways I can now only begin to understand, I did not feel worthy to ask God. At the hardest, most challenging time of my life thus far, I received an answer in a way that would begin a new chapter in my life and life would never be the same again.

At my mom's viewing at the funeral home, I requested that her rosary beads be put in her hands. These rosary beads turned from crystal beads and links and crucifix to a beautiful rose gold from 8:05 to 9 P.M. My pastor, Fr. Ward, who was at the funeral home that evening, said that it was a message from the Blessed Mother, telling me my mom was OK and not to worry about her. This was witnessed not only by family, but friends there that evening. Truly, Heaven touched earth that evening and I turned into a "little child" of God feeling loved as never before.

This experience, coupled with continued gifts of spiritual phenomena through Our Lady, led me, very ill, to Medjugorje in June of 1994, not seeking a physical cure, but to thank Our Lady for the gift of the rosary beads.

So very much happened since that time, and I truly learned that God so much wants to touch us, heal us, speak to our soul in so many miraculous ways. The gifts of the Holy Spirit are being poured forth, I believe as never before, to a world so urgently in need of healing at the darkest time in history as I see it.

It was at this time I was called to Medjugorje by my Heavenly Mother, who had heard all of my prayers and could see as only Jesus' Mother could, all of the pain I was in. That first pilgrimage was truly heaven on earth for me and I came home and asked Our Lady to please let me share Medjugorje with the whole world, and I didn't want anyone to heal me but Her Son, Jesus. My spiritual director said to be careful of what you ask for – because you might just get it. At that time, I truly did not understand what I was asking – it was just loving words to my Heavenly Mother who I came home from Medjugorje more in love with than ever before.

Much has happened spiritually in my life since the onset of my illness and my first pilgrimage to Medjugorje in June of 1994. It is only through God's grace, Our Lady's constant care, and spiritual direction since 1995, and Pope John Paul II, in a most special way that I am here today. The fruits of these years, and the suffering I was asked to endure, I believe, are blossoming in "Mother's Prayer Family" – prayer group, "Mother's Hope Foundation" – an organization aiding sick and disadvantaged children, and "Mother's Pilgrims" – a travel group to Medjugorje. These were established while I was homebound and in bed, and each, I believe, directed by Our Blessed Mother and the great gift that I received on First Friday, October 5th, 2007, in Medjugorje.

In 1994, after I returned from Medjugorje, I was given the spiritual gift of inner locution, which is an inner voice written on my heart and at times heard in my ears. It took me many years to understand and accept, claim and feel comfortable with this gift, and to share this gift in THIS WAY is truly a miracle for me – one in which I truly believe Our Lady wishes to be shared at this time. My spiritual director always discerns these inner locutions. When I asked him years back, amid many tears and physical pains, and seeking much needed spiritual guidance, why God was asking me to start a prayer family and lead Mother's Hope when I was so sick, something I would have never chosen for myself, he said simply, *"God never asks us to do what we want to do, but what He wills us to do – thus it is a cross for us!"*

Holding onto my mom's rosary beads and Our Lady's hand, that cross turned into Easter joy on October 5th, the feast day of St. Maria Faustina, Apostle of Divine Mercy, who came into my life in a very special way years back. On October 2nd, Mirjana Soldo, one of the six visionaries in Medjugorje had her monthly apparition from Our Lady; Mother's Pilgrims is always present and graced to be very close to Mirjana at the time of her apparition. I was taken back when asked to lead a decade of the Holy Rosary and truly felt we were all in Heaven's arms. During the apparition I heard the words very clearly and softly written on my heart. "Climb Cross Mountain." I immediately felt it to be Our Lady's request. I told our spiritual director on our pilgrimage what I heard written on my heart, and knew I must try to do it because Our Lady asked me to do something I would never have thought to do on my own. Two days later, our group was scheduled to climb Mt. Krizevac. This was my 14th pilgrimage to Medjugorje and the majority of the time I spent back at my room. A couple of times I waited at the bottom of the hill and prayed. I remember feeling very scared as we all gathered at the bottom of Cross Mountain and saying to Our Lady, "I'm scared, so You have to hold my one hand." And with my mom's rosary beads held so tightly in my other hand, I said to Our Lady, "And my mom has to hold my other hand and we have to climb Cross Mountain for Jesus." With a body that could not climb Apparition Hill alone, I embarked on another part of my spiritual journey trusting what I believe I learned through so much suffering and yet so much joy at times led by Our Lady. I let go of my fears and thought with my heart and not my head, and gave them to Our Lady. I made it to the top of Cross Mountain. No words can describe the feelings I felt and still do, as I remember kissing the palm of my hand and touching the cross, then closing my eyes and putting my head on the cross for a long time. We were one, the Cross and me. The huge white Cross loomed ever so high, and the sweetness I felt in my soul was indescribable. That big Cross and all the endless huge boulders on the way up reflected all of our lives. At that moment, I felt like I had made peace with my cross of poor health, and it was taken from me. But I had to learn, one must climb the mountains of life, one step at a time, never looking up, as I had been taught ever so gently by the Mother of God, and was able to do that special day.

The sun shined so brightly and the blue sky and clouds seemed to lead me back down the mountain, taking one rock, one step at a time, like I had done it many times before. With inexpressible joy I found myself running over to St. James Church that morning and gazing up at the statue of Our Lady in front of the church. We had been through so much together, Our Lady and me, all my life. We climbed so many mountains together and at times, so many times, She and Jesus carried me. I went inside St. James Church; the Italian Mass had just begun and I was able to walk easily up front and stand right in front of Our Lady's statue. After I received Jesus, I knelt looking up at Her – feeling blessed beyond words, and as the miracle of my physical healing had been given me, I felt for a moment sadly, "What could I now offer to Jesus that would be worthy?" I felt compelled after Mass to go to the rectory to tell Fr. Svetozar, the assistant pastor at St. James Church in Medjugorje. Father and I have become very close since 1995, and he knew well about my ongoing illness and my physical limitations. When I told him what I had experienced at Mirjana's apparition, and my climb of Cross Mountain, he said, "Praise be Jesus and Mary! Only Heaven could have done this!" He also said, "What I respect the most about you is your courage and for just being Cathy." I said, "Father, it is not my courage but was given to me by Jesus and Mary, truly."

After I climbed Cross Mountain, the energy I had not had for 26 years was instantly given back to me and I knew that deep inside of me I could stop taking all of my medications. After returning home, my husband and I went to a prescheduled check-up with my oncologist at Hillman Cancer Center. I felt compelled to bring him rosary beads, medals, a picture of the Infant Jesus, and Our Lady, and a rock from Medjugorje. After sharing my experience in Medjugorje with my doctor, and the reality of the symptoms I had experienced for so long all being gone, the doctor told me he would write on my chart that "Today the patient shows no signs of disease and is in remission." I said, "That is not true because there is no cure for mastcytosis and my malignant non-Hodgkins lymphoma has not come back." He said, "You are right – there is no cure, and I know I did not do anything." I said, "I know it is a MIRACLE," and he said, "Well, I guess you could say it is a miracle, but I want you to come back and see me in one year." I believe it is gone, never to come back.

EVERYONE who goes to Medjugorje receives a miracle, and one is not bigger than another. I learned the greatest healing God can give you is a spiritual healing. I learned that you don't have to climb any mountains for God. If you can climb Apparition Hill or Cross Mountain, that's great, but some people climb mountains everyday of their lives. A very wise priest told me that, in 1994, when I felt so sad and sick and everyone in our group was going to climb Cross Mountain and I couldn't. If God had healed my body in 1994, I would not have understood what He did or why He did it.

I learned healing comes in steps and God works in each person differently: spiritual healing, which, if we cooperate, can continue on forever; the healing of peace and joy; and physical healing if Almighty God deigns it. Medjugorje is an Oasis of Peace, where miracles flow like an unending river for all who seek to know Jesus and Mary and Their loving embrace.

I just returned home from Medjugorje, and just like Our Heavenly Mother, She embraced me once again as Her dearly beloved chosen daughter. Medjugorje visionary Mirjana invited me to kneel beside her at her second of the month apparition. Again, no words can describe the peace and joy I felt as I thanked Our Lady with each beat of my heart.

Our Lady is calling us to be Her "Dear Little Children." Don't ever be afraid to answer Her call. Please share what Our Lady has done for you, as people need to know that miracles exist. I believe more today than ever before.

Editor's note: You can visit Cathy's websites, www.mothershope.org, and www.motherspilgrims.com.

(3/05)
A Rose Petal from Our Lady of Grace

By Mike Golovich

In October of 2004, I went on a pilgrimage to Medjugorje with a group of fourteen. On Sunday, October 10, we left our pansion around

8:15 A.M. to go to the church in Tihaljina, where Fr. Jozo had a statue of Mary placed. When I entered the church, I saw the beautiful statue of Mary. I knelt before her and said some prayers. I got up and walked around a little and came back to the statue, and kneeling down before her again, I glanced at the floor in front of her and there was a rose petal, bright red. I picked it up and placed it in a wallet insert with a picture of Mary which I had in my shirt pocket. I said some prayers and then I took some pictures with a one-time use camera which I had with me.

After the others gathered in the church, our spiritual adviser, Fr. James Graham, had Holy Mass for us. It was special, our own Holy Mass in a far-off country. After Mass, we had some time to spend in the church, after which we went outside. I went before the statue of Mary outside the church and knelt before her. I felt prompted to pray a Rosary, so I did.

As I was praying the Rosary, I noticed another group member near me, and I heard the bus motor. But something was telling me, "Schedules can be broken; finish praying the Rosary." I again felt another member of the group near me, and I just showed I had a little to go. She waited till I finished. She understood. I showed the rose petal to the others once I was on the bus. After going to the Oasis of Peace, we returned to Medjugorje. Later on in the day, I realized that the date was 10-10-04, the same as my home address, 1010-4th St.!

That afternoon I met Michael, Mary and Judy from Ireland. Michael had a stroke about seven or eight years ago and was in a wheelchair. I shared with them regarding my stroke five years ago. On Tuesday, October 12, we were invited to a concert by David Parkes in the yellow building behind St. James. To my surprise, Michael, Mary and Judy entered. I had noticed what seemed like facial features of Jesus on the rose petal, so after the concert I went up to Michael, Mary and Judy and showed the rose petal to Mary. She showed it to Michael and bent down to him and he whispered something to her. She told me that he said it was Jesus. I didn't know what to think. David Parkes, who was cured of Crohn's disease was about 10 feet from me, so I went over and showed him the rose petal. He said, "It's Jesus! You're blessed!" After this I showed it to others.

After I returned to the States, I had my film processed. Even though I had taken about 15 pictures in the church, only three came out of the statue of Our Lady of Grace. They were beautiful, almost lifelike. Even my doctor thought it was a real person.

Medjugorje is beautiful and there is something happening there! I still treasure my gift from Mary.

Editor's note: If you would like a wallet-sized picture of the rose petal and Our Lady, you can contact Mike at (724)869-8284 or write to him at 1010-4th St. Baden, PA 15005. Mike has distributed over 30,000 of these cards since this story was originally written.

(11/09)
My Personal Pilgrimage

By Susan Tassone

How did I get involved with the holy souls in Purgatory?

I want to share why I got involved and tell a little bit about how God is working in my life to help you understand what I experienced.

On August 11, 1983, the feast of my patron, St. Susanna, I was hit head on and injured by a cab, which left my left leg damaged. My doctor told me that my leg was permanently damaged, and that I would have constant bouts of painful swelling and tenderness of the leg for the rest of my life.

The date was even more significant. Fifty years earlier, on that very same day, my great aunt, known as "Little Mary," who was ten years old at the time, was also injured in a car accident. She died. I survived. A priest told me that my life was spared and that I had a mission. He said that sometimes a sacrifice is made in the family for a greater cause. It shook me up.

I have had a special bond with the Blessed Mother since I was a child. My mother was very active in the parish, and we were very young when she planted the seed for the love of Our Lady in our hearts. (I remember, for example, we had the Pilgrim Virgin statue in our home.)

In 1993, with the permission of my doctor, I decided to go on a pilgrimage to Medjugorje, to pay a visit, experience closeness with Our Lady, and to return home. Our Blessed Mother had other plans. During an apparition on Good Friday night, 1993, I saw an image of Our Lady within a cobalt blue color. I knew it was Her. They say the white flashes are angels that appear before Her. My knees shook. I "knelt" to steady them. I was in amazement and awe.

My rosary links turned to gold and my leg, my "permanently damaged" leg, was healed on Mt. Krizevac (Cross Mountain). My doctor said it was a miracle and I was blessed. However, he waited three years before he would document the healing. He wanted to be sure it was real. Three years later, I flew back to Medjugorje to deliver the letter. It is one of the documented medical cases of registered healings in Medjugorje. Fr. Slavko Barbaric interviewed me for "Mir Magazine," the local magazine of Medjugorje.

When I returned home, I realized Our Lady had other surprises for me. Someone gave me a booklet called *Read Me or Rue It*. It was about the plight of the holy souls in Purgatory. I was fascinated with the stories about the holy souls and how they intercede for those who relieve their sufferings. These souls were in desperate need of our Masses. The Mass is the most powerful means to relieve and release the holy souls in Purgatory, especially Gregorian Masses – 30 Masses in a row for one deceased soul. Put Gregorian Masses in your will!

The booklet said the holy souls would repay you 10,000 times. I liked the idea. I needed all the friends I could get! It was like quid pro quo: You help me, and I will help you. I wanted all my family and friends to reach God. I identified with the holy souls. I don't like being cooped up. I am a free spirit. I like my freedom. Why not help release them so they can reach Heaven? Free them!

I took it upon myself to become a missionary for our holy heroes. In my journey, I began to understand how critical the doctrine of Purgatory is to our faith, how Purgatory is a very positive and consoling part of that faith.

I began collecting Mass stipends for the holy souls in Purgatory. People of every faith gave donations. I soon realized that they were hungry for God. I collected $763 and brought the donation to my pastor. To my surprise, he was unable to accept the donation because he was the only priest in the parish and his Mass-intentions book was filled. For the first time, it personally struck home how we need to pray for vocations to the priesthood. The priest sent me to the Catholic Missions Office – or, as it's officially called, the Propagation of the Faith. Every diocese has one. Its purpose is to support our missionary priests all over the world through our prayers and donations.

I visited the Missions Director and learned again how desperately our Catholic missionary priests needed Mass stipends. Many times those gifts are their sole income because the people of the countries where they serve are too poor to donate financially.

Since 1993, I have waged a crusade for the holy souls in Purgatory, collecting Mass stipends – anything I could do for our missionaries and suffering friends in need. I tried to promote this through television, radio, Internet print media, public speaking, and writing. To date, more than two million dollars have been raised for Mass stipends for our missionary priests because of readers like you. I like to see it as two million souls released from Purgatory. Who do you miss the most? Who do you wish you could have done more for? Have a Mass offered for them! Include Masses for the living, too. Remember, the Mass heals the living and the deceased!

My journey has deepened my faith tremendously, allowing me to better see the goodness and mercy of God, and to join with my fellow supplicants in celebrating the beauty of our faith. My heartfelt thanks to Our Lady, my life, my sweetness, and all my hope.

Editor's note: Susan answered Our Lady's call to "give the joy of the Holy Mass for the holy souls . . ." Susan has authored several books on Purgatory. She is recognized as leading the "Purgatory movement" in the United States. Susan is a popular speaker and is a frequent guest on radio and television shows. Visit www.spiritualtreasury.com for Masses and Gregorian Masses.

(6/08)
Testimony of Zeljka Rozic

By June Klins

Two years ago, when I went to Medjugorje for the 25th anniversary, we were blessed to have as our guide Zeljka Rozic, who is visionary Vicka's cousin. Because it was anniversary time and there were so many groups there, Zeljka had to do double, and sometimes even triple duty, so we did not see her as much as we would have, had we gone at a different time. Zeljka was very apologetic about the situation, but it could not be helped and we all understood. We were just happy to have her as our guide. When Zeljka was with us, I took notes when she said things I thought would interest our readers and videoed her speaking a couple of times. Since we are approaching anniversary time again, I thought this might be a good time to share some of Zeljka's testimony.

It was Sunday evening, when we arrived in Medjugorje, and because of delays we were too late for Mass at St. James. We had a priest with us, though, so we figured he would just have Mass for us at our pansion. However, there was a glitch. Zeljka told us that a number of years ago the bishop there had said Masses could not be said at the pansions. They had to be said in the Adoration Chapel or in St. James Church. So off she went to get special permission for us to have Mass in the chapel. She told us that the chapel was only open for Adoration till 6 P.M. because at that time everything on the church grounds closes so that people can join in the evening Croatian Mass. Zeljka and Father Doug, our spiritual adviser, obtained permission and we had a beautiful Mass.

On our first full day in Medjugorje, Zeljka spoke to us near the shade of a tree in front of St. James. She gave us some tips about staying safe and cool in the unusual heat wave they were experiencing that year. Then she shared some interesting stories with us.

Zeljka told us that her aunt, Vicka's mother, once told a story about when she and Vicka were in a train car with six people as Vicka's apparition time approached. Vicka got quiet and was preparing for Our Lady to come. Vicka made the Sign of the Cross. She did not react to any poking or anything during the apparition. After the apparition was over, she made the Sign of the Cross again, and then went right on talking as if nothing had happened. She later told her mother that she was embarrassed, and did not want to call attention to herself.

Zeljka said that the visionaries no longer have their apparitions on the church grounds in obedience to the bishop. When the visionaries were having their apparitions at the church, Our Lady would bless all religious items with Her Motherly Blessing during the apparition. But now since so few people would be able to be present for an apparition and have their items blessed by Our Lady, She would bless the religious items people brought to the church during the time of the apparition, 6:40 P.M. anyway. What a wonderful Mother to provide for Her children like this. (She always stresses that religious items should be blessed by a priest also, which is the greater blessing.)

Zeljka talked a little about Vicka's suffering. She explained that Vicka had recently had back surgery and could not see pilgrims. Vicka was the only visionary not able to participate in the 25th anniversary celebrations on June 24th and 25th. It must have been quite a cross for her, but Zeljka told us that Vicka willingly suffers for Our Lady's intentions and has always had health problems of one kind or another.

Zeljka said that one day she was looking over Vicka's shoulder reading the notebook that tells the story of Our Lady's life that Vicka will publish when Our Lady gives her the go-ahead. But when Zeljka turned around she could not remember one thing that she had read!

Pointing to the statue of St. Leopold Mandic by the confessionals, Zelkja told us that when St. Leopold's church was bombed in Italy, the only things that were left standing were the statue of Our Lady and the confessional.

A holy hour of Adoration is held every Wednesday and Saturday night, and Zeljka told us that on June 24th there would be all night Adoration for the anniversary.

We walked with Zeljka to the Risen Jesus statue behind St. James and Zeljka shared some interesting information about the statue that I did not know. She said that the statue was sent to Rome before it came to Medjugorje in 1998, and Pope John Paul II blessed it. She said that the liquid mysteriously coming from the knee of the statue has been scientifically tested to be human tears. She said that a pilgrim from Poland wiped her cloth on the tears and it came out on the cloth looking like blood. It too was tested and found to be human blood. She emphasized that the parish of St. James has made no official statement on this phenomenon.

In answer to the question of a pilgrim, Zeljka said that Ivan had an apparition of Fr. Slavko after he died just like he had of Pope John Paul II the night of his death. And in answer to another question, she said that locutionist Jelena still gets locutions occasionally, but not as frequently as before.

The next day. Zeljka told us some more stories from the earlier days of Medjugorje and answered some questions the group had. She talked about how hard it was to live under Communist rule and how especially hard it was on the visionaries. There were times when the visionaries' relatives and acquaintances were ordered by the Communists to be among the visionaries and to spy on them. Zeljka recalled one occasion where a young man came to be there during the apparition. He was a friend of the family and Our Lady told the visionaries he was there for a purpose, so after the apparition they said, "Someone is here not because of a good reason, and we would like that person not to show up again." Then he got up and left, quite embarrassed.

Then Zeljka told about the time that the visionaries were kidnapped by a social worker. They were begging her to return them to Medjugorje as it got close to apparition time, but of course she was told not to. So she kept them there during the apparition time, and they were praying as apparition time got close. They were able to see a great light coming from Medjugorje, and Our Lady appeared to them at the waterfall. They were sad and crying and She consoled them and told them not to be afraid.

One of our pilgrims asked Zeljka if it were true that the social worker who kidnapped the visionaries was converted after that. Zeljka said, "She always was a believer, but she was working for the government, and she was told, 'You do this today or you're fired, and not only that, you will be in trouble.' She was forced – not that she wanted to do that, because she lived here and was their cousin and neighbor. She really had no choice. She did not mean anything bad, and it's not like she was a bad person. She was always a believer, but she just had to do that."

Then Zeljka told us about Vicka's father: "As for my uncle, Vicka's father, he was in Germany when the apparitions started, and he didn't know anything. One day he opened the papers they were getting there in Germany on a regular basis from here, and he saw his daughter was in there and that's how he learned about the apparitions! He read the paper that his daughter was seeing Our Lady, and you can imagine how he felt! They had eight children, and he was the only one working in Germany. They were working in the fields and he was afraid to come home because he knew if he came they would take away his passport, and he would not be able to go back to his work. So poor him! You can imagine how he felt. He knew they were going through persecution and everything, and he wouldn't dare to come because the officials would take his passport."

Another pilgrim asked Zeljka if the parents of the visionaries had trouble believing in the apparitions in the beginning. Zeljka said, "All of us couldn't believe in the beginning, but when we saw changes in them – like imagine Jakov was not yet 10, and try to make a 10 year-old come to church and pray three parts of the Rosary, stay for Mass and for the apparition and pray seven Our Father's, Hail Mary's and Glory Be's, and the others were teenagers, and just seeing the change in them, that was the best proof to us that something supernatural was happening to them."

The Risen Jesus statue behind St. James

(4/09)
Gifts Exuding from the Statue at Medjugorje Increase During the Hour of Mercy

By Andrea Toto-Walshe

I met my husband in April of 2005 during a pilgrimage with Penny Abbruzzese and Fr. Moyna to Fatima, Lourdes, and Garabandal. Both of us booked relatively close to the date of departure unbeknownst to each other. There was a special calling that we both felt we needed to respond to, not realizing that a unique bond was being created by all of heaven for us to be joined. From our very first trip many unexplained happenings occurred, sometimes on a regular basis.

We were married on December 10, 2005, and since my husband's family traveled from Europe for our wedding, we postponed our honeymoon till February, 2006. As we wanted to consecrate our marriage to the Blessed Mother and give thanks, we went to Medjugorje with Our Lady Queen of Peace Prayer Group from February 11th until February 19th. The gifts that we were showered with from our Blessed Mother were incredible.

There is a castle in Medjugorje that is owned by a couple named Nancy and Patrick Latta. Nancy is Fr. Jozo Zovko's translator. Fr. Jozo is the priest who saved the children from the authorities when no one believed that they were seeing the Blessed Virgin. We were invited for breakfast Saturday morning, along with some priests and sisters in our group. After a wonderful breakfast, Nancy asked us if we would stand in the middle of the kitchen, close our eyes, and open our hands. We thought we would be given a special blessing. We were known as the "newlyweds" and Patrick (my husband) was always asking priests for special wedding blessings. Nancy told us that the Blessed Mother appeared on Apparition Hill holding this heart made of red baby roses. The Blessed Mother gave it to one of the visionaries, who in turn gave it to Nancy and told her, "You will know who to give it to." To our utter surprise, Nancy gave it to us! We received a wedding gift from the Blessed Mother! Needless to say we couldn't find a scraper large enough to peel my husband Patrick off the ceiling!

That afternoon we went to the site of the Risen Christ. This is a fifteen foot bronze statue of the 'Cross of the Risen Christ' that has been exuding a substance that drips from the knee. This has been happening since the apparition's 20th anniversary in 2001. A friend of ours was here about six months prior and she had this liquid tested. It came back "human tears." We believe that when Jesus was crucified, our Blessed Mother was holding Him around the knees, and that these are the tears of Our Blessed Mother. We wanted to bring home some of the handkerchiefs with the tears to those who were sick.

It was approximately 3 P.M. when we went, and we brought with us ten white and ten blue handkerchiefs to absorb the liquid. Also note that at times this liquid smelled like roses. My husband tasted the liquid and said it had a salty taste, like tears. We noticed that between 3 and 4 P.M. (the hour of Divine Mercy), the liquid ran out instead of shedding several droplets every ten seconds.

Patrick was taking each handkerchief and soaking it with the "tears." When he handed one to me, we both noticed there was blood on it! The first thing Patrick said was "bronze does not rust." It looked like blood and water mixed.

We took it back to the house where we were staying at to show everyone. We were still in shock. When we arrived home I had no idea where we were going to keep the heart and the blood soaked handkerchief. By accident I noticed a small hat box and mentioned to Patrick I must have purchased this during my compulsive days, because I do not remember buying it. Patrick commented that it would be perfect for our heart and handkerchief. What I did not notice was the top of the box was a blue butterfly (seen at other sites of apparition). Perfect !

Mary's Mantle, Winter Issue 2007

(5/09)
The Gift of My Cross

By Donna McMaster

When I was a child, I didn't know God. I was raised by atheists, I went to public school, never heard of the Bible, and I didn't know what the words, "sin" or "saint" meant. To me, Jesus was a baby statue people withdrew from their attics at Christmas time, laid Him in a bed of straw for a school play, then wrapped Him back up until the following year. Christmas meant presents delivered from a jolly man in a red suit, and Easter meant one thing: chocolate. For those raised in religious families, it is difficult to understand how anyone wouldn't know about God. But for those of us raised without Him, how could we know? If no one at home or school or on the playground ever mentions Jesus, then it is quite easy to remain ignorant.

My first exposure to the word, "Catholic" came when I planned to marry a Catholic man. As required by him, I got baptized and received

Holy Communion on my wedding day. Back then, we didn't have R.C.I.A. classes, so I was not prepared properly. The elderly priest who gave me the Sacraments was retiring, so I suppose he thought the new priest would instruct me. The new priest must have thought the former priest had already enlightened me. Either way, I didn't understand what I was doing and I didn't care, as long as I pleased my spouse (who didn't seem to know much more about God than I knew). We attended church off and on, but the homilies about unknown people in long ago times bored me. Eventually, I quit going altogether.

Although having several children gave me great joy, my marriage seemed doomed from the start and eventually fell apart. I was drowning in financial troubles and developed serious physical ailments. I didn't feel like I could walk one more step through life. One night, alone in my upstairs bedroom, I walked over to the sliding patio door, looking down. I contemplated jumping, head first. Too painful, I decided. Then, for some unexplained reason, I looked up. With rivers of tears soaking my nightgown, I cried out, "God, are you real? If you are, please help me! Show me a reason to live!"

The next morning, a neighbor came with a stack of papers and shoved them in my hand. "Here," she said, "my mother went to some place overseas and brought me these. I'm not interested, but I know you like to read, so I thought you might want them. It's something about Mary appearing in a place called Medjugorje."

I didn't ask where Medjugorje was. Instead, I asked, "Mary who?" My surprised neighbor shook her head. "Just read them. They're self-explanatory."

I was so hungry for truth and a meaningful purpose in my life, I would have eaten those pages if I could have! I read them over and over again. As my eyes rolled across the pages, something inside me stirred. A flicker of hope grew stronger and I felt like a magnet being pulled towards something, someone. I couldn't resist. Before I knew what happened, my mouth suddenly blurted, "God, I believe! I believe this is true!"

That night, I had a dream: Mary came. She told me that it was no coincidence that I received the Medjugorje messages. It was She, Herself, who brought them to me. She introduced me to Jesus who had been killed because of my sins. The look of sadness in Her eyes pierced my heart like a hot dagger. I cried as I asked Her to forgive me. Brilliant rays of light glowed from Her smile. She explained about sin, about the soul, the Catholic Church and many things. Somehow, She communicated with me without moving Her mouth, except when She called me Her "daughter." My heart melted as a beautiful warmth covered me. Then, She invited me to Medjugorje. I had no money. How could I go?

The next few weeks were frustrating. I was so excited to find God, to discover Mary and to fall in love with Jesus, that I told everyone I encountered about my experience. Most of my six children didn't believe me. Their father didn't believe me. My parents insisted I had lost my mind. I went to a priest to seek spiritual direction. He didn't believe me, either. I complained to God, and asked Him to send me to someone who could help.

I found Father Leroy Lee. He had been to Medjugorje several times and knew the visionaries. He gave me the instructions I had missed. He taught me the Ten Commandments, gave me the Sacrament of Reconciliation, bought me a Bible and arranged for my husband and me to go to Medjugorje with him! Unfortunately, Father Lee died of cancer before our trip, but it was his dying wish that we go on the pilgrimage anyway, so we honored his request.

On the first morning after arriving in Medjugorje, our group sat behind Saint James Church, listening to our guide. Something prompted me to move away from the crowd. As I sat alone on the ground, suddenly, something dazzling white caught my eye. I heard a male voice say, "Pick up your cross and carry it always." I plucked the small grey stone from the earth and noticed sparkling white lines in the shape of a cross running through it. I stuck it in my pocket, thinking that I was supposed to keep this stone with me. The next morning, again alone, I asked Jesus, "How do I follow You? It has taken me so long to find You, I never want to lose You." Again, I heard a male voice, "If you want to follow Me, you must follow the path of the Cross. It is a road of suffering now that leads to glory later." Then, I understood that carrying my cross meant my suffering in life, not the physical stone I was given. As I turned the stone around in my hand, I saw the shape of a large shoe and inside that shoe, right before my eyes, a tiny footprint appeared, while I heard the words, "To follow Me is not to lag behind or race ahead. Put your footsteps in Mine and walk *with* Me." To my surprise, I looked up to see a member from our group standing over me, watching. He had witnessed the footprint appearing, although he did not hear the words I heard. Deeply touched, I showed the stone to others. Most of the people did not believe me.

A group of us witnessed the cross on the mountain glow bright red. I watched someone's rosary turn gold as they held it. I even found miraculous images on developed photographs I took, that I hadn't seen at the time. All of these physical signs, though, were not the most important things to me. They were like small necessities along the path to Heaven, pointing out the way, much like a compass and map assist someone on their earthly journey. I asked for none of these "special" things. I only asked God to show me His love and to help me to love Him.

I'd like to say that my marriage was repaired in Medjugorje and that my health improved. I wish I could relate how my family came to believe in our loving Lord, and how my financial problems disappeared. But the truth is none of that happened. It has been thirteen years since my trip to Medjugorje. During that time, the Catholic Church annulled my marriage. My health worsened and my financial problems increased. My parents and most of my children have disowned me. I lost my house, my friends, my car, and I was picked apart cruelly by mental health experts during a child custody battle. One important element remains, though, that no one can ever steal, misplace, borrow or kill: my faith in God!

Not everyone who goes to Medjugorje receives exactly what they ask for, but I am convinced that everyone who goes there does receive gifts from God. He gives according to our needs, not our desires. In truth, the precious treasures I gained more than compensate for what I lost: My heavenly Father gave me the gift of *writing*, to share with others on paper whatever He wants the world to know. I have had many articles published in various Catholic magazines and I continue to make use of this talent. I am currently working on a couple of books. I also received the gift of *understanding*, so that when I read scriptures, I can understand how God wants me to live my life, full of meaningful purpose. I received the gift of *joy* in knowing Jesus and Mary, and sharing that love with others. I received the gift of calm *acceptance* during my trials. Patience and perseverance have become my close friends. Faith, hope and charity fill my heart. I received a deep desire for Heaven, rather than earthly goods. These graces are worth more than all I suffered, and if I could go back in time, I would endure it all again. There is absolutely nothing I wouldn't give, just to be with my Lord forever.

To some extent, I do understand how saints can bear sufferings for Christ. (Not that I am a saint!) When God takes from us with one hand, He gives sevenfold with the other hand. The type of perseverance and faith we receive that enables us to continue, while we focus on Jesus is a supernatural gift from God. We cannot do it alone, but we can do all in Christ. How could Peter walk on water? How could the apostles cure diseases? They, like we, did nothing on their own account, but God accomplished His works through them, by infusing His loving power into them. I compare this to someone gasping for air. When a paramedic infuses oxygen, the patient can breathe. I used to say, "I can't." Now, I say, "With You, Lord, I can!"

I carry the little stone with me, a physical reminder of the love of Christ and His Mother. Even though I still suffer, I am at peace. I don't know whether I am destined to live out my life one step ahead of bill collectors (I hope not!), and I'm not sure how long it will take for my health to improve (soon, I hope!), and I doubt I will ever marry the good Catholic man I dreamed of (no white knights riding up to my doorstep, yet!). Nonetheless, with God's powerful gift of acceptance that I received in Medjugorje, I can bear whatever God gives or takes away, and I feel truly blessed that I, a sinner, have been welcomed into the Immaculate Heart of Mary and Sacred Heart of Jesus.

Now, for the rest of the story . . .

I have been praying all these years to reconnect with the organization that gave me those first messages, those first glimpses of hope from the stack of papers through my neighbor. I am certain that those people prayed for me, and I wanted to thank them and encourage them to continue prayers for non-believers like me. Their prayers are being answered! I couldn't remember the address, but I would never forget the blue and white pages, since blue is my favorite color. I also remembered the general place they were from: Pennsylvania. Last year, I was invited to a "Medjugorje Mass" offered at a local place by our parish priest, who made a pilgrimage to Medjugorje. While there, a friend offered me copies of the monthly messages she received and suggested I write for my own copies. I did, and am now receiving "The Spirit of Medjugorje" newsletters from Pennsylvania – the very same messages from the stack of papers that first set my heart ablaze, beginning my journey from atheism to Catholicism! So, to staff and readers alike, a very big THANK YOU from the bottom of my heart! Please continue your prayers and good work, and be assured that God truly is listening! Helping one soul is priceless.

For any of you who have not yet made a pilgrimage to Medjugorje: Please believe firmly that God will shower His blessings upon you. He may not give you what you ask for. He might just give you more than you ask for. And I'm sure Heaven will be more joy than any of us can ever imagine! May God bless and reward each of you abundantly.

Editor's note: Donna is from Ontario, Canada. She recently wrote the following update to her story: "Fourteen years after God gave me the gift of acceptance in Medjugorje, to carry my cross alone, Our Lord surprised me with another gift of acceptance – the opportunity to accept a marriage proposal from a loving, Catholic man whose name was written into my heart in high school. On November 1, 2010 (All Saints' Day), Phil Tamburino and I were married in St. Mary's Church, Welland, Ontario, Canada. I am now writing a book about our long journey towards God and each other."

(5/05)
Our Miracle Baby

By Cindy Homan

My husband and I went to Medjugorje in April of 1991. We were 23, and we went to prepare for our marriage. In April of 1993 we went back and asked for a baby. On our first trip, while we were climbing Mt. Krizevac, I took a picture of the rocks to show people back home how the people would climb barefoot up the mountain.

All the way up Krizevac are the Stations of the Cross. When I got the pictures developed you could see Jesus' face with crown of thorns with the rocks in the background. Many miracles happened in our pictures on the first and second trip.

We were married the following September. We had a Medjugorje wedding – we exchanged our vows on the crucifix. We tried to have a baby, but I had extensive stage-4 endometriosis. I was on my fifth round of lupron injections to put my body into a temporary state of menopause to help my body heal.

When we went back to Medjugorje in April of 1993, not many pilgrims were there that Easter because of the war in Bosnia. We were blessed to go up in the choir loft with Marija and Ivan for the apparition. As soon as the Blessed Mother appeared you could smell the most powerful scent of roses. You knew She was there at that time. My husband and I both asked the Blessed Mother to ask Jesus for a child. That July I found out I was pregnant! The doctors felt this was impossible because of the lupron injections. They did an ultrasound, and I had a complete placenta previa. I was bleeding throughout my pregnancy.

Brian and I had started a Medjugorje prayer group in May of 1991, and that prayer group prayed daily for me and the baby. Brian Scott Homan was born on March 3, 1994; he was seven weeks premature. The day he was born I started hemorrhaging and had an emergency C-section. Prior to the surgery they give me three steroid injections because his lungs were not developed. I was told afterwards that Fr. Ferraro prayed before the tabernacle and kept a light on next to the tabernacle for me and the baby. Brian had no lung difficulties. He did stay in the special care nursery for two weeks, and he came home on 3/17/93, 4 lbs. 6oz. He was a healthy baby. Thank God for everything.

We tried to have another child and couldn't. I went into the hospital for a procedure, and I was told at that time I had a very large complex mass (endometrioma) on the ovary connecting to the colon. I had to see a gynecologist and colon rectal surgeon to perform the surgery. They told us that they don't know how I could have conceived or carried a child. We know it was the grace of God and the Blessed Mother. We can never thank Them enough for what They have done for us.

A postscript to this story – while we were there [in Medjugorje] in 1991 we made a cross out of twigs and tied it together with my husband's miraculous medal and we had placed all our petitions under the rocks. When we climbed Krizevac two years later I said to my husband, "Can you imagine if our cross is still there?" The cross WAS still there with his medal still tied to it. What a gift!

Editor's note: Cindy is from Billerica, MA.

(3/09)
My Miracle

By Kathy Cook

In December, 2006, I made an appointment with one of our local ENTs for what I thought was a blocked left ear. I assumed it was blocked with ear wax and had to be flushed, as I have had this procedure in the past and was told that I would be "prone to this." I was surprised when one of the "young maverick" doctors, after looking into my ear, told me I had fluid behind my eardrum and he would have to "drain" it. I was moved to a different location in the office and he performed a myringotomy on my ear (which hurt beyond belief) and told me I would be fine in a couple days and my hearing would return in full.

Post surgery, my ear starting "leaking" during the night when I was asleep and I would find my pillow and nightgown soaked in fluid. I called the MD who performed the surgery and he saw me right away and told me I had developed a "post-op" infection, which would require antibiotics and steroids. This continued for two years total and five surgical procedures later, in addition to nine courses of the "top of the line" antibiotics and steroids to heal my ear over the next 18 months. The expenses incurred trying to fix my ear were immeasurable.

Needless to say, the "leaking" continued, and a new horror – it was also leaking during the day while I was at work. I am a local hospital customer phone representative and my daily duties included the answering of phones all day long for customer disputes with their bills. Not only could I not hear the patients' complaints and respond accordingly, but my clothes were now dotted with wet spots from my leaking ear. In March, 2008, I was officially discharged from my ENT with the second doctor of the particular group of specialists, stating, "I am officially out of options." I made an appointment in April, 2008 with the head of our ENTs at the hospital that I work for, thinking he could help me. He also prescribed meds and told me to call him if I needed to.

In August of 2008, I was referred to one of our "oldest" ENT specialists in my area. He was a down-to-earth, "old-school" Jewish doctor in practice for over 40 years who pulled no punches. He performed another myringotomy on my ear, and when yet another post-op infection developed, he brought me and my husband into his office on a Sunday afternoon, and prefaced the consult saying, "I don't want you to worry, I will be with you every step of the way for what I am about to tell you." He went on to say that he thought I was suffering from a "cerebral spinal fluid leak," and he was referring me to specialist at HUP (Hospital of the University of Pennsylvania) immediately, due to the fact that I had an open pathway to my brain and could contract meningitis which could be fatal, if not taken care of immediately. He went on to say that the only way to "fix" this problem was a dual surgery by an ENT and a neurologist simultaneously to patch the leak in the dura of my brain.

I could ramble on and on about the horrors incurred by me personally as I met with the ENT and the neurosurgeon in Philadelphia; however, I will tell you that during my November 3, 2008 visit with Dr. Kevin Judy and after an MRI at that facility, I signed the OR consents with many, many risks which could occur during the surgery which included: a heart attack on the table, a stroke on the table, inability to speak after severing my facial cranial nerves, inability to close my left eye, inability to walk, blood loss requiring blood transfusions, which included its own set of risks, inability to hear, chronic infections, and the fact that there were no guarantees associated with this surgery, etc, etc, etc. The reality was – if I did not allow the surgery, I could die within days due to many types of brain infections and brain abscesses. I felt I had no choice but to undergo this risky surgery to plug up the hole in my head. For the sake of my husband and children, I signed all forms. Surgery date was to be in December sometime.

About November 5, 2008, my aunt Kay (no blood relative – my mother's best friend) called me and told me she wanted to see me. My husband and I went to her house and she presented me with "the cloth of Medjugorje" and explained to me what it was and what she wanted me to do with it. She advised me to keep it as long as necessary, but when I was finished, I was to return the cloth to her for the next person that needed it. I went home immediately and read over all the material she included with the cloth and commenced using it that day. My next visit to Philadelphia was December 3 with the surgical ENT who would be performing my surgery. I had used my prayer cloth every morning. On my knees I would pray to Jesus and the Blessed Virgin to please release me from this suffering and pending surgery. I developed a renewed deepening of my faith, which I had lost after the death of my beloved mother in the year 2000 – the usual selfish feeling of "Why did God have to take my mother at age 69, when she had so much more love to give us and her grandchildren?"

To my complete surprise, and also my family's complete relief (my sisters are all in the medical field and knew full well the risks of the surgery), Dr. Bigelow told me that day, following his examination and many tests, that *my CSF Leak had spontaneously sealed over and there was no need for the surgery at this time*! He was not promising, however, that this leak would not re-occur, but that at this time, and without his surgical intervention, my "leak" had healed over and he would not have to see me until March, 2009, for follow-up. Dr. Bigelow also revealed to us that day, that this had "never" happened to one of his patients and he could not medically explain how this occurred. He seemed completely stumped. I asked him at the end of the visit if he was a religious believer and went on to explain what I had been doing the past month (my prayer cloth) and he just shook his head and responded – he believed in whatever worked for me.

I have recently been back to my "old-school" doctor, Dr. David Barras, and he too, could not believe that the hole in my head had sealed on its own. I also advised him of what I had been doing (my prayer cloth) and he was astounded to say the least. I just had a follow-up visit with him, and his examination revealed no leaking and my left ear looked perfectly "normal." I do have a slight hearing impairment and have some headaches at times, but other than that, feel great. I also need to use my ear drops everyday due to the multiple tubes put in my ear.

I have continued to use my prayer cloth every day since, and during the course of thanking Jesus and Mary for favors granted, I also include other people I know in my daily prayer and ask for relief of their suffering also. I know of quite a few successes and, of course, I attribute their healing to my "prayer cloth" prayers.

I eventually returned the cloth to my aunt and obtained one of my own. Due to this "miracle" of mine, I have felt compelled to share my "medical secret" with as many people as I possibly can, and I feel that God wants me to tell my story, so that others will also have this very deep spiritual healing and renewed faith.

I find it ironic that my "leak" stopped thanks to another "leak" – the liquid coming from the Risen Jesus statue in Medjugorje. I hope to travel there someday in thanksgiving. Blessed be God and the Virgin Mary.

Editor's note: Kathy is from Wilkes-Barre, PA. As of this writing, her ear has never leaked again.

The Confessionals in Medjugorje

(3/07)
The Confessional of the World

By Louise Lotze

Last March I was inspired to write to my mother's former pastor, Father Paul Tobin, who was now assigned in Campbell, OH, and encourage him to look into joining a group with whom I would be making a pilgrimage to Medjugorje for the 25th anniversary. I knew that Father Paul could speak Croatian and that he was a very pro-Marian priest. Later he told me that he had to pray about this trip. Fortunately the visionary Ivan was coming to Randolph, OH, and Father Paul heard about this and went to hear Ivan speak. It was after this that Father Paul was convinced he should go. It so thrilled him that he understood every word that Ivan spoke in Croatian. Father Paul did not need the English interpreter. With his pastor's permission, Father Paul made his plans for June.

Upon arriving at the Cleveland airport I was just approaching the check-in line when Father Paul arrived with a big smile and his luggage in tow. He commented to me that he still wasn't sure why he was going or why I had suggested it to him. I told him that the Holy Spirit had inspired me to invite him, and of course Our Lady had a big part in wanting him there, too. Little did he know the plan Our Lady had for him in Medjugorje.

On the morning of the 24th, Father Paul concelebrated with 60 priests inside Saint James Church for the English Mass. That afternoon our combined group of about 35 walked to the visionary Mirjana's house in Bijakovici where she spoke to about 60 of us crammed into her pilgrim basement dining room. She spoke about the early days of the apparitions and answered all our questions. In the evening, since it was June 24th, and the anniversary of the first day of the silent apparition, the Mass behind the church was packed with pilgrims and with 252 priests concelebrating at the outdoor altar.

In the afternoon of June 25th, the day of the anniversary, we walked to the Cenacolo and heard testimonies by two of the drug addicts who needed to be healed from this great evil. Sister Elvira, an Italian, founded this community and brought it to Medjugorje. It is now an international community. A group of young Sisters danced and sang for us and we all were enjoying their program. Father Paul noticed the large icon of the Resurrection displayed in the room, painted by the members of the Cenacolo. The men explained the symbolism and the figures for us. Father Paul later purchased a copy at the gift shop to take back to his pastor. That evening was the awesome Croatian Mass and the Feast of the Queen of Peace. Five of the six visionaries were present at this Mass and later sang with the pilgrims. It was such a joy-filled evening.

In the meantime, Father Paul was busy with Mary's plan for him. While I thought he was one of the priests concelebrating at the Croatian Mass, he was actually hearing confessions and could only hear the Mass as it was broadcast outside the Church surroundings. Father Paul was a devoted confessor who would not get up and walk away from a line of penitents. Since he was also fluent in Italian, his language plaques on the ground said English and Italian. He discovered he had three Italian penitents to every English one. I called him "our Saint Padre Pio," but later I decided he was also like Saint Leopold Mandic, patron of confessors, and the first Croatian saint, whose statue is near the outdoor confessionals.

While we were at the Cleveland airport on June 22nd, I had told Father Paul that Medjugorje has been called "the confessional of the world." Several days later he asked me to repeat what I had told him about Medjugorje. He said I had given a prophecy which he was indeed living. Not only did he hear confessions every evening, but pilgrims were snagging him after the morning English Mass and asking him for confession. Father Paul was told by them that he was "getting a reputation." His lines were long and he always stayed until the last one was heard. Some evenings he even went early and started confessions at 5:00 P.M. Several evenings he heard confessions until 12:30 A.M. Early into our pilgrimage he made the comment, "I've never done anything like this in my life." He heard confessions standing in the field in the sun because they had no other place for him, also in the hot confessional boxes where the air conditioning wasn't working, and frequently alongside the stone church wall in the outdoors.

Once a French woman came to him and asked him to hear her confession. He said, "I know a little French; of course I will." One man approached him and said, "Father, I am Italian." Father Paul responded, "That's not a sin," and they both burst into laughter. A lady asked him when she finished her confession if she should find a therapist when she returned home. Father Paul said, "Absolutely not! Jesus is your only therapist." Another lady returned to him two more times that evening just to show her gratitude after she had phoned home. The most unusual occurrence however was the note he received from a lady. After her confession she went to a bench and wrote a small message and brought it to him. He opened it, and to his surprise it said: "I love you, Father Tobin." She had signed her name. He said, "I've never received a love letter before this one." The day we met to go to hear Father Jozo at Siroki Brijeg, we couldn't find Father Paul. Well, of course, he was unexpectedly hearing confessions and missed this trip.

On June 29th, the Feast of Saints Peter and Paul, we had a surprise birthday party for Father Paul at our pansion. It was his 68th birthday, and the cake had "Happy Birthday" written in Croatian on it. It was later that evening that he received the "love letter" from a penitent, an unexpected gift. Father Paul wasn't keeping track, but in my daily journal I had recorded the hours each day he spent in hearing confessions. (We would ask him each morning at breakfast how late he had heard confessions the previous night). Our Lady's plan for him was fulfilled, I feel confident.

During the return flight to Cleveland I asked Father Paul for his impressions of his first pilgrimage to Medjugorje. He said, "I never felt like I was in a foreign country. I felt so at home since I could speak and understand their language." He also commented on how very humble and hospitable the Croatian people are. Olga and Milenko, the owners of the pansion, treated him like a relative and he could speak to the taxi drivers in Croatian, also. He was so thankful for this opportunity. He said that one of his memorable moments was being present at the Cenacolo for Mirjana's monthly apparition. It amazed him how very quiet and well-behaved all the young children were who were literally sitting at his feet. I then told him that I felt the reason he was called to go to Medjugorje was to save souls. He responded, "I certainly hope so."

A few weeks after being home, Father came to Assumption Church, his former parish, and celebrated a morning Mass. His homily was focused on Mary, since Saturday is Mary's special day. Father Paul is already giving witness to Our Lady. He related two stories concerning Medjugorje and concluded by saying, "I think Our Blessed Mother is very pleased with what She sees there." I agree with him wholeheartedly!

Father Paul, in writing about his experience in Medjugorje, noted, "I was privileged to be there for the 25th Anniversary of the apparitions and to be present on July 2nd for Mirjana's message at the Cenacolo in Medjugorje. The greatest spiritual experience was my time in confession. During my 42 years as a priest, never did I spend six to seven hours hearing confessions for two weeks straight. The power of prayer and the call to conversion are very real and powerful in Medjugorje. Truly, Medjugorje can be called 'the confessional of the world.'"

Editor's note: Louise is from Ashtabula, Ohio. Louise later added, "Although Father Paul missed the June visit to hear Father Jozo's talk in Siroki Brijeg, he was blessed, not only to hear Fr. Jozo, but to concelebrate Mass with him in Pittsburgh, PA, on Nov. 9. Father Paul was overjoyed! God provides in wondrous ways!"

(10/07)
Angels at the Youth Festival

By Sam Longenecker

My friend Mike and I went to Medjugorje for the Youth Festival this year, thanks to the generosity of one of the subscribers of "The Spirit of Medjugorje." We had some awesome experiences while we were there. Mike and I were chosen from the thousands of American pilgrims to represent the United States in a procession. What an honor that was!

On the second night we were there, we saw the clouds form around the moon in the shape of Mary holding Baby Jesus. It was so amazing and we could not stop watching. Even better is when the clouds went away and the moon started to dance, it went up and down repeatedly.

Then, one day we were there when Mirjana was having her apparition (August 2). Right when Mary appeared to her, everything went silent. All of nature outside just stopped. Then all of a sudden there was this man who started to swear and cry and throw himself around. Apparently he was possessed by the devil and he couldn't take the Blessed Mother's presence there. I was freaking out because the man scared me. But then he stopped and cried.

That same day at night time, we made friends with a nice group of British kids. We were going to see Ivan's special apparition on Apparition Hill. When his apparition started, the same thing happened. All of the sounds of nature stopped. Then all of a sudden, Elizabeth, one of the British girls, and I saw what looked like white doves fly over the statue of Mary. We were in awe and it was just so amazing. Then I noticed they were not doves. But they were actually angels. They were two angel wings together and the ends of the wings looked like the texture of your eye color, like the lines. It is hard to explain. They kept coming from the sky. They could appear and then glide above, then disappear into thin air. Then after awhile of that we saw this huge shooting star that almost took the shape of Mary and it looked like it fell into the city.

Then after the apparition was over, we all stayed up on the mountain praying for awhile and we could still see these angels fly above us. Then across from us on Cross Mountain, we saw these flashing lights everywhere. We saw this one red light that would lead the other white, yellow, and blue lights around. We learned soon after that the red light was St. Michael, and the others were other angels. They were protecting all of us I guess. They were guarding both mountains and watching over us. So then we decided to leave, and on our way the angels would fly over us and lead us home because we got a little bit lost.

So it was an amazing trip and I will look forward to going back again and bringing someone. I know my girlfriend would be amazed to see all these miracles. Now, time to time, I will still see the flying angels. I have seen them twice since I have been back to Erie. I wonder if I will see them on October 2, the feast of the Guardian Angels!

Editor's note: Sam lives in Erie, PA, and had just started his sophomore year of high school when he wrote this. He returned to Medjugorje in May, 2011.

(10/08)
My Experience in Medjugorje, May 1996

By Alice DiCarlo

Our daughter, Maria, first introduced me to Medjugorje after she attended a talk by Wayne Weible. She purchased his book, The Message. She told me that Wayne, a Protestant, said that the Blessed Mother was appearing in Medjugorje. After the talk, he gave Maria a medal. He said, "The medal was blessed by Our Lady," and that She wanted Maria to have it. I was skeptical.

I read The Message and could not get the events happening in Medjugorje out of my mind. My husband Mario also read the book. I thought I would love to go there someday. However, how could I ever afford a trip to a Communist country? It seemed absurd.

At that time, I was driving an old 1976 car. We decided it was time to sell it. I told Mario that I wanted to advertise the car for the price of a ticket to Medjugorje, $1,500. He said, "You will never get that price for that old car." The first call that I received was from a man who lived quite a distance away from our home. He and his wife came, looked at the car, never opened the hood, and said he would take it. I said, "Don't you even want to test drive it?" He said, "OK" and took it just to the end of our street, about a block, and came back. We came into our house and he counted out $1,500 in cash, in 100-dollar bills. Was this the confirmation that I needed to go to Medjugorje? I obtained an application form for the pilgrimage, filled it out and had it in my purse, but didn't mail it. Still, I was hesitant.

I started praying the Rosary daily, sometimes all three Mysteries. The Lenten season was approaching, so I decided to attend daily Mass, praying, asking, our Blessed Mother if She was calling me to Medjugorje. Our parish did not have daily Mass every day of the week, so I decided to attend a weekday Mass at a neighboring parish, one that I had never attended before. I'll never forget that day. After Mass, while still sitting in the pew, a lady that I had never seen before came to sit beside me. She said, "Our Blessed Mother told me to give you this." She placed a rosary in my hand. It was the most beautiful rosary that I have ever seen. It had filigree around each bead, in gold, except for the crucifix, which was silver. She said her husband had given her the rosary, it turned gold in Medjugorje, and that I was supposed to have it. I was stunned and tears welled in my eyes, and I couldn't speak. She left, and I didn't even ask her what her name was. I remembered I still had the application to Medjugorje in my purse.

I told Mario of this encounter. How much more confirmation than this did I need to affirm that I was supposed to go to Medjugorje? We mailed the application for the May pilgrimage, to spend eight days in Medjugorje, then leave the tour group, and visit Mario's sister in Italy for another seven days. I invited my 81 year-old father, who had recently recovered from prostate cancer surgery, to come on the trip. He thought he would like to see Italy, but could not quite understand Medjugorje. He was slow in making a decision and did not have a passport. He applied for one, but I thought it was too late to receive it in time for the departure. The passport arrived within 10 days! Usually it takes 4-6 weeks. I went to a Catholic religious store and purchased a black rosary for Dad to take on the pilgrimage.

My dad was Catholic, but did not go to Confession or Mass in 30 years, since my mother died. For many years I prayed that Dad would return to the Sacraments. That April, he called us to come to his house and attend Mass with him on Divine Mercy Sunday. I was a little surprised, but thought that he might be preparing for his trip. We attended Our Lady of Refuge Church. (What an appropriate name.) At Communion time, he came out of the pew right behind me. I turned around shocked, and he kept following me. Then, I realized that he would never receive Communion without first going to Confession. He knew Holy Communion was the Body and Blood of Jesus, and would never commit a sacrilege. Tears ran down my face, as I received Holy Communion. After Communion, I gave him a big hug and kiss. In the parking lot, he told me that he went to Confession to the priest privately in the rectory a few days before. He wanted to surprise me.

That same month our daughter and son-in-law were expecting their first baby. I was present, with my son-in-law, during the delivery of our grandson, Joshua. Our daughter, Maria, held the golden rosary in her hands, during the labor pains and delivery. I stood behind the doctor, as she quickly worked to remove the umbilical cord, which was wrapped tightly around the baby's neck three times. Joshua was fine, a strong and healthy baby boy.

Soon we were off to Medjugorje. After a long flight, we arrived in Medjugorje with our group of 17 people. The minute you come into the village, you feel peace. Dad attended daily Mass, climbed Apparition Hill, and then early the next morning climbed Mt. Krizevac. It was a very hard and difficult climb. My dad made it up both mountains. And it was a miracle that all of us felt no pain at all, even in our legs. We walked around the village until 10 P.M. that same evening. The following day, all of us went to Confession, before the evening Mass, during the Rosary, after the apparition at 6:40 P.M. We were outside, standing next to the Adoration chapel. Someone said, "Look at the sun. It is spinning!" We could look directly into the sun, without harming our eyes. All different colors were spinning around the sun, pulsating. It looked like the Host was covering the center of the sun. Some people saw the face of Jesus in the Host. Other people saw Our Blessed Mother's face in the center. My dad was the only one who saw a large cross above the sun. It lasted about 50 minutes. My dad sat down on a park bench, outside the Adoration chapel, crying. The only other time that I ever saw Dad cry was at Mom's funeral. He took the black rosary from his pocket and started praying. I walked over to him and knelt down in front of him. He told me that this was the first time he had prayed the Rosary on his own. I cried too. Then, I asked him to do something. I asked him to bless me. Kneeling before him, he took his thumb and made the sign of the cross on my forehead.

The next morning, our group was waiting outside St. James Church. The 10 A.M. English Mass was soon to begin. One member said, "Look at my rosary – it is turning gold, right before our eyes." All of us looked at our rosaries, and the silver links had turned to gold also, for almost every person there. I purchased my rosary three years before at the Vatican gift shop, and the links were silver for three years, and now they were gold.

It was May 18, Pope John Paul II's birthday. Our group decided to buy a bouquet of flowers to place at the statue of Our Lady of Medjugorje, in front of St. James church and to pray the Rosary all together. We were all there except for one person. We decided to wait for her, before beginning the Rosary. While waiting, I looked up in the sky all around me. No clouds were visible, except for one tiny little cloud, far in the distance, in the back of me, near Apparition Mountain. The sky was so very blue and clear. Finally, we were all together, praying the Rosary. Just as the Rosary was about to end, I opened my eyes and looked up at the sky, and a perfect shaped dove was made with clouds directly above the statue of Our Blessed Mother. It was huge. No other clouds were around it. Unfortunately, I did not have a camera with me. We were praying the last decade, so I couldn't tell anyone to look up. When the decade was finished, the clouds dispersed and floated away. I told no one. Tears came to my eyes, as I whispered, "Thank you."

Our group left for the U.S. and we continued onto Italy for another week. It was not until I returned home, about two weeks later, that I would cry at home for no reason at all. I cried every time that I would think of Medjugorje. I felt lonesome. It is so hard to explain the feeling – a loss. I started to attend daily Mass, learning more about my faith and reading good Catholic books. Before Medjugorje, I was a Sunday Mass person only, and Confession perhaps twice a year, if that. Now TV programs did not interest me at all anymore, and I have a complete dislike for TV. I did not like the music that I liked before. I purchased the video called "Beyond the Fields" and would cry all through it, because it took me back to Medjugorje.

In March of 1997, one year later, I had the feeling that I should return this beautiful golden rosary back to the lady who gave it to me, because my own rosary turned gold. I went to the church to find her. She was there. After Mass she stayed in her pew to pray. I didn't want to interrupt her. I loved this rosary, and I kept praying, asking, "Do I have to give it back?" I said to Jesus, "If she is still here when I come out of the ladies' room, then I'll give it back." When I came out, there she was, right in front of me. I took her hand, and placed the rosary in it, and said, "Thank you." Tears came to her eyes. I knew then that this rosary meant as much to her as it did to me. It must have been very hard for her to give it away to me. Through her tears, she said, "Thank you" and said that it was her birthday that day. What joy I felt! God is so good.

My life changed completely. I guess that is what is called a "conversion of heart." Medjugorje also changed my dad's life. He would tell everyone of his experience there. He even talked to people in stores while shopping, at the bank, and at the car dealer. He brought tears to the eyes of strangers, non-Catholics, when he told of his pilgrimage. When his cancer came back and spread to his bones, he still attended Mass, until it was so painful to sit through it. I gave him Holy Communion at home until he was called Home at age 86 in 2001. He was buried holding the black rosary in his hands.

In February of 2006, Mario and I made a pilgrimage to the Holy Land and met some very wonderful people. While waiting in the lobby of the Notre Dame Hotel in Jerusalem, a lady and I started a conversation about some of the places that each of us had visited previously. I told her just a little bit about Medjugorje, and said, "What a wonderful peaceful place it was." She said she would like to visit someday.

This year, 2007, she emailed me, and said that she was planning to visit Rome and would also spend three days in Medjugorje. When she told me that she was going to Medjugorje, I wanted to ask her to purchase a rosary for me, made from the stones from the mountain. But, I didn't ask. I realized that she only had three days in Medjugorje, and I did not want to impose shopping for me, and interfere with what she was to experience. When she came home, she emailed me that she sent me a gift in the mail. When I opened it, it was a rosary bracelet made from the stones from the mountain! Wow! Isn't it amazing that Our Lord knows what is hidden in the recesses of our heart?

I realized that the miracle of Medjugorje is NOT the spinning sun, or rosaries turning gold, but the **conversion of hearts**, millions of people returning to the Sacraments, with a deep love for the Holy Eucharist. Our Lady of Medjugorje is asking five things of us: Prayer from the heart (the Rosary daily), fasting (each week), monthly Confession, reading Holy Scripture, and receiving Jesus in the Holy Eucharist. The Queen of Peace, our Blessed Mother, is coming to Medjugorje to lead Her dear children back to Jesus.

I really believe there is no such thing as a coincidence. People are placed in our life for a reason, from God. Every encounter or chance meeting has a purpose. Thank you Jesus, for placing all these people in my life, to help direct me back to You.

*Editor's note: Alice is from Clarkston, MI. Alice has been an email friend since her son went on a pilgrimage to Medjugorje with my son. She first emailed me after reading of my son's Rosary miracle on September 8, 2001. Another encounter from God! That story is in Volume II of **The Best of "The Spirit of Medjugorje."***

(12/09)
The Cross and the Family

By Richard Reilly

After visiting Medjugorje in September, 1995, I came home feeling that Our Lady and Our Lord were asking me to do something. I did not feel the same as before, and was filled with much peace. I felt drawn to start a prayer group, and eventually this happened.

Almost from the first prayer meeting, as I would be praying, an image would come to me. I would picture Our Lady at the foot of the big cross behind the altar in our church. She was kneeling, facing the cross. It was so wonderful, as She stayed until the Rosary was over. One evening, as we were all praying the Rosary, Our Lady did not show up alone. The scene changed to the Holy Family. Yes, there was the Nativity scene, directly below the cross of Our Lord. I had never seen this image before, with the birth of Our Lord and the Blessed Mother and Joseph in the Nativity scene below the crucified Lord together.

As this beautiful and unknown presentation was given to me other times, I started to think there was more to this, and that there must be a picture or story or scene somewhere that this represents. I started to ask around and looked at as many books as I could. When there was an art showing on various TV stations and on EWTN, I did not find a picture that resembled this scene.

In September of 1996, I again was called to Medjugorje. Although it turned out to be as unbelievable as the first time, with many blessings, I found no information there that would bring to mind any help on this scene that Our Lady and Our Lord let me see and remember. No one that I could find had ever seen or heard of the image I described.

In September of 2000, I went to Medjugorje with a friend of mine. While shopping in the religious stores there, we went to a store called "Charly's." The owner's real name is Joseph, although many people call him "Charly." We had gone to Charly's store a couple of times to look around, so it was nothing for us to drop by and say hello. Toward the end of our pilgrimage, we went to Charly's again, and my friend purchased a nice amount of merchandise, so Joseph went to find him a little thank you gift. After he found just what he was looking for, Joseph turned towards me and said, "This is for you," and handed me an 8" porcelain crucifix. The crucifix had the nativity scene of Jesus, Mary and Joseph below the crucifix, with God the Father holding up the arms of Our Lord on the cross, with the Holy Spirit above. What a surprise!

To this day, I have not seen another one or anything like it. After my return, I had the crucifix professionally photographed and cards made up for distribution. On the back of the cards it says:

The Cross and the Family
Jesus, Mary and Joseph

The Holy Family had personal and family crosses. But they placed their trust and faith in God, that God would bring the greatest good from the crosses. Pick up your cross. Follow and trust in God to see the good from your crosses. The Cross of Jesus brought the opening of the gates of Heaven, forgiveness of original sin, and a place in eternity with God, but you must carry your cross and live the Word of God. Work and pray to rid the world of abortion and contraception; to restore the dignity of life from conception to God's time for death; for the forgiveness and love for all members of Christ's family and y.. so all can live in peace. Pray for the healing and unity of all families. May Christ have mercy and bless our families.

An image of the cross was received by someone praying the Rosary at St. Martin's Roman Catholic Church, and the cross you see was given in Medjugorje to that same person. He was led to believe that the cross and the family go together for salvation. What matters is not what crosses we receive, but how we carry them and offer them to God. If we offer them to God, they become lighter, and if we fight them, they will become harder to bear. When we place our trust in Christ, we come closer to Him and His mercy. Jesus, I trust in You!

Editor's note: Richard is from Decatur, IN. You can contact him at rcrmatthew@hotmail.com, but he asks that you put the word "cross" in the subject line.

Special Crucifix from Medjugorje

(3/05)
Lessons, Laughs and Love from Medjugorje

By Dawn Curazzato

Medjugorje is often referred to as "The Edge of Heaven," where many gifts and graces are received. My trip, itself, was a gift due to the generous response of family and friends at a surprise fiftieth birthday party. I had wanted to go to Medjugorje for a long time and was fortunate to be able to go in October of the Jubilee year. As I looked forward to a peaceful and praise-filled trip, my mother was diagnosed with advanced bladder cancer. To make matters worse, I was scheduled for surgery upon returning from the trip and was advised not to climb or walk around too much – a ridiculous thing to tell someone going to Medjugorje!

The day before I was to leave, I held my mother's hand at her hospital bed and cried, telling her I couldn't go. She said, "Don't you dare cancel this trip! You can do more for me there than here, and your sisters will be with me." As I boarded the bus to Toronto early the next morning to get our flight, I left with a heavy heart. When seated, I turned towards the window and I began to cry. A hand reached out from behind me and a voice said, "Don't cry. Everything will be alright." Apparently the woman behind me saw my reflection in the window. She introduced herself and then handed me a first class relic of Blessed Margaret of Castello. I nearly fainted, as I was on this trip with my prayer group, The Ladies of the Lord, and we were just given Blessed Margaret as our Patroness, suggested by the Dominican nuns! In a spirit of generosity, Maria told me to keep it, and she told me she worked at Roswell, the same hospital my mother was having her surgery in, as we spoke! She assured me, my mom was in good hands and I marveled at the God-incident that had just transpired!

Many people speak about mystical happenings in Medjugorje, but I believe a pilgrimage should always be made in the spirit of faith, and prayer should be the central part of it, not the supernatural. If you are graced with such an experience, you should give thanks and praise to the Lord and share it with the express desire to save souls and build up the church. It does not mean you are special, as we are ALL special to God, and in all likelihood you may be one of His weaker children, whom He is bestowing this gift on that you may grow in faith!

Upon arriving in Medjugorje, I felt prompted to run to St. James Church as everyone else unpacked. As I went up some steps I noticed there was a tremendous racket coming from a small grouping of trees. There must have been thousands of birds. I didn't see them, but I sure heard them. All at once the birds stopped, in unison and when I looked at my watch it was 6:40 – the time Our Lady appears to the visionaries! Does nature sing upon Her arrival and then honor Her with complete silence? It was getting dark and I quickly ran back to the home we were staying in, pondering what had just happened. It would not be the only unusual experience I would have while there. On our third night, my roommate and I opened our window which faced Cross Mountain and we saw the huge cross encased in a reddish glow, as if on fire. When we told our guide about it the next morning, she told us there are no lights up there. When we became insistent about what we saw, she smiled and said some pilgrims report seeing the cross totally disappear and others have seen it lifted into the sky in flames. We also experienced our rosaries changing from silver to gold. Perhaps the highlight of the trip came when many of our group made a side trip to Dubrovnik and I stayed behind with several others. We went to the Croatian Mass, but the church was full, so we heard Mass outside. In a short while, people began pointing to the sky, and when I looked up I witnessed the Miracle of the Sun! Everything stopped for me and I was taken back to a place in time, when as a child, after seeing the story of Fatima, I told my father how I wished I could have been there to see the sun dance in the sky and visit the Blessed Mother! Here I was some 40 years later doing just that! God is good! I will always remember and be thankful for these mystical experiences, but for me, Medjugorje was about something else!

Human nature exercises itself even in the holiest of places. I am Irish and humor is important to me. Laughter is the music of the soul, and I believe it is an important element in the healing process. I had brought the manuscript to the book I had just written to be blessed in Medjugorje. I had looked in the Bible for humor to include in my book but found no specific instance of it. No belly-roll there! This disturbed me and I thought of the apostles Our Lord chose. There were some doozies! Our Lord must have laughed sometimes even though His mission was serious! I have trouble praying the Sorrowful Mysteries of the Rosary. The inhumanity displayed to our Lord troubles me. One day while praying I said aloud, "Lord, when I die, I do not wish to see Your sorrowful face. I want to see You smile!" I had all but forgotten it when I left for Medjugorje, but if Our Lord can read hearts, He certainly can read minds.

One night after getting all soaped up in the shower, the water stopped! We were told this sometimes happens in Medjugorje. I hollered to my roommate to hand me some wipes which were less than adequate for the job, kind of like washing a car with a q-tip! I'm a beautician and I prepared for this situation by bringing a wig. We had quite a bit of fun with that wig and got some pretty silly pictures, causing hearty laughter! One friend thought we got a little carried away and thought we should maintain a more prayerful posture. I went to Confession the next day. There are very long lines for Confession, something one never sees in the West and yet, Our Lady has stressed this will be the "Remedy for the West." When I went in, I told the priest my sins, and then I told him about the wig incident. He told me it was not a sin, and I left feeling pretty good.

Two days later, we were at dinner with our group and there was a person who always took her food first and was a bit inconsiderate. I leaned over to my friend telling her if that was the case tonight I was going to stab that person's finger with my fork – just kidding. But my other friend who sent me to Confession the first time heard me, and said that called for another trip to Confession!

"Bless me, Father, for I have sinned; my last Confession was two days ago." "Two days ago?!" I said, "Yes, Father," and I proceeded to tell him I like making people laugh, but I do not have holy humor. He asked me what I meant, and I told him they used to call me "Dawn Rickles" in High School. He told me he was from Ireland and had the same type of humor, and it is not a sin. When giving me the blessing he told me God made me this way and He gave me my humor! As I was leaving, I began to think what a wonderful sacrament Confession is, and I wonder why it is feared instead of revered. It is a dialogue of love, a circuit of grace that brings us the forgiveness of Jesus Christ through the priest. It is our continuing education, which brings us back to holiness and opens our hearts to receive gifts and graces from Our Lord. The Lord uses the lips of the priest to say the words each of us need to hear.

My life has a Trinitarian thread woven into it, as everything seems to happen to me in threes. This would hold true for Confession too! On the day before we left, our group went up Cross Mountain. It can be treacherous, especially when slippery and there are many rocks and steep inclines. It is an exhilarating and spiritual event to reach the top! When it was time to descend, I helped one of the older ladies in our group. Several people went rushing ahead of us. One of them was the person I made the remark about which sent me to Confession. As we got half way down the mountain, I saw that person slide and take a tumble. My friend and I went over to see if everything was all right and we were assured there was no injury, so we went on our way. When we reached the bottom, we had a fit of laughter and when my friend, who had sent me to Confession the other two times, asked what was so funny, my companion proceeded to tell her how funny the other person looked when she fell. Before she could finish, I got "The Look." This time I piped up and told my friend I would go to Confession, but whatever this priest says, goes. I had to wait 45 minutes, and when I told the priest this was my third Confession in a week . . . he asked me if I knew of scrupulosity and I answered, "Yes Father, she sent me here!" I went on to tell him how ashamed and humiliated I was and how my humor is so different from what is in my heart. Then I cried, feeling I may have insulted the Mother of God with my humor. In very heavy Irish Brogue he said, "Oh my child, this is NOT a sin. It is a GIFT!"

When I went back to the house, it was almost time for dinner. I told my roommate what the priest said, and she fell on the floor laughing. She asked me to please wait for her because she wanted to see our friend's face when I told her it's not a sin, but a "gift." We had great fun with the "gift" and I thank God for it!

Upon my return from this special trip, I had much to be thankful for: I had witnessed several mystical events; my book, *Memoir of a Miracle*, was published; my surgery was successful; and my mother was completely healed of her cancer.

A few months ago my mother died of a heart attack and this has been the most difficult year of my life. Still I thank Our Lady of Medjugorje for Her intercession and Our Lord for allowing us to have her for four more years. The lesson I received on humor, through the confessional, has left a lasting impression on me. Though the pain of her loss is oppressive, I know when my tears dry, humor will replace this sadness. I know someday I will see my mother again and I will see Our Lord smile!

Editor's note: Dawn lives in Williamsville, NY.

(7/08)
Fr. Bill Kiel

By Wendy Ripple

William Joseph Kiel was born on the Feast of St. Ephraem, June 9, 1943. St. Ephraem was described as a man of small stature who, during his lifetime, was known as a great teacher and defender of the faith; he was called to the deaconate and ordained late in life. Similarly, Father Bill was ordained into the priesthood later in life after a successful career as a high school biology teacher.

Father Bill grew up with a family devoted to the Blessed Mother; he prayed the Rosary nightly with his brothers and mother, and was always very active in the Church. Throughout his early life, he would periodically have thoughts of becoming a priest, but chose to continue enjoying all that the world had to offer: a successful career, a house and land in the country, dating, and money. Over time, however, God's call began to make its way deeper into Bill's heart. It was finally during a teacher's strike at age 44 that he began to look for, and pray about, a "better way to make a living." His prayers led him to Saint Vincent's Seminary in Latrobe, Pennsylvania – and eventually to Medjugorje.

Academically, Father Bill had no difficulty during seminary. However, physically, he suffered. Fifteen years prior to entering St. Vincent's, Father Bill had hurt his back while clearing his property. Despite consulting every appropriate medical specialty, he suffered chronic pain from the bulging disc in his back and from very frequent, severe migraine headaches. Because of the back pain, though, he had particular difficulty reverencing the altar and serving at Mass. He asked God over and over to heal him from his back pain – not for his own relief, but so that he could sit and stand reverently at the altar. Almost unknowingly, he prayed to become a holy priest. Father Bill recalled how his prayers were answered in quite an unexpected manner: "I was back (home) for my brother's birthday, and he said that there was a man that would be speaking at St. Pius Church about his conversion through the Blessed Mother in Fatima, Lourdes and Medjugorje. He asked if I would want to go with him. I said, 'Sure.' So I went. After he was finished speaking, this man offered a Special Blessing from the Blessed Mother from Medjugorje to all people in the church. The blessing was, 'Receive the Blessing of the Blessed Mother and be filled with the Holy Spirit.' I was sitting in the pew watching people receive blessings, and I saw people resting in the Spirit, and I thought, 'What the heck is going on in this Catholic Church? He can't be Catholic! This just doesn't happen in the Catholic Church!'"

Father Bill continued, "I waited until the very end of the blessings because these people in the church knew I was in the seminary. They knew me, and I was afraid that if I would go for the blessing I would cause a scandal if this wasn't a real Catholic thing. I was nervous. I said, 'Okay, Lord, whatever You have for me; I am open to whatever.' The man put his hands on me, prayed for me, and the next thing I know, I opened my eyes and I was lying on the floor looking up at the ceiling lights thinking, 'What in the world happened?' I got up and was walking back to the pew and I kept looking at my feet because I couldn't feel them. I knew they were there, but I couldn't feel them or the floor under me. It was just like I was walking on air. I went back to the seminary and went to bed, got up in the morning, and, for the first time in fifteen years, I had no back pain. I thought, 'Well, something must have happened last night.'" He realized that his prayers had been answered, and just in time for his ordination to the diaconate. He was able to sit, stand and move about the altar reverently and without pain.

Father Bill received the Sacrament of Holy Orders in May of 1993, and was assigned to the duties of a diocesan priest. For over a year he continued to wonder about the events that were reportedly occurring half way around the world in a small village between two mountains, Medjugorje. He felt connected to these events; after all, he was healed through a blessing that had originated in that village. Perhaps his lifelong devotion to the Blessed Mother was leading him in another direction. Father Bill began to feel called to Medjugorje. Responding to that call, he inquired about joining a pilgrimage scheduled for November of 1994, led by the man from whom he had received the Special Blessing. He not only joined the pilgrimage, but went to Medjugorje to serve his fellow pilgrims as their priest and spiritual director, and unbeknownst to him, to be called into a deeper relationship of service to the Lord.

Once in Medjugorje, for the first time, Father Bill had three profound spiritual experiences that forever changed his life. He described this experience which had occurred while listening to the testimony of Vicka, one of the visionaries: "I was standing about eight feet away from her. Her eyes just locked into my eyes, and when that happened there was a feeling of warmth that went all through my body. It was such a peaceful warmth! At the same time that was happening, my lips got fiery hot, really fiery hot! I didn't know what was going on here." Father Bill pondered these happenings as he walked back to town to celebrate Mass at St. James. He questioned whether, like the prophet Isaiah, he was cleansed of his sins by a spiritual ember.

As the pilgrimage continued, Father Bill joined his group in climbing Cross Mountain. While praying and climbing, Father Bill began to worry a bit. He knew that the climb ended at the foot of the Cross where each pilgrim was to surrender to Jesus the greatest obstacle, the burden that placed distance between him and Christ, but he did not feel that he had any such burden. Father Bill clearly remembered the conversation he had with God as he made his way up the rugged path. He said, "Okay, Lord, look. I have been ordained a little over a year, almost a year and a half; I feel that I have been truly blessed. I don't know of any burdens that I have. I don't know of any, but if you know of a burden that I have, let me know and I will give it to you." He reached the foot of the Cross, looked up, and without any hesitation opened his mouth, "Lord, I give you my greatest burden – my lack of trust in you." He no sooner heard these words coming from his own mouth when he asked, "What did I just say? Why did I say that?"

He stood motionless at the Cross for what seemed to be a very long time, long enough for his entire life to be replayed in his mind. He saw his life in a different way. He suddenly understood and exclaimed to himself, "Hey Kiel, you didn't trust; that was the burden!" He realized that all of his life he had taken control – as a teacher, in business, while building his home, and even with prayer. He had always asked for God's help, but if God did not answer Bill's prayers Bill's way and in Bill's time, then Bill took matters back into his own hands. Ber. Cross, Father Bill for the first time made the connection betv need for control, the stress in his life, and the migraine headacl he suffered for years. He saw that his lack of trust harmed his spiritual well-being which then resulted in his physical symptoms. At that point, Father Bill, by the grace of God, surrendered his 'Type A-have-to-have-everything-done-yesterday' personality. He surrendered control and gave it back to God. He prayed, "Lord, give me the grace to surrender my will to Your will, and let me put all my trust in You." Father Bill was transformed that day on Cross Mountain; he was renewed spiritually and, again, healed physically, for some months after the pilgrimage he suddenly realized that he had no more migraines. His short prayer of surrender from the base of the Cross has since become a part of his morning offering.

The Blessed Mother had called Father Bill to Medjugorje; Her small priest had been witness and recipient to many miracles and graces. In Medjugorje, he was spiritually purged and renewed, and physically healed. God was surely, in hindsight, preparing his servant to receive the challenge of an even greater gift – the Gift of Healing. Father Bill received the Gift of Healing during that same pilgrimage, he believes, through the hands of Father Jozo. His pilgrim group traveled to hear Father Jozo speak; after the talk, Father Jozo invited the priests in the audience to concelebrate Mass. Three priests and a deacon joined Father Jozo at the altar; Father Bill was one of them. This was the only time in all of his eighteen pilgrimages that Father Jozo invited priests to concelebrate Mass! After the Mass had ended, Father Jozo stood and began speaking in Croatian. Father Bill understood Father Jozo's words that he would bless the priests, and then he would have the priests, in turn, bless the people. As he was listening, and understanding Father Jozo, Father Bill caught himself and said, "Kiel, you don't understand Croatian!" Shortly thereafter, the interpreter appeared and explained to all exactly what Father Bill had heard in Croatian.

Father Jozo then directed Father Bill to the back of the church where people were in line to receive a blessing. Father Bill recalled what happened next: "I started laying hands on people, and people started to rest in the Spirit. I thought, 'What in the world is happening?' I'd blessed a lot of people, and they had never rested in the Spirit! I finished all of the blessings; I had several people come up to me to thank me for the blessings and thank me for the healing that they felt they had received. At that point, it was just an instant thought in my mind, that what I was taught in seminary was true. The priest doesn't do anything; God works through you as a priest. So, all I could say to the people was, 'Thank God! All I did was pray for you!'"

It wasn't until actually returning home from Medjugorje, though, and discussing the events with others that Father Bill realized that he had been given the Gift of Healing. In his heart he knew that God had given him a gift, and that gifts are not meant to be hidden, but to be shared. Father Bill continued blessing people and began celebrating Healing Masses, a ministry that continues today to heal many – spiritually, emotionally and physically.

Father Bill has been to Medjugorje, now, eighteen times, as spiritual director and pilgrim. Interestingly, though, he does not focus on the apparitions of the Blessed Mother, the spinning sun, the golden rosaries or other such supernatural phenomena. These, he knows, are little gifts from God that help us to increase our faith, but his faith is not based on these. He is, however, witness to the fruits of Medjugorje – the countless conversions and healings that have originated from the grace of God poured out onto the holy ground between two mountains. Father Bill believes, also, that the Virgin Mary, our Mother, is the mediator of God's grace not only in Medjugorje, but everywhere! He believes that it is Mary who has led him, not only to Jesus, Her Son, but to the Trinity.

Editor's note: Wendy lives in Fairview, PA.

(6/08)
My Pilgrimage to Medjugorje

By Rose Mary Chamberlin

My dear friend who brings me the Holy Eucharist also brought me several issues of "The Spirit of Medjugorje." I have been reading and absorbing the wonder of Our Lady's messages and the stories of those whose lives have been forever changed by a pilgrimage to Medjugorje.

This glorious newsletter renewed all the memories of my pilgrimage in June, 1990. My journey was a miracle.

I had been chosen as a finalist in the New York State Beef Cook-off. The Holy Spirit inspired my recipe for "Beef Simply Divine." I asked for prayer – I wanted to win so I would have a nest egg to go to Medjugorje.

In April I attended a mini-retreat at the House of Prayer in Plainview, NY. A lovely lady walked up to me and placed $1000 in my hands. She told me that when she woke in the morning, Jesus gave her instructions on where to go and what to do. When she heard me share my story and ask for prayer, she knew I was "the one." I immediately gave the money to Sr. Marcia for the June trip. Then I came in second place in the Cook-off and won $280 – the EXACT price of the trip was $1280!

My twelve days in Medjugorje were "Heaven on earth." Mary welcomed me with all the love of Her Mother's heart. I saw Her in prayer atop Mt. Krizevac. My adventures were many and glorious. I am forever grateful.

I have been ill for many years – suffered my first heart attack at 48. My mother was dying from a massive heart attack and was hospitalized and in ICU. We hurried to her. While there, I also had a heart attack. The nurses said it was a first time event. That was the summer of 1989. I went to Medjugorje in June of 1990. Despite many physical limitations, I was able to climb Mt. Krizevac and Apparition Hill. Blessed Mother kept a seat open for me near Her statue in St. James Church – no matter how crowded the church was.

I stayed at the Stanka's house and you could clearly see the cross atop the mountain. Early one morning several of us saw Gospa praying at the foot of the cross, dressed all in white. My room-mate and I went to our room and watched and prayed the Rosary. I also saw Her disappear. She was lifted up above the cross in a globe of light, higher and higher, and then it shattered. Heart-stopping!

One day I spent hours in church. I heard Mass in English, German and Italian. About 1:00 P.M., via inner locution, I was told to walk along the street and I would know the restaurant when I come to it. I was to order something to eat and wait. The Lord was sending someone to me. I did exactly as I was told. Soon a very poorly dressed mother and daughter came up to me and asked if they could eat with me. The restaurant was nearly empty. Their names were Brigitta and Olga. Olga was 13, mentally-challenged and blind. They were from Czechoslovakia. Brigitta had been held in a mental institution as a prisoner and Olga had been taken from her. I told them to order lunch. We spent hours together. I gathered clothing, soap, money for them while they sat under the trees in front of St. James. Brigitta told me it was the first time she was not afraid in years, and she wept. She and Olga sang folk songs to me – so hauntingly lovely. We wrote for a time after my return, but her last letter that reached me said my letters were not getting to her. I don't know what happened to them.

My time in Medjugorje was filled with joy and love and indescribable emotions. Fr. Jozo – Fr. Slavko – heavenly Masses – Rosaries – the Eucharist, glorious – penance, often.

I walked through the fields and kissed the hands of the women. I drank in the pilgrims from around the world. I met the first integrated group of Catholic women allowed to travel together out of South Africa. We exchanged rosaries and they turned gold before our eyes!

I was taken by Vicka into the room of apparitions in her home with two other ladies and she prayed over us. She placed her hand on my head and I seemed to be pushed downward, and I hear the Holy Spirit say, "You have been marked by a heavenly sign."

I can still feel the utter silence when Our Lady appeared. Even the birds by the hundreds came and settled down – the air was permeated by Gospa.

My journal is full of the colors, sounds, tastes and mystical phenomena with which I was graced. But most of all – above all – was Jesus and Mary. I – I who am nothing – was loved, held, and loved more by my heavenly Father.

Now, due to my poor health, I seldom leave my home. I have a ministry writing to prisoners in the US, and I also write to Christian prisoners in Asia, Pakistan, Indonesia, etc. I also write a monthly newsletter to my parish prayer intercessors. A prayer cell meets at my home on Tuesdays and we pray for the problems that plague our world and our dear ones. We belong to the Apostolate of Suffering, the association of the Holy Face, the Prayer Crusade for Priests, and the Universal Living Rosary Association.

I will never forget living the miracle of Medjugorje.

Editor's note: Rose Mary is from Stony Brook, NY.

Our Lady of Tihaljina

(2/06)
Our Lady's Darkened Hands

By Annmarie Wright

Little did I know what was in store for me when my Medjugorje pilgrimage group led by Steve Shawl stopped at the Immaculate Conception Church in the town of Tihaljina near Medjugorje. We were on our way to the airport, but almost as an afterthought we had stopped at Tihaljina to see Father Jozo Zovko, OFM. Unknown to us, he was by this time stationed in the town of Siroki Briej, a short distance away.

I was grumpy and wanted to get to a restaurant and have a bite to eat as well as to take a smoking break. God, who has such interesting ways of dealing with us, had other plans for me. I wandered around the church, and I took numerous photographs of all the pretty statues. One statue in particular caught my attention because it seemed familiar to me, and yet nothing seemed out of the ordinary about it. The statue of Mary has become known by several names – "Immaculate Conception," "Our Lady of Grace," "Our Mother of Mercy," and "Our Lady of Tihaljina." However, most pilgrims recognize the statue as the one in the photograph that Fr. Jozo Zovko gives to pilgrims who attend his presentations at his church. Some people believe that when you stare at the photograph in a meditative frame of mind for a period of time, that the features in the photograph actually change.

When I returned to the United States, I sent some of the photos that I took to friends, but I did not send the photo of Our Lady of Tihaljina. I said to myself, "Everyone has seen this one." I did not give the photo another thought because I had seen it so much in various places, and yet I knew little about its interesting story. Later I learned that the statue, created in Italy by a talented artist, came at great monetary cost to the people of the parish, who hold it in high regard. Some pilgrims have related unusual accounts in regard to this statue and its impact on their lives.

Meanwhile, several years after my trip, my life continued as usual as though my Medjugorje pilgrimage, though a pleasant interlude, had not intervened in my life. Then I started reading a book entitled *Abandon Yourselves Totally to Me*. That's when I began to ask myself about the reason for my pilgrimage, and how I had been affected spiritually. I concluded that there was a part of me that I was holding back from God. I had not totally surrendered, for example, my smoking habit.

I stumbled across an account of when the visionaries of Medjugorje had asked Mary at Apparition Hill if others could touch Her, and She agreed to this request. After many hands had reached out to Her, the visionaries noticed with distress that Mary's clothes had turned a dirty color as a result of those people who carried unconfessed sin in their lives and who had touched Her. What I read prompted me, for some unknown reason, to dig out the photo that I had taken of Our Lady of Tihaljina. That's when I noticed that the hands in the photograph seemed a sooty color. I asked myself, "Wow, why didn't I see this before?!" I grabbed a magnifying glass and looked at the thumbnail photo that clearly showed the darkened hands. Then I enlarged the small photo to 5 x 7 and then 8 x 10. Still the hands appeared a darkened color.

Many people, including myself, have asked how the hands could have become darkened in the photograph. Thus far no one has come up with a satisfactory explanation. However, what I know for sure is that my life has changed since I took that photograph, and I no longer smoke!

Editor's note: Annmarie is from Portland, Oregon.

(9/07)
Mystical Events in the Little Village of Medjugorje

By Louise A. Hogg

For many years I had wanted to go to Medjugorje. My sister and niece went several years ago and brought back many wonderful pictures and souvenirs. One souvenir that was given to me was a doily made by a woman in this small village. It was Our Lady with "MIR" crocheted at the bottom. Every day I would pray that someday I would be able to make this trip to visit with Our Lady and see the wonders of this spiritual place. But due to medical problems, the trip was next to impossible (I thought). Plus, the fear of flying was heavy on my mind.

Last year I was invited to make a pilgrimage in April with my sister, niece and a friend of ours. Checking with all my doctors, they said there was no reason for me not to go. Would I overcome the fear of flying, especially over water???

While arrangements were made for the pilgrimage, I prayed continually that I would overcome my fear and also be well enough to make this journey.

The day finally arrived. On April 26, 2006, a pilgrimage group of 31 people made the journey to Bosnia. I was one of them!!! In fact, Jesus and Our Lady held me in the palm of Their hands, for there was no anxiety whatsoever – an overwhelming peace had taken over my body. The fear of flying over water was gone. It took us 28 hours to reach our destination, but it was well worth it.

Upon arrival, the first thing on the agenda was to go to St. James Church and give a prayer of thanksgiving for our safe arrival. St. James is a beautiful church filled with spirituality, holiness and awe. There is a statue of Our Lady in the church to the right of the altar. She seems to say: "Welcome. Thank you for responding to my call. I will give you many blessings during your trip, for you have come to me."

On Tuesday, May 2, we were able to go to an apparition. Mirjana, one of the visionaries, was to speak with our Heavenly Mother that day. We were not able to go inside the building where Mirjana would have her apparition, for there were thousands of pilgrims and the building was overcrowded. As Mirjana was about to arrive, the sky started to clear from the morning rain. Upon looking up at the sky, I could see a huge rain cloud starting to drift away, and the sun was peeking from behind it. As the sun started out from behind the cloud, it was spinning. I took a picture of the beautiful sight. After the picture was developed, I could see a dove, representing the Holy Spirit, and rays coming from the dove. At the time the picture was taken, one could not see the dove or the rays, just a cloud and the spinning sun.

Once Mirjana arrived and entered the building, everyone was anxious with anticipation. When the music stopped, we knew that Mirjana was speaking with the Blessed Mother. Outside there was only silence. The traffic stopped, the people were at a hush, the dogs quit barking, and even the birds quit singing!! When nature stops you know something special is happening.

At this time, I was prompted to take a picture of the sky above the building where Mirjana and our Heavenly Mother were conversing. I looked up, saw some clouds in the sky and asked myself, "Why should I take a picture? There is nothing in the sky." But the inspiration kept prompting me to snap. So I did. Once again, after the picture was developed, there was a spectacular vision – our Heavenly Mother showed Her presence. In the sky is an image of Our Lady wearing a crown.

After Our Lady left, everything turned back to normal. The birds seemed to have broken into songs of joy, for the songs were even more beautiful than before.

What I learned was that when prompted to do something, I should never doubt myself. I would have missed two wondrous photos if I would not have followed my inspirations.

Later I was able to climb Apparition Hill. It had rained earlier, leaving the stones a little slippery, but it was not too bad going up the small mountain. At the top is a beautiful statue of Our Lady. She seems to say, "Welcome, I see you made it." To the left of Our Lady is a statue of Jesus on the cross. It was hard climbing to the cross, for the rocks were bigger and more slippery, but it was attainable. Coming down was the hardest part. Gravity seems to pull you down, and the rocks were more slippery. I sprained my left foot, so now I was limping. But with the grace of Our Lady I did manage to get through the rest of the pilgrimage.

Although climbing Mt. Krizevac was out of the question, the day before we left for home, I climbed partly up the mountain. I found a nice comfortable rock to sit on, and started to pray the Rosary. At this same moment the bells of St. James started to ring, and then the pilgrims started to pray the Rosary in Croatian. What a spiritual feeling! I finished my Rosary and listened as the others at St. James finished theirs. I felt a gush of warmth envelope me, and something caught the corner of my left eye. As I turned my head, there was something pink close to my head. Upon examining it, I found it to be a small pink rose. Looking at the bush closer and all the bushes around, there were no other flowers and hardly any green stems – just the one right next to me. There was once again a feeling of blessings being bestowed upon me – a true blessing from God. God shows us His love, but we have to open our hearts and our eyes so that we can feel and see His love.

An extraordinary event during this trip was the change of the Host during Adoration. We were all praying in the Adoration chapel, when for me the Host changed from white to red, then into the shape of a heart! I later asked if any had witnessed this moment and they all said no. Were my eyes playing tricks on me? Deep in my heart I know this event to be true. Another blessing!

Throughout my pilgrimage journey from Mirjana's home to listening to sermons and hearing other speakers, one thing became perfectly clear to me – pray for priests and the Church for they are under attack. Our Heavenly Mother wants us to pray the Rosary often for priests, for they represent Her Son on earth. We are not to condemn or judge them, but to pray for them. When a priest gives us his blessing, Jesus stands behind him. Pray to our Heavenly Father and Mother that They may bestow special graces, blessings and protection upon each of Their chosen ones who represent Their Son on earth.

In the newsletter that came before our trip (the April, 2006, issue of "The Spirit of Medjugorje"), there was an article about the Divine

Mercy Shrine in Surmanci, about 15 minutes from Medjugorje. I told my sister that I wanted to visit the church, for I have a great devotion to the Divine Mercy. We did have an opportunity to visit the church. Oliver, the taxi cab driver, knew the location and took four of us there. When we reached the church, I knew this was the church I had been looking for since 2001.

During one of my hospital stays, I had befriended a girl about 24 years old. The day that she left the hospital, she drew a picture on a piece of cardboard and handed it to me, saying: "Someday you will go here." I asked her where it was, and she said she did not know, but that she felt she had to draw it for me, and that one day I would go there.

The picture was of a church with a steeple, a bell tower and a cross on the top of the tower. Behind the church it looked like a cemetery with gravestones. At the very top of the picture was a large cross with rays coming out from it. On each side of the large cross was a smaller cross. The crosses were on a hill.

Before we got to the church, I took a picture from on top of a hill that looked down on Surmanci and the Divine Mercy church. When developed it showed that there was a building behind the church which we found out later was once a school. The building had windows that could have been mistaken for gravestones. It looked just like the picture in the drawing. The cross with the rays at the top of the drawing I am assuming was the Mt. Krizevac cross, and the two smaller ones, the crosses on top of St. James towers.

Upon entering the church, one comes to a painting of the Divine Mercy image. We kissed the feet of Jesus, and said a prayer. Then we found a relic of St. Faustina and said a prayer.

I later went back to the painting and prayed the Divine Mercy Chaplet. As I got up, I kissed the feet of Jesus, and when I looked up, the painting had one tear coming from the left of Jesus' face. Upon touching the liquid, I found it to be very oily and blessed myself with it. Another blessing! I waited for more liquid to form, so that I could call others to see. None formed.

Always ask for blessings, for on the first day of my trip, I asked Our Lady to bless me – help me see what I need to see, hear what I need to hear, feel what I need to feel. Do what I need to do. Our Lord and Our Lady truly blessed me with the mystical events in this little village of Medjugorje.

If you ever once said to yourself, "I would like to go to Medjugorje," Mary is calling you to come to Her. Please answer Her call. She will guide you to happenings that will enrich your life. Do not let medical problems or fears stop you from being with our Heavenly Mother, the "Queen of Peace," and Her Son Jesus.

Editor's note: Louise is from Belle Vernon, PA.

Inside the Divine Mercy Shrine in Surmanci

(4/08)
The Risen Christ Miracle

By Liddy Fordham

In October I was blessed to be able to go to Medjugorje for a week. As I am aware that "The Spirit of Medjugorje" lends the "blessed healing hankies," I purchased hankies, had them blessed, and went to the Risen Christ.

As usual, there was a queue there, so I decided to sit down and wait, but this queue got longer. One really has to stretch to get to the part where the liquid (which has been tested and found to be human tears) is oozing in droplets. I waited and suddenly felt rather sad. I started speaking to God and saying that I didn't have anyone tall to help me with all these hankies, but I waited. Then I noticed a man walk to the right leg of the Risen Christ and look at the back of the leg, he wiped his hankie. I quickly got up and stood behind him. I couldn't believe it – liquid was oozing from behind, by the hamstring!!! Tears welled in my eyes and my heart wanted to shout with joy . . . he left and this wonderful healing liquid actually trickled quickly from one point and I wiped all the hankies that I had bought . . . what love and joy filled me. My God had heard my prayer – it was for "The Spirit of Medjugorje" to help others. Others came and stood behind me and when I finished, I knelt and praised, thanked, kissed and held the legs of the Risen Christ.

At Mass again I held the packet with the hankies for more blessings. This was one of my miracles for me. May the hankies bring healing and/or comfort to those who pray with them.

Two days later I decided to buy more hankies to send to South Africa, or for anyone in the family who would want one. Obviously I immediately went to the right leg and kept looking, praying, but nothing. So patience is what my Lord wanted me to learn. Now I had to stand in the queue, which I eventually did do, and had to stretch and place each hankie when the liquid trickled out. I do so love Him blessing me.

On my last day the rain was pouring and I felt rather heart sore at not having climbed Mt. Krizevac, and during Mass asked our Blessed Mother to please stop the rain or at least let there be a light drizzle to enable me to climb, as early the next morning I was going home, and it is rather dangerous climbing when it is pouring with rain. When Mass finished, I walked out and there was a light drizzle, I thanked Our Lady.

Maree, a friend I had met, walked to where we were staying to collect our walking sticks and head towards Mt. Krizevac. By the time we arrived at the foot of the mountain, the sun was breaking through the clouds. I was so happy. We did the Stations of the Cross all the way up. It never rained again until early the next morning when we were on the bus heading towards the airport; the rain poured down. Another miracle for me.

Editor's note: Liddy lives in London, England.

(11/05)
AWOL in Medjugorje

By Andy Gibbs

Last year I had an interesting experience as I climbed Apparition Hill in the rain. Although this hill is much smaller than Cross Mountain, it would still be a challenge to climb in the rain. I was looking around seeing if any elderly people needed help climbing, and didn't notice any.

As you climb this hill, you pray the Rosary at Stations as you go up. We started our first prayers at the base of the mountain. When we started to climb, I had taken about two steps, and someone caught my eye to the right. A little old quiet lady named Gloria (not her real name) was starting to climb the mountain, and looked very unsteady. I got behind her, and another lady got beside her and we started helping her up the hill. Given how feeble she looked, I didn't think she had a chance of making it up the hill.

Step by step, she made progress. The rest of the group would wait at each station for us before starting the prayers. Gloria stopped several times to rest, but she got right back up to continue her climb. I was prepared for the rain with all of my waterproof gear. I also had on a thin plastic poncho to protect my backpack. With the extra exertion required to help Gloria, I started sweating, and sweating, and sweating. By the time I got to the top, I think I was as wet inside as I was out.

I could not believe it, but Gloria made it all the way to the top of that mountain. She reached the statue of the Virgin Mary and just relished in the moment. Later, she mentioned to someone that she "escaped" from the assisted living complex where she lives. She knew if she told anyone where she was going, they would try to talk her out of it. So, she just packed her bags, and left. Imagine the stories she had to tell her friends when she got back! She told us that God sent her here to climb this mountain, and she was determined to get to the top.

I told her that through her example, she was helping us climb our spiritual mountain. Later, she said that God sent her two angels to help her up the mountain. I don't know about that, but I can say that it was the highlight of my trip seeing her reach the top. She said that she would pray for us every day for the rest of her life.

Editor's note: Andy is from Westminster, CA.

(9/06)
A Family Trip to Medjugorje

By Tony Pellatt

A family trip to Medjugorje was just a dream earlier this year for me, my wife, Sherry, and our two sons, Brian, seventeen and Tom, twenty. We knew the expense was not within our financial means, so Sherry and I planned to make the trip without them. That was, until we received an Easter gift from Sherry's parents, who knew nothing about our plans or dreams at the time. It was a check large enough to completely finance a trip to Medjugorje for the four of us.

Almost immediately we contacted Stipe Vasil, a native of Medjugorje, who now lives near St. Cloud, Minnesota, with his wife, Lisa, and their five children. Ten years ago, on the fifteenth anniversary of the apparitions, I joined Stipe and five others on a pilgrimage to Medjugorje. That trip left such a lasting impression on me, that I knew someday I would return. It turned out that Stipe was already planning to join a group from St. Elizabeth Ann Seton Parish in Hastings, Minnesota, including Father Jim Perkle, the pastor. A few phone calls and one month later, our family became an integral part of a group of thirty pilgrims headed to Medjugorje.

It became apparent from the start that this group was deeply spiritual and highly emotional. Three within the group had recently lost their spouses, whom they had planned for years to include in this trip. What I didn't know in the beginning, was how close we would all become by the end of this pilgrimage. We all stayed with Stipe's brother, Simon, a professional host, who has wonderful accommodations, excellent food, and lots of delicious wine from his very own vineyard at no extra charge. I strongly recommend his place to aspiring pilgrims!

I was amazed with both our sons and how quickly they embraced the holiness of Medjugorje. Normally reserved, they seemed to be in awe at the sites surrounding them, particularly Cross Mountain, Apparition Hill, the Redeemer Statue, and St. James Church. Tom snapped photos with his new digital camera of nearly everything he saw, including, but not limited to roosters, chickens, geckos, butterflies, flowers, & vineyards. However, he took particular interest in photographing those holy reminders of Jesus and Mary, who were the two main reasons for us being there. However, it was a single photograph taken by Brian one night that stole the show.

We had all decided earlier that same day to climb Cross Mountain in the afternoon. There was some concern among us that certain individuals within the group might not be physically able to make the entire journey to the top. One such person was Kitty, a full-figured woman who had both her knees replaced not too long ago. Kitty was determined to reach the summit exclaiming, "Jesus died for us, this is the least I can do for Him." There were ten males in our group. Six of them assisted those women who needed an arm to hold onto as we negotiated the rocks and boulders that make up the path. It took us about two hours to complete the fourteen Station of the Cross. When we reached the top, there was complete silence for awhile as we took in the breathtaking view of the surrounding area. My thoughts were also about what devotion those Croatian people must have had to the crucified Christ in order to endure the physical demands involved in building that huge concrete cross. Following about an hour of prayer and meditation, we began our decent of Cross Mountain. Most of those paired up during the climb up the mountain stayed together on the way down with the exception of Kitty. Somehow, she remained until last and required at least two strong men to help steady her legs while declining the slope. The only two men left were Jerry, in his mid-fifties, and seventeen year old Brian.

Three hours later they appeared inside Simon's house, along with two other women who also helped bring Kitty down the mountain. Almost in unison, they all recreated the perilous journey for the rest of our group. Following dinner, our pilgrimage leader, Jerry, had all of us sit in a large circle, in Simon's dining room, to discuss the day's events. The first to stand in the center of that circle was Kitty, who broke down crying as she stated how much she appreciated everyone's help in climbing up and down Cross Mountain, but was especially overcome with emotion, as she recognized Brian who, "At just seventeen years of age, would care so much for me every inch of the way down that mountain, pointing out every little obstacle along the way! I'm sure that Mary is smiling down on him now." Looking over at Brian she stated, "I will never forget you as long as I live."

We broke up the group after about forty-five minutes, at which time some walked outside onto the patio. There was a full moon visible in the Medjugorje sky, with intermittent cloud cover. Brian decided that he would capture a photograph of the moon with his mom's digital camera. When he looked at the result, he was amazed that the moon appeared to be in the shape of a heart. Whether it was the result of overlapping clouds or maybe Brian's unsteady hand while snapping the night time photo, we all felt that Mary truly was smiling down at him.

Editor's note: Tony is from Eau Claire, WI.

Brian's special photo

CHAPTER FOUR

Living the Messages

"Live my messages and put into life every word that I am giving you. May they be precious to you because they come from Heaven" (6/25/02).

(11/06)
Our Eternal Home is in Heaven

By Fr. Slavko Barbaric, OFM

"Dear children! Do not forget that you are here on earth on the way to eternity and that your home is in heaven. That is why, little children, be open to God's love and leave egoism and sin. May your joy be only in discovering God in daily prayer. That is why, make good use of this time and pray, pray, pray; and God is near to you in prayer and through prayer. Thank you for having responded to my call" (July 25, 2000).

DO NOT FORGET THAT YOU ARE HERE ON EARTH ON THE WAY TO ETERNITY AND THAT YOUR HOME IS IN HEAVEN.

It is a truth of our lives that we are pilgrims here on earth. We know from where we have come. God has created us out of love and we also know where we are going – to our eternal home. This life here on earth is really only an introduction and a preparation for eternal life. That is why it is important for us to remain on this path, that we keep the right conditions on this path which is Jesus Christ, and the conditions are what He said about Himself: "I am the way, the truth, the light and life." Without light we cannot see, without truth we take wrong paths, and without the life that He gives, we are dead. For the path here on earth it is important that we retain inner freedom and that we do not get stuck to anything or anybody, and here there are many dangers that people close themselves and then hang onto themselves or onto other people, other ideologies and the material. All this hinders the path toward our eternal home.

When we remain really conscious that we are on this path, that our life here on earth will someday come to an end, and that death is only a transition, then it will be much simpler to remain on the right path. Then it will become much easier to forgive, to love, to be merciful, to be good, because we know that everything is transitory, but when we forget this, then we will lose ourselves somewhere. Everyone who hates, who is selfish, who is dependent has already lost himself and will not be able to keep going. That is why so many people today are really empty internally or sad or depressed and no longer can find the purpose of life, because they do not wish to take the path that Jesus has shown us.

When Mary asks us to fast and to fast with bread and water, She is trying to awaken us and make us conscious of and help us to cross that bridge, because over the centuries and throughout the history of the Church it was always the pilgrims who over weeks, months or even years passed from town to town as pilgrims. Pilgrims are those who travel to places where God showed Himself, and on these pilgrimages the people could only take food that lasted, and that was bread and along with it also water. So when we hear that we are supposed to fast with bread and water for two days, then we may deduce from this that Mary's intention is, in this fashion, to make us freer and so that we also behave like the pilgrims that we are. In this Jubilee Year (2000) and in all the years since the beginning of these apparitions, the Pope has often spoken about all of us being pilgrims and then called all Christians to visit holy places and especially the Holy Land and Rome in this Jubilee Year.

Mary, as the one who comes to Medjugorje every day, is in a manner of speaking, also a pilgrim and through Her being a pilgrim, She has also moved many people to knowingly become pilgrims, and we must again be grateful for these 19 years and one month of Her presence here, and that many people by way of Her presence have really accepted this way of the pilgrim because they have accepted the path of our faith. And we must really remain conscious that our eternal home is in Heaven.

Editor's note: This excerpt from Fr. Slavko's reflection was written on July 27, 2000, four months before he went to his eternal home, Heaven. He died unexpectedly on Cross Mountain on November 24, 2000, after having prayed the Stations of the Cross. The next day, Our Lady said in Her monthly message that he was in Heaven.

Fr. Slavko's grave, a place of prayer in Medjugorje

(4/06)
Forgiveness

By Carolanne Kilichowski

What is forgiveness? *The American Heritage College* dictionary defines the word – forgive: 1. To excuse for a fault or an offense 2. To renounce anger or resentment against 3. To absolve from payment or debt.

Every day, in prayer, I pray with my heart, as Christ has taught us, "Forgive us our trespasses as we forgive those who trespass against us." I can remember being a child learning the Our Father and thinking about what this really means, and wondering if my heart could seriously forgive if someone really hurt me deeply. At times, this was not always an easy task. It sometimes takes much patience and prayer to overcome a heart that has been deeply hurt.

My latest test came on December 19, 2005, a few days before Christmas. As I walked out of work and got into my car, about to place the key in the ignition, which would lock my doors the minute that I put the car in reverse, my back door opened. I was startled and looked to see this young man beginning to seat himself in my back seat. I jumped out of my car, not knowing what he was doing, and having a sense of danger, as this young man had a very sly smile on his face. I saw that he was grabbing two bags from my back seat, so I realized he was robbing me. I yelled at him to give me back my bags, and asked him what he was doing. He looked surprised that I confronted him. He made some signal, and two very young kids came running to take the bags from him and they handed him a towel. In this towel was a gun which he pointed at my face and told me to "Shut up" . . .and called me a nasty name. At this point I looked around to scream, but no one was around. Where are people when you need them? I began to shake, as I felt my life was in jeopardy. I was never this close to a gun before. If he indeed made any motion to hurt me I would have done what I could to save my life. In my heart I prayed to Our Lady to help me. The gun was to keep me quiet so they could get away. As they ran, I took the cell phone out of my pocket to dial the police, but it was not working, as I was shaking, and somehow could not push the right button to make the call. He took the Christmas present I was just given, a bag of prayer books and a rosary, my checkbook and some receipts from bills. My purse was in the front seat and I thank God he did not notice. I was afraid they would run back when they discovered no money in the bag. I got into my car and went back to work to the security people for help. I felt strength from God at this time, a real grace!

I spent the next days praying for all these very young people who are leading a life of crime. I asked God to forgive them and to help them to feel His love. I was very surprised to find people asking me why I am praying for the guys who stole from me. It only made sense to me. The only way I could help them was to pray for them. Will I press charges if they are found? Yes, I will, to stop them from hurting others and hopefully help them to curtail a life of crime. In my heart I have truly forgiven them, as they do not know what they are doing.

A true example, most of us remember, is that of John Paul II. After being shot in the chest by his would-be assassin, he went to visit him in jail to forgive him and pray with him. Often I think what an impact this made on this man. To be truly forgiven by a man he wanted to kill!

I remember reading about the early days of Medjugorje and how Father Jozo challenged the people in church to forgive their brothers and to stand up and say, "I forgive you." At that time there were many problems between the Croatians and the Serbians. It was heart-warming to know that the parishioners took his words to heart and stood up voicing forgiveness for their brothers and sisters.

In this season of Lent, it is time to examine all of our hearts. My prayer for all of you is that when you pray those words of forgiveness, your heart will feel free of hard feelings. My prayer is that your hearts of stone will change to a heart of flesh. Free yourself of hard feelings and forgive your transgressors. If you sincerely have a problem with this, ask God for the grace of forgiveness. You will find that your heart will be light and happy when you can give that to God and feel that your heart has let it go. One practice I recall from a retreat, was to take a stone and carry it around for a week, or however long it takes you to let go. During this time take it with you everywhere, feeling the weight of the stone and feeling the rough edges. Imagine how the weight bears down in your own heart with these feelings of hardness. Imagine the rough edges being the hard times in your life when you were hurt by others. Take this stone or rock to church to pray. Ask God to relieve you of this heavy burden. Go to Confession and talk it over with a priest.

The graces you will receive in Confession will help you to overcome your heavy weight. Don't be afraid to cry, for tears are cleansing and healing. Let us all pray for one another. We all have hurts and times in our lives where we need to forgive others. Let us throw those stones away and begin again with a new heart of flesh, filled with love . . . one that Jesus would want us to carry.

"Pray that God gives you true peace. Live peace in your hearts and you will understand, dear children, that peace is the gift of God. Dear children, without love you cannot live peace. The fruit of peace is love and the fruit of love is forgiveness. I am with you and I invite all of you, little children, that before all else forgive in the family and then you will be able to forgive others . . ." (Our Lady of Medjugorje, 1/25/96).

Editor's note: Carolanne lives in Hamburg, NY, and is a Felician Franciscan Associate.

(10/05)
The Holy Sacrifice of the Mass

By June Klins

Ten years ago my "fairy tale" life came to a screeching halt with a force akin to Hurricane Katrina. The tool I needed to begin rebuilding sat dormant in my dresser drawer since my childhood years. I took out my rosary and dusted it off and began to use it every day. Within a few months Our Lady, through the Rosary, led me to daily Mass. I became addicted. I cannot imagine living without daily Mass. Our Lady ALWAYS leads us to Jesus.

At Medjugorje Our Lady asks us to make the Eucharist the center of our lives. She does not say this for Her sake, but for OUR sakes. She knows that we need Jesus in the Eucharist to strengthen us in our "Katrina" times, and also to sustain us in everyday life. Our Lady tells us that when there is a choice of whether to go to an apparition or to go to Mass, we should always choose Mass.

My son and his friend attended World Youth Day in Germany this year, and they had just found a perfect spot to see the Pope, when someone invited them to go to Mass. They declined, as they did not want to lose their spot. When the Pope rode by, my son's camera malfunctioned until after the Pope passed by. My son soon realized that God was telling him that they should have gone to Mass! When there is a choice to see Our Lady, the Pope or go to Mass, we should go to Mass. It only stands to reason that given the choice between ANYTHING and going to Mass, we should choose Mass.

So why is attendance at Mass dwindling, especially during this Year of the Eucharist, which ends this month? I surmise that it is because people do not understand the Mass. For if people really and truly understood the Mass, every church would be like St. James in Medjugorje, where people line up an hour ahead to get into the church.

During this Year of the Eucharist I have read much and heard many talks on the Mass, and although all were wonderful, what impressed me the most was the emphasis that was placed on the Mass being a "sacrifice." For the last few decades there has been more of an emphasis of the Mass being a meal, which, of course, it is. BUT, the Mass is also a sacrifice, and that is why it is called the "Holy Sacrifice of the Mass."

To understand this, we need to review what is meant by sacrifice. Fr. Albert Shamon in his enlightening book, *Behind the Mass*, explains it in simple terms. "A sacrifice is giving up something you love for a greater love. . . . Therefore, a sacrifice has two parts: (1) the giving up part; and (2) the love behind the giving up. What one gives up can usually be seen; we call this the *exterior* sacrifice. The love behind the giving up, the *why* one gives up generally cannot be seen, for you cannot see the heart. This is called the *interior* sacrifice. Of the two elements of sacrifice, the more important is the second element: the interior sacrifice . . . So giving up something without the proper motive renders the gift useless . . . All God asks of us is our hearts. When Cain and Abel offered their sacrifices, God considered not so much the gifts as the spirit of the giver. God was pleased with Abel's sacrifice, because He was pleased with his spirit. He rejected Cain's sacrifice because his heart was not good. Later, Jesus rejected the sacrifices of the Scribes and Pharisees because they were offering only lip service to God . . . On the contrary, when God asked Abraham to sacrifice his son Isaac, He did not demand Isaac's death once He saw Abraham's heart was ready to do God's will in all things. As you can have prayers without words, the Blessed Sacrament without Cathedral walls, so one can have sacrifice without destruction. The ideal, however, is to combine both the exterior and interior sacrifice. Jesus did this on Calvary."

Father goes on to say that what happened on Calvary is still going on in Heaven, and that Jesus made it possible to bring to earth what is going on in Heaven when He commanded His apostles and their successors to do what He had done at the Last Supper in remembrance of Himself. Thus at every Mass priests bring Christ to the altar where He continues what He is doing at the right hand of the Father. "The Mass is a little bit of Heaven breaking through on earth; the Mass perpetuates the sacrificial offering of Calvary."

Fr. Shamon goes on to explain how at Mass the Passion of Jesus is represented by the separate pronouncements of the words of Consecration. There is a pause between the words, "This is My Body," and "This is the cup of My Blood." To separate body and blood would inflict death, but since Christ can die no more, this does not happen. However, the heart of the Calvary sacrifice is RE-presented at Mass. The obedient descent of Jesus to the altar at the words of Consecration prove that the same *obedience to the Father's will* lasts forever.

Fr. Shamon writes, "The Mass is not just His sacrifice, but the Church's. That is why the two most important words after the Consecration are, 'We offer,' because they designate OUR sacrifice." We offer all our heartaches, problems, the "Katrinas" of our life, which we accept as Jesus accepted His cross, and bring them to the altar to offer to the Father with Jesus. Then at Communion, God the Father gives back to us what we offered to Him in the form of Food. Jesus comes to us to strengthen us, so that when we have the "Katrinas" of our life – and we all will; there is no escaping it – we will know that we are not alone. Let's make every year a "Year of the Eucharist."

(1/05)
Mirjana's Special Message

By Sr. Emmanuel

On December 2nd, the visionary Mirjana received her monthly apparition under the green tent of the Cenacle, in Medjugorje. For years, on the second day of the month, Our Lady has been appearing to Mirjana in order to intercede for the non-believers. Usually, Mirjana does not communicate a message following the apparitions of the second of the month. But this month, to everyone's surprise, Mirjana wrote the message she had received and she asked that it would be translated right there, in front of the people present. Here is the text of the message:

"I need you! I am calling you! I need your help! Reconcile with yourself, with God, with your neighbors. In this way you will help me. Convert the non-believers. Wipe the tears from my face!"

The Gospa calls us to reconcile with ourselves first. Sometimes, we see people who are devastated by a lack of inner peace even after they have confessed their sins, though they completely believe in the forgiveness of God. When they see that peace is escaping them, they often confess again the same sins from the past, hoping that God's mercy will at last work on their hearts and bring them the peace they so desire. But to no avail! Very often, this torment comes from the fact that, even though God has forgiven them, they haven't forgiven themselves. It happens a lot in case of abortion.

For example, a 56-year-old woman had been suffering from severe internal turmoil for 30 years. At each confession, she mentioned this sin that she committed at the age of 26, but the peace of God always eluded her. She came to Medjugorje for help and we asked her if she thought her child had forgiven her from Heaven. She answered: "Yes." Then we asked her if she had forgiven herself. Horrified, she cried out, "How could I ever forgive myself for doing such a horrible thing!?" Right there, we had the key to her trouble. Invited to review her state in the light of God, she accepted to recognize humbly that, yes, she was capable of such an act, and even worse: the only thing she really possessed was her own misery, (as Jesus told St. Faustina). She admitted that this abortion had humiliated her and ruined the good opinion she had of herself. The lack of peace actually came from pride, subtly disguised as a virtue. When she realized this, she accepted to apply to herself the mercy that God had given her without measure. To reconcile with ourselves does not mean to call "good" the bad we have done or to deny the sin. On the contrary! It is to call it "bad" and to throw it away forever in the heart of God, in the depth of His Mercy. After this breakthrough, the woman finally found peace in her heart. She had changed glasses and was no longer afraid of her misery: she was not focusing on herself anymore but on her Savior, and only saw herself in the light of mercy. She had transformed her remorse into repentance.

It is good to be constantly ready to welcome Jesus, who will come as a thief. I will never forget my friend, Jakov. He was a man from the village of Medjugorje who owned vineyards, a large storage of wine; and had a strong liking for alcohol, (especially after he returned from Germany where he had worked very hard). Because of this tendency, his behavior was sometimes difficult to put up with, despite his wonderful, big heart. One day, he developed cancer of the stomach; but it did not stop him from doing all his chores in the fields and elsewhere. He remained cheerful. One morning, out of the blue, he called one of his sons and said: "Go and get all our neighbors, friends and family members, I need to talk to them." His son was surprised but he did as he was told. Then, Jakov sat in his bedroom, where he invited everyone to come one by one. He asked each of them for their forgiveness, for any harm he may have done to them, knowingly or unknowingly. He did likewise with his sons. He made sure he reconciled himself with everyone and paid all his debts. Then, he went to church and made his confession. That evening, during dinner, he was happy. Had he guessed what was to come? That night, he went to bed as usual and fell asleep, never to wake up, filled with peace.

Children of Medjugorje, www.childrenofmedjugorje.com

The Blue Cross – where Mirjana currently has her apparitions
on the second of the month

(6/09)
Prayer to the Mother of Goodness, Love & Mercy

The following prayer was dictated by Our Lady to Jelena Vasilj, one of the two Medjugorje locutionists, on April 19,1983. Jelena was only 10 years old when this prayer was dictated to her.

O Mother of mine, Mother of goodness, love and mercy, I love you infinitely and I offer myself to You. By means of Your goodness, Your love and Your grace, save me. I desire to be Yours. I love You infinitely, and desire You to protect me. From the depth of my heart I pray You, Mother of goodness, give me Your goodness. Let me gain Heaven by means of it. I pray You, by Your infinite love, to give me the grace, so that I may love every man, as You have loved Jesus Christ. I pray You to give me the grace to be merciful towards You. I offer myself completely and desire that You follow my every step, because You are full of grace. And I desire that I will never forget this. And if, by chance, I should lose grace, I pray You to restore it to me once more. Amen.

(*The phrase "I pray You to give me the grace to be merciful towards You" means "give me the grace to love Your will which is different from mine.")

(2/07)
The Bible – a Catholic Book!

By June Klins

Recently I was discussing Our Lady's January 2006 message about reading the Bible with a friend, and she mentioned that among her favorite books of the Bible are Tobit and Sirach. I said I loved those books, too, and what a shame it was that the Protestant Bible does not have those books. Many Catholics do not realize that the Catholic Bible has seven more books than the Protestant one, while some people think that we added those books to the Bible, which is not true at all. If we are living Our Lady's messages I think it is important to be educated about this.

The Bible did not exist until the 4th century. The Church came FIRST, then the Bible. The Bible is a CATHOLIC book. There is not a single article of the Catholic faith that is opposed to anything in the Bible!

The Bible, as we know it, with its 73 books was approved by the Pope in 382 A.D. at the Council of Rome. The Councils of Hippo (393 A.D.) and Carthage (397 A.D.) ratified the Canon of Scripture, which means the list of books in the Bible. It stayed that way for over 1200 years until the 16th century when Martin Luther chose to remove seven books: Sirach, Tobit, Wisdom, 1 Maccabees, 2 Maccabees, Baruch, and Judith. These seven books had references to the Resurrection in them, and originally the Sadducees had taken those seven books out of the Hebrew scriptures. Since Martin Luther believed in salvation by faith alone, he took out the second book of Maccabees which has verses which refute his belief. 2Maccabees is part of the apocrypha (the seven books the Sadducees took out), so he took out all of them. He also removed James, Jude, Hebrews and Revelation, saying they were not the inspired Word of God. The 17th century Lutherans put the New Testament books back in though, so the Protestant New Testament is the same as the Catholic one.

The Bible is a Catholic book. "All scripture is inspired by God and is useful for teaching, for refutation, for correction, and for training in righteousness, so that one who belongs to God may be competent, equipped for every good work" (2Tim 3:16). That is why Our Lady wants us to read it every day. Just do it!

(3/05)
How Does Fasting on Wednesday and Friday Bring Us Closer to Jesus?

By Sr. Emmanuel

A few members of the prayer group (the young people's prayer group formed in the 80s in Medjugorje) disclosed to me that Mary requested that every Thursday of the year we commemorate the gift of the Eucharist and the Priesthood.

One way to live this commemoration is by fasting with love on Wednesday and Friday. We remember in joy, in faith and in thanksgiving that Jesus gave His Body and His Blood to us as food and drink. Our Lady is so much in love with the Eucharist, the Bread of Life, that She gives us all day Wednesday to prepare ourselves for this commemoration. It does not mean that we should attend Holy Mass on Thursday only! Starting on Wednesday, She wants to eliminate the distractions of food, grocery shopping, cooking, and the worries related to food. That way we become immersed in the flavor of bread, the bread that will become the real Body of Jesus, since Jesus chose bread to be transformed into His Body. On Wednesdays, we should not think, "I can't wait to eat." Rather, start fasting with joy and with the heart and begin enjoying the reality of bread. We prepare ourselves like the Hebrews in the desert during the Exodus. God gave them manna, the bread that came down from Heaven. He was preparing His people to receive the mystery of the Eucharist. In the same manner, Our Blessed Mother is preparing us today. On Thursday we celebrate and commemorate the institution of the Bread of Life.

When I listen to the visionaries in Medjugorje I am always surprised to learn that Our Lady never mentioned fasting on Friday as a remembrance of Christ's death on the cross. They never mention that! Instead, Friday is the day after Thursday. Our Blessed Mother doesn't want us to quickly return to the distractions of food. She wants us to remain focused and not go right back to Lobster Bisque, Chicken a La King, prime rib and all those special dishes. On Friday, She wants us to savor the taste of bread and remain immersed in His mystery as long as possible. It's the same attitude the Jews have toward the Sabbath day. It is their holiest feast day, and when the sun sets on Saturday evening at the end of the Sabbath, Jews continue to sing and recite hymns as if they could keep the Sabbath from ending. To the Jewish people, the Sabbath day is like a fiancé to his beloved – they just don't want to let it go! Similarly, when we fast on Fridays we do it to savor the taste of bread as long as possible, the bread that reminds us of the Bread of Life.

I always imagine the Virgin Mary remaining on earth after the Ascension among the apostles. When She entered into the kitchen, after the Last Supper, how could She look at bread as She had before the Last Supper? As soon as She saw bread, something must have made Her motherly heart throb. No doubt She thought, "My Son placed Himself in bread. This is the substance that became my Son!"

When we look at a single grain of wheat from which bread is made, we have before us the whole story of Christ, the story of the Redeemer. When Jesus speaks about the grain of wheat in the Gospel, we see that the grain of wheat must fall on the ground, be buried and die. It's through this death that life will come again and produce fruit in abundance – thirty-fold, sixty-fold, or one hundred-fold. This is the whole story of the death and the resurrection of Christ, and of the fruit of His Redemption. For the grain of wheat to become bread, it has to be crushed to produce flour. Jesus also was crushed: His body, His heart, His soul, His whole Divine Being. The story of the grain embodies the story of Jesus' love for us. He let Himself be crushed so that we might be nourished by Him and sanctified through His food. When Jesus spoke about the Bread of Life, He said, "He who eats this bread will have eternal life."

That's why we can welcome Wednesdays and Fridays with love for bread, with love for our Redemption. The Blessed Mother wishes to engross us in it, not only spiritually, but also in practice. As a very sensible Jewish woman, She immerses us in bread so that we almost have to be with Jesus. Through fasting, She focuses our attention on the loving presence of Jesus. She allows us to marvel at the fact that, in an utmost gesture of humility, Jesus transformed Himself into bread. Here, we have the real meaning of fasting: it is a matter of loving the Eucharist. Everything that She says and directs us to is centered on Jesus. And if we fast in this way, with a love for the Bread of Life, our fasting changes. It becomes a joy! This is why Our Lady says, "Dear children, fast; but fast with the heart." We'll gain a great love for the Eucharist. And this is an incredible grace because as a great French mystic, Marthe Robin, said, "Our glory in Heaven will be proportional to the fervor we put into our Holy Communions on earth." The more we receive the Bread of Life with care, love and deep gratitude, the greater our glory will be in Heaven.

*From the book **Freed and Healed Through Fasting**, © Sr. Emmanuel Maillard, 2004. Used with permission from Children of Medjugorje, www.childrenofmedjugorje.com*

The Adoration chapel next to St. James in Medjugorje

(7/05)
The Healing Power of the Eucharist

By Donna Arnson

History is full of events that show the power of the Eucharist to change lives and there are numerous miracles that God has performed through the centuries to demonstrate to us His real presence in the Eucharist. The phenomenon of bleeding hosts, often reminding us of the bleeding heart of Christ, anguishing over the sin of mankind, is one that is occurring in Worcester, Massachusetts.

This Miracle of the Eucharist, involves Audrey Santo (known as "Little Audrey"), a victim soul now age 21, living in Worcester. She was involved in a near-drowning accident when she was three years old. She remains confined to her bed in a state called Akinetic Mutis – non-moving, non-speaking, receiving care 24 hours a day from her family and a staff of nurses. This silent, suffering young girl has been used by God in a special way. Since her return from Medjugorje in 1988, many alleged miracles and mystical experiences have surrounded her and many healings have been reported by thousands who have visited her. And in a special way, Little Audrey is God's instrument to bring us to the Eucharist and to experience the awesome healing power of the Eucharist.

Little Audrey has received Holy Communion, by mouth, every day since she was five years old, her only solid food since that time, as she is fed via a gastrostomy tube into her stomach. For most of her life, she has been lying in bed before the Blessed Sacrament in her bedroom, with permission of the local bishop. There are five consecrated Hosts that have exhibited human blood that are kept in the tabernacle in her room. It is clear that the Eucharist has been the focal point and center of her life. She has manifested marks on her body resembling the wounds of Christ. It is believed that Little Audrey offers up and unites her suffering to Christ and her suffering becomes redemptive suffering. It is redemptive suffering that brings the healing.

My daughter Katie and I visited the chapel in Little Audrey's home in May and were invited to celebrate in the Adoration of the Blessed Sacrament. The priest brought out the monstrance, and it contained a bleeding Host. (The blood was dark brown and in the shape of a rugged cross.) We were experiencing Eucharistic amazement and an awesome revelation, "I am here." One pilgrim burst out crying. I immediately felt so much love! I was in the presence of LOVE! And Katie and I also felt a tremendous peace. Jesus' presence was before us, the LIVING body, blood, soul, and divinity. It was so awesome! Here was the miracle of divine love for us, here His majesty, His grace, and His goodness shining forth in a most extraordinary manner. We were encountering the glory of God. Jesus has shed His precious blood and was showing how much He cared about us by dying on the cross for the forgiveness of sins, and He wants us to be healed. The Lord was showing us the reality of His presence in the Eucharist. A true sign of His presence to build up the faith of the people, in the bleeding Host, to visually help us believe and to draw us to Him. We met Jesus in the Eucharist and were experiencing Eucharistic wonder and profound amazement and gratitude. It was a "WOW" moment!!! We could unburden our hearts, release our feelings and emotions to Him, and give Him every situation that was beyond our control and that threatened our peace. His love was consoling, encouraging, radiating peace and healing. We were experiencing joy, in this spiritual intimacy with Jesus.

The Blessed Mother's message to the Medjugorje visionaries on September 25, 1995, spoke of coming into a spiritual intimacy with

Jesus that will be a joy for us. "Today I invite you to fall in love with the Most Holy Sacrament of the Altar. Adore Him, little children, in your parishes and in this way you will be united with the entire world. Jesus will become your friend and you will not talk of Him like someone whom you barely know. Unity with Him will be a joy for you and you will become witnesses to the love of Jesus that He has for every creature. Little children, when you adore Jesus you are also close to me."

Jesus is showing us that He wants us to be with Him and come to Him in the Eucharist. When you sit in His awesome presence you are going to change. Even if your heart is cloudy, just sit there. Even if you don't know what to say, or your mind is blank, or your heart is broken, just sit there, presence to Presence. The healing power of the Eucharist will transform you, mentally, physically, and spiritually. By being present before the Eucharist, you will have your faith restored and by making the Eucharist the center of your life, as Our Lady requests at Medjugorje, you will find life and joy, peace and mercy, hope and restoration, in the Eucharistic heart of Christ. You are not alone, forgotten or abandoned. You are His, and He is with you. His Presence is a beautiful gift of love, powerfully affirming His compassionate care for you. Praise God that we have been given the greatest treasure of all, the gift of JESUS CHRIST! Now that's quite AMAZING!!!

Editor's note: Donna lives in Birmingham, AL.

(10/08)
Teaching the Rosary to Protestants

By June Klins

One year on the feast of Mary, Mother of God, my pastor announced that we were going to start praying the Rosary before Mass every Sunday. In his homily he said that we MUST pray the Rosary every day! AMEN!

After Mass, a lady who was sitting several rows in front of me approached me and asked me if I pray the Rosary. I laughed to myself, and thought, "Of all people to ask – I give away rosaries!" She told me that she wanted to ask a different lady, but that the Holy Spirit had directed her to me. Dee (not her real name) said she had left the church at age 15 and had been Protestant for 35 years and was now returning and joining our parish. She said she still had a problem with Mary and the Rosary though. She said that when Father said we had to pray the Rosary every day, she felt he was speaking directly to her. Usually Mary brings us to Jesus, but in this case Jesus brought Mary to her!

I reached into my bag to get Dee a rosary. I usually carry rosaries with me that are in prescription bottles (I have written about this several times – but for the new people – the Rosary is a prescription for what ails you and for our world.). I also wanted to give her a pamphlet on the Rosary. Wouldn't you know – I forgot to replenish my supply after giving my last ones away and did not have either one with me! Of all times . . .

BUT the Holy Spirit had a better plan. As I reached into my bag for a copy of my son's miracle story with the Rosary, something was bulging in the pocket of the folder where I keep the story. I looked to see what it was and lo and behold – it was a little book of the Scriptural Rosary. I felt the Holy Spirit prompt me to give it to Dee. I have to admit that I did not want to because this book had been a gift from someone and I loved the book and used it all the time. But I gave it to her anyway. She was so excited as I showed her the Bible verses for each Hail Mary. I know the Holy Spirit put that book in that folder like that just for her. I have never had that happen before!

Then Dee asked me if I could meet with her the next day to teach her how to pray the Rosary. We did meet and she told me that she LOVED the idea of the scriptural Rosary. It all made sense that this way of praying the Rosary would appeal to her more because of her Protestant background, which is usually very Bible-oriented. So my suggestion is that if you are trying to present the Rosary to Protestants, this may be the way to go. Meet them where they are at.

Editor's note: When I asked Dee what brought her back to the Church, she replied that it happened as she was preparing a lesson to teach at her Protestant church. As she read over all the scripture verses about the Eucharist, especially John 6, she said she knew something was amiss with her church. She said that she felt that Jesus would not have made such a big deal about the Eucharist if it were just to "remember Him." Dee said that the story about the men on the road to Emmaus

*was a turning point for her. Wow! Jesus revealed the scriptures to her
just as He did for the disciples on the way to Emmaus!*

(9/09)
The Triumph of the Cross in the Home

By Father Angelus Shaughnessy, OFM, Cap.

There is a town, Siroki Brijeg, of 13,000 inhabitants in Bosnia-
Herzegovina that has not had a single divorce in living memory. The
town has suffered for decades at the hands of the Communists and
for centuries from the Moslems. They attribute the success of their
marriages to the crucified Lord.

When a couple think they have found their lifelong partner, they
don't say, "I have found the perfect man; I have found the perfect
woman." No, they say, "I have found my cross." And when they come to
church for the marriage ceremony, they bring their own large crucifix
with them. This is how they exchange their vows: the crucifix is placed
upon the altar. She places her hand on the corpus of the crucifix. He puts
his hand on top of hers; and the priest wraps the stole over everything
on the cross. They know that if either one leaves the cross, the marriage
is in danger.

So when they have their problems (as they will), they do not rush
off to a counselor or an attorney or to some psychologist or psychiatrist.
They go to the crucifix which is mounted in their home. As soon as the
marriage ceremony is over, that is where they pray together and learn
to solve their differences, and they teach their children where to turn
as well.

*Editor's note: The above was excerpted from "Mother Love," a
newsletter published by the National Office of the Archconfraternity
of Christian Mothers, Winter 2008. Father Angelus is the National
Executive Director of the Archconfraternity of Christian Mothers. You
can visit his website at www.fatherangelus.com.*

(11/05)
Penance in Heaven?

By June Klins

Not long ago a non-Catholic lady was telling me about her father, now deceased, who abandoned the family and later reunited with her only to disown her. Then she said something I found very interesting for someone who is not Catholic. She said, "God must be having him do penance somewhere." This very sweet lady could not fathom that her father went to hell, even though he would not win any "Father of the Year" awards, but she knew that his actions did not warrant him in Heaven. She hit the nail right on the head. We call it Purgatory.

Watching the horrible situation at the Superdome in New Orleans on TV after Hurricane Katrina, I felt as if I were viewing Purgatory on earth. Just as the people who were stuck in New Orleans NEEDED OTHER PEOPLE to come and rescue them, so too the souls in Purgatory cannot pray for themselves and NEED US to pray for them. Some of the people were complaining that help was not coming soon enough. Don't you think that this is the way the souls in Purgatory feel? How often do we ignore the souls in Purgatory, or how often are we in denial that a certain person could possibly be in Purgatory? Our Lady has said that most souls go to Purgatory and that very few go directly to Heaven. She tells us to pray for the souls in Purgatory every day.

The visionaries, as well as some saints, have said that there are levels in Purgatory. When the busses in New Orleans came to take people to a better area, it reminded me of when the souls move up a level in Purgatory because of our prayers. They are not quite home, but things are somewhat better. Likewise, when I saw the people who were air-lifted to safety I thought of how Masses, especially Gregorian Masses, are like an "air lift" to Heaven for the souls in Purgatory.

"Today I wish to call you to pray daily for souls in purgatory. For every soul prayer and grace is necessary to reach God and the love of God. By doing this, dear children, you obtain new intercessors who will help you in life to realize that all the earthly things are not important for you, that only Heaven is that for which it is necessary to strive" (Our Lady, 11/6/86).

(9/08)
The Miracle Praye

By Fr. Peter Mary Roo

Say this prayer faithfully, no matter how you feel. w ...
to the point where you sincerely mean each word, with all your hea...
something good spiritually will happen to you. You will experience
Jesus, and He will change your whole life in a very special way. You
will see.

*Lord Jesus, I come before You, just as I am. I am sorry for my sins,
I repent of my sins, please forgive me. In Your name, I forgive all others
for what they have done against me. I renounce Satan, the evil spirits and
all their works. I give You my entire self, Lord Jesus, now and forever. I
invite You into my life, Jesus. I accept You as my Lord, God and Savior.
Heal me, change me, strengthen me in body, soul and spirit.*

*Come Lord Jesus, cover me with Your precious blood, and fill me
with Your Holy Spirit. I love You, Lord Jesus. I praise You, Jesus. I
thank You, Jesus. I shall follow You every day of my life. Amen.*

*Mary my mother, Queen of Peace, St. Peregrine, the cancer saint,
all you angels and Saints please help me. Amen.*

Fr. Jozo

(5/07)
Fr. Jozo Speaks about Rest

The following is Fr. Jozo's reflection on the July, 2006 message.

"Dear children! At this time, do not only think of rest for your body but, little children, seek time also for the soul. In silence may the Holy Spirit speak to you and permit Him to convert and change you. I am with you and before God I intercede for each of you. Thank you for having responded to my call."

In the human nature God also created a need for rest. During creation, the Lord Himself created a day of rest and named it the Lord's Day. It is the day in which the Church places the Eucharist as a sign of a meeting with the Risen Lord. It is the day in which our body rests and the soul gets filled with grace. It is wisdom to harmonise the rest of the body and the renewal of the spirit. After the first missionary journey, Jesus sent His disciples to rest. The Apostles gathered around Jesus and reported to Him everything they did and taught. He said to them; "*You must come away to some lonely place . . . and rest for a while*" (Mk 6:30).

In human nature there is a need to find a harmony between the body and the soul. Even pagans said: "A healthy spirit in a healthy body." Care for the body is necessary, it is from God. However, anguished and excessive concern for the body is a deviation and develops into an unhealthy state. Today, the culture of the body and of what is physical is over exaggerated. Physical pleasure has become a goal. The promotion and the cult of the body has become the content of television programs, newspapers, films and other media. Man has lost his security and feels attacked because he has lost the harmony. It looks as if the truth in man has fallen, stumbled and disappeared. Unfortunately priority is given to error which gains ever more space and suppresses the truth.

What is this truth? It is a virtue to protect the soul. It is a virtue to find time to rest our soul, as Our Lady calls us to in this message. It is vacation time which is a time to renew the physical and spiritual strength. With leaving our home and our parish we must not leave behind our faith, prayer and spiritual life. We must not become the same as those who identify their rest with a repulsive life, entertainment and the like. Unfortunately, many Christians spend their rest in vain, without Holy Mass and without prayer. Today, the tourist centers, unfortunately, try to bring new content to the summer programs such as new forms of entertainment and uninhibited activities. In this way, during summer holidays many fall to the very bottom in a moral and Christian sense. Instead of returning home with a rested body and soul, they return with wounded hearts and devastated spirit, marriage and life.

In a Motherly way, Our Lady calls us to every day find time to dedicate to our soul every day. Therefore, I must reflect on how this is possible. Here are several practical suggestions.

I need to go to my rest with the following:
1. with the Bible,
2. with my family Rosary,
3. with a book of Christian content,
4. with a decision to regularly go to Holy Mass,
5. with a decision to resist and avoid unchristian programs I come across,
6. with a decision to begin each day with prayer and to end it with prayer.

On vacation it is necessary to strengthen our family unity by taking walks together and speaking with our children and friends.

We must know how to seek silence. It is the Holy Spirit who wondrously speaks in silence. We need to become open to the inspirations of the Holy Spirit who changes and ennobles us. If we were just to look at a sunset and the wonderful colors created in the sky – such wonderful experience of what is beautiful frees us from our burdens and frustrations. Rest is wonderful and beneficial when the Holy Spirit gives it to us. Then there is no frustration or overburdening and our soul is rested and free. As the prophet said: "Only in God is your rest my soul."

What is Our Heavenly Mother saying to us and what is She teaching us? She is telling us that rest must build us and help us grow in faith, peace and love. She teaches us not to lose face and our soul on vacation, instead to use it for a benefit and the good of both our soul and body. It is Her desire that rest be an occasion for our growth and for our moral, intellectual and spiritual enrichment.

Dear brothers and sisters, I pray for all of you who do not have a possibility of going to rest and for all those of you who do. May the Queen of Peace accompany you all and protect you with Her blessing.

(1/06)
Being Polite While Answering Our Lady's Call

By June Klins

Fasting is by far the hardest of Our Lady's messages to follow. But it is very powerful, and Our Lady has told us on numerous occasions that we can stop wars and change the course of nature by prayer and fasting. Sometimes, however, we can find ourselves in an awkward position, such as being invited to dinner on a fast day. We want to be polite, but also honor Our Lady's request to fast. Also, some people who have health problems may not be able to fast on bread and water. When these situations were posed to my internet prayer group, the following suggestions were made.

1. Fast on either the day before or after.
2. Eat only a little or half, if you have to eat.
3. Eat something you do not like.
4. Fast that day from something you like, such as coffee, sweets, TV, cigarettes, etc.
5. Fast like we do on Ash Wednesday and Good Friday, with no eating between meals.
6. Fast from complaining.
7. Join your friends with a cup of hot water.
8. Tell them the truth when fasting – great way to witness.
9. If the fast has been broken, don't beat yourself up.
10. Watch out for patterns – is it happening mostly on fast days and is it the same people who call you out on these days? It is possibly the work of the evil one.
11. Pray, pray and pray for guidance, strength and endurance. Our Lady needs our help for Her peace plan.

For those who have trouble fasting, repeat often the words of St. Paul in the bold print. "In every circumstance and in all things I have learned the secret of being well fed and of going hungry, of living in abundance and of being in need. **I have the strength for everything through Him who empowers me**" (Philippians 4:12-13).

(2/09)
Time for Scripture

By Brother Craig Driscoll

It is very good to read Sacred Scripture each day. Many people already do this. Many great spiritual writers have recommended this. As always, it is good to pray to the Holy Spirit before reading Sacred Scripture. Some Bibles have a prayer printed at the beginning or, if not, you could make up one of your own.

Make time (we do not *find* time – we *make* time) even if it is a short amount of time for reading Sacred Scripture daily. Here are some helpful hints that I hope you can use to make time for daily reading of Sacred Scripture:

- Set aside the same time everyday for this reading.
- Begin with the beginning of the Old Testament or the New Testament.
- Begin with your favorite book of the Bible.
- Decide to read a chapter of Sacred Scripture each day.
- Set aside a certain amount of time to read Sacred Scripture.

Brother Craig, the Founder of The Monks of Adoration, studied theology at the Angelicum in Rome. You may contact him a monkadorer@verzion.net.

(8/05)
The Two Precious Vessels

By June Klins

Our Lady, in Her messages, tells us that we should make the Eucharist the center of our lives. When I first began to follow the messages of Medjugorje, I mistakenly interpreted this to mean that Our Lady says we should go to Mass every day. Nancy Latta, who translates for Fr. Jozo, explained that Our Lady would never say that because some people cannot go to Mass every day, and Our Lady would not want these people to feel guilty that they are not living the messages. Once we had a missionary from Mississippi come to our church to talk, and he said that in his diocese there are so few priests that they can only have Mass one Sunday a month. I was flabbergasted that this situation would exist right here in the United States. And given that this is true in other areas of the United States, it is certainly true in other areas of the world. We who have access to daily Mass often take it for granted that everyone has this privilege. I am very blessed to be able to live in a city that has daily Mass available in the morning, at noon and after work. "Much will be required of the person entrusted with much, and still more will be demanded of the person entrusted with more" (Mt. 12:48). But for those who are not blessed to live in an area with daily Mass or cannot get to daily Mass because of a schedule conflict, the Lord has provided an alternative.

That alternative is called "Spiritual Communion." St. Liguori, in his book, *The Holy Eucharist,* wrote: "A Spir... Communion, according to St. Thomas Aquinas, consists in an ardent desire to receive Jesus in the Most Holy Sacrament, and in lovingly embracing Him as if we had actually received Him." St. Thomas Aquinas and St. Alphonsus both taught that Spiritual Communion produces effects similar to sacramental Communion, according to the dispositions with which it is made, the greater or less earnestness with which Jesus is desired, and the greater or less love with which Jesus is welcomed and given due attention.

"How pleasing these Spiritual Communions are to God," St. Alphonsus wrote, "and the many graces which He bestows through their means, was manifested by Our Lord Himself to Sister Paula Maresca, the foundress of the convent of St. Catherine of Sienna in Naples, when (as it is related in her life) He showed her two precious vessels, the one of gold, the other of silver. He then told her that in the gold vessel He preserved her Sacramental Communions, and in the silver one her Spiritual Communions."

"All those who desire to advance in the love of Jesus Christ," St. Alphonsus continued, "are exhorted to make a Spiritual Communion at least once in every visit that they pay to the Most Blessed Sacrament . . . This devotion is far more profitable than some suppose, and at the same time nothing can be easier to practice. Blessed Jane of the Cross used to say that a Spiritual Communion can be made without anyone remarking it, without fasting, without the permission of our director, and we can make it at any time we please; an act of love does all." Isn't that an awesome thought?!

The little blue *Pieta* book of prayers gives the following prayer that can be said when making a Spiritual Communion: "O Jesus, I turn toward the holy tabernacle where You live hidden for love of me. I love you, O my God. I cannot receive you in Holy Communion. Come nevertheless and visit me with Your grace. Come spiritually into my heart. Purify it. Sanctify it. Render it like unto Your own. Amen. Lord, I am not worthy that Thou shouldst enter under my roof, but only say the word and my soul shall be healed."

The Cure of Ars said, "A Spiritual Communion acts on the soul as blowing does on a cinder-covered fire which was about to go out.

Whenever you feel your love of God growing cold, quickly make a Spiritual Communion."

How awesome our God is, to provide us with Spiritual Communion. Of course, Sacramental Communion is the preferred means to receive Our Lord. I can't help but see the similarity of the silver and gold vessels to the silver rosaries which turn gold in Medjugorje and elsewhere. Could the message here be that frequent reception of Spiritual Communion will eventually lead to a more frequent reception of Sacramental Communion? St. John Bosco once said, "There are two things the devil is deadly afraid of – frequent Communions and frequent visits to the Blessed Sacrament."

In this Year of the Eucharist, may we take advantage of all the Eucharistic treasures Our Lord has provided for us. "Let holy Mass be your life" (Our Lady, 4/25/98).

Editor's note: I was prompted to write this article after I received the story of the two vessels in the mail from two different people in the same week, and then read in St. Alphonsus' book a day or two later – a story I had never heard before three times in one week! The Holy Spirit made it pretty clear that He wanted our readers to know about this!

(7/08)
Forgiving Yourself

by June Klins

One year on the feast day of Mary Magdalene, July 22, I was attending a St. Ann novena, and the priest, Fr. John, spoke about forgiveness. He said that Mary Magdalene trusted God enough to accept forgiveness, and she also moved ahead to FORGIVE HERSELF. He said that it is very important in the spiritual life to forgive yourself, and that many people torture themselves with their sins of the past.

Father John said we must forgive ourselves so to accept God's forgiveness and love, so that we can respond to God's love. He said that we are all guilty of doing things we regret, but God's mercy and forgiveness are beyond our comprehension. He gave seven steps to self forgiveness:

1. Decide to forgive yourself. This is the hardest step. No one can do this for you. It is an act of the will, not a feeling. No matter how horrendous the sin, you need to take this first step.
2. Forgiveness of self is tied to the image we have of God. Two thirds of the Gospel is about forgiveness. God forgives us if we forgive each other. If we see God as a loving Father it is easier.
3. Make use of the sacrament of Reconciliation – no matter how long it has been or how bad the sin(s).
4. You need to deal with guilt in a healthy way. If you still feel guilty for something you did 30 or 40 years ago and have confessed it, that is not healthy. When we deal with guilt in a sensible way it leads to self forgiveness. Healthy guilt can actually bring us closer to God.
5. When the steps above are difficult, always take it to the crucified Jesus. Ask for the grace to forgive yourself and forget forever. Say things like "Father, forgive me for what I have done." The grace is already given, but we have to ACCEPT it.
6. In the New Testament Jesus tells us we will be forgiven as we forgive others (not an Old Testament virtue). Some of us should bite our lips when, during the "Our Father" we say that part.
7. Forgiving ourselves is a PROCESS, and we have to be patient with ourselves. We have to persevere. This is especially hard for people who have committed sins against life, such as abortion. It CAN be forgiven in the sacrament of Reconciliation and this is the place to start the process of self forgiveness.

In summary, Father John said to forgive yourself for the sins of the past because it is essential for a healthy spiritual life. On June 25, 1988, Our Lady said, *"Surrender yourself to God so that He may heal you, console you and forgive everything inside you which is a hindrance on the way of love."*

(3/07)
My Boring Confession

By Brian Klins

"Your sins aren't exciting enough anymore," my friend sent to me in a text. It was a reply to a message I had sent him about the confession I had just left. I broke away from work today for a quick stop into the confessional booth at Westminster Roman Catholic Cathedral (in London). It's the only church I know that has Confession everyday from 11:00 A.M. to 6:30 P.M. It's the "drive-thru" to forgiveness.

Mass was being celebrated as I waited in the queue and carefully considered each of the sins I had committed throughout the past week. After about nine other evildoers, I entered the confessional booth and began, "Bless me, Father, for I have sinned . . ." I continued on with my transgressions while an old white haired priest remained with his eyes closed, seemingly pondering over what I was saying. His head was propped up against the frame of the confessional window while he listened intently to each of my sins. On completion, there was a long silence. I waited. I cleared my throat. I breathed heavily. I waited longer. Finally, after about half a minute, a startled priest woke up, gasped for air, grumbled, and stumbled around with some words, "Thank you for a good confession . . ."

Luke was right; my sins aren't what they used to be. It's a good thing.

Editor's note: Brian's sins are not "exciting" anymore because through frequent Confession and living Our Lady's messages, we receive the grace to overcome our sins, including the "exciting sins." "God allows me every day to help you with graces to defend yourselves against evil" (Our Lady, 10/25/84). Brian lived in Beckenham, England when this was originally published. He and his family now live in Erie, PA. Brian's miracle story of how his life was saved through praying the Rosary is in Volume II of **The Best of "The Spirit of Medjugorje."**

(2/09)
A Different Fast

By June Klins

Our Lady asks us to fast on Wednesdays and Fridays. She says that the best fast is on bread and water, but it may be wise to fast from something else first and then work up to the bread and water fast. Our Lady says you can fast from TV, alcohol, cigarettes, etc. Fasting from complaining is also a good one.

Another idea came to me one day as I was reading St. Augustine's *Confessions:* to fast from "idle curiosity." In his *Confessions,* Book X, St. Augustine writes about "idle curiosity." He gives examples of running over to look when there is an accident ("ambulance chaser" we would say), or going to the circus to see the freak show, or just watching some animals chase each other (unless you were praising God for them). He says, "When our hearts become repositories piled high with such worthless stock as this, it is the cause of interruption and distraction from our prayers." We are wasting valuable TIME. Time is a gift given to us by God to use for His glory.

Of course there is a healthy kind of curiosity that should even be encouraged such as the curiosity to learn more about the Bible, the saints or about this wonderful world God has created for us. But "idle curiosity," as St. Augustine describes, is a different matter. In some cases, curiosity could even be a serious sin, such as pornography, or could lead us to sin if, for example, we ask too many questions about someone else's business that may cause us to be judgmental or to gossip.

As I read from the *Confessions* I became aware of how curious I really am. I am not the type to go through someone's medicine cabinet, or to peek out the window at the neighbors, and never considered myself to be a "nosey" person, but it is the little things. One example is that if I am reading in the Adoration chapel and someone walks in, I sometimes look to see who it is. Or if I am writing an article on the computer and hear that I got an email message I might check right away to see who it was. That breaks the flow of what I was doing and it was not necessary. I could give lots of examples, but see how our curiosity

– even something so small – can keep us from doing what God wills for us at that moment?

St. Augustine also speaks of a spiritual curiosity – wanting to see signs and wonders just for the pleasure of the experience. Do we look at the sun more than we should, looking to see if it will spin? Are we "apparition chasers" – reading the messages of every alleged visionary? Are we curious to read Our Lady's monthly message, but not make it part of our lives? This list goes on . . .

For those who may be looking for something different to fast from this Lent, try fasting from idle curiosity. It is not as easy as you might think, but with God's grace you can do it!

(10/09)
Rosary Distractions

By Lisa Potts

I am very dedicated to saying my Rosaries. I find them comforting and deeply moving. They are, in the very best way, a true devotion to our Blessed Mother and Our Beloved Savior. While saying them, I kept getting distracted, and I was constantly drowsy while I was saying them. I finally decided that maybe I wasn't being as devoted as I should be and, rather than being disrespectful, I should put them away to give myself a break.

Big mistake! I found the following on a website dedicated to the Rosary and discovered what was REALLY going on . . .

"Distractions"
By Saint Louis Marie Grignion De Montfort

"Being human, we easily become tired and slipshod, but the devil makes these difficulties worse when we are saying the Rosary. Before we even begin, he makes us feel bored, distracted, or exhausted; and when we have started praying, he oppresses us from all sides, and when, after much difficulty and many distractions, we have finished, he whispers to us, 'What you have just said is worthless. It is useless for you to say the Rosary. You had better get on with other things. It is

only a waste of time to pray without paying attention to what you are saying; half-an-hour's meditation or some spiritual reading would be much better. Tomorrow, when you are not feeling so sluggish, you'll pray better; leave the rest of your Rosary till then.' By tricks of this kind the devil gets us to give up the Rosary altogether or to say it less often, and we keep putting it off or change to some other devotion.

"Dear friend of the Rosary Confraternity, do not listen to the devil, but be of good heart, even if your imagination has been bothering you throughout your Rosary, filling your mind with all kinds of distracting thoughts, so long as you tried your best to get rid of them as soon as you noticed them. Always remember that the best Rosary is the one with the most merit, and there is more merit in praying when it is hard than when it is easy. Prayer is all the harder when it is, naturally speaking, distasteful to the soul and is filled with those annoying little ants and flies running about in your imagination, against your will, and scarcely allowing you the time to enjoy a little peace and appreciate the beauty of what you are saying."

I've heard that the more powerfully you pray, the harder the devil works to get you to stop. Our Holy Rosary is a very powerful devotion to the Blessed Mother and Her Beloved Son, not to mention how powerfully they affect us. This must be why Our Lady is so encouraging us to pray, and to pray the Rosary. We are saying VERY powerful prayers, so if the devil is on our tails, it sounds like we're doing just what we're supposed to be doing. Let's keep up the good work!

Editor's note: Lisa is from Pueblo, Colorado.

(9/05)
Confessions at Walmart

By June Klins

If you have ever heard visionary Mirjana speak, you would have heard her say that Our Lady says there is not a man on earth who does not need to go to Confession once a month. Then she pauses and says, "But She does not say anything about women!" The first time I heard her say that, she and Jakov were speaking together and she looked at him and smiled as she said it. The whole crowd laughed. If I remember correctly, Jakov jested back that women needed to go to Confession MORE than once a month, which got another laugh.

I remember the good nuns telling us in grade school that the Pope went to Confession every day. I always wondered, "What in the world could the Pope do wrong that he had to go to Confession so often?" Fr. Bill, a Redemptorist priest, clarified this point at a novena I attended this summer. He said that we should still go to Confession even if we have no serious sins because every time we receive the sacrament of Reconciliation we obtain graces to help us fight temptation. It makes us stronger.

Chances are, however, that most people have something that needs to be confessed. Once the visionaries told about a time when Our Lady said that the people who were with them were allowed to touch Her, even though they could not see Her. Before long Our Lady's gown became blackened, and She explained that the darkening of Her gown had been caused by the sins that had accumulated on the souls of the people touching Her, and She recommended that they go to Confession.

Fr. Bill said that often people say they do not need to go to a priest to confess. But Father explained that in the other sacrament which takes away sin – Baptism – we need someone to baptize us. We cannot baptize ourselves. It is the same with Confession. The grace of forgiveness is a "ministered" grace. It comes through a minister. We cannot do it ourselves. Isn't it such a relief to hear those words, "I absolve you . . . ?"

Father Bill said that when we repent of our sins, it is like putting the garbage out for the garbage collector. Likewise he said that when we hold back on certain sins and do not repent, it is like keeping the garbage in the house. After a while it is going to stink!

Father said a good way to examine our consciences is to go through the seven capital sins. To find our main faults he said we should ask our families and the people at work. That is where our main faults show up – with family and at work. He said to be very careful about what you watch on TV or look at on the computer. He said, "Garbage in –garbage out." He also cautioned about what we read, that we should not read trashy books.

Then Father spoke about forgiveness. He repeatedly said that there are no "buts" in forgiveness: "I would forgive so-and-so BUT . . ." He said forgiveness is not a feeling –you don't have to like the person to forgive him. He said forgiveness is a decision and to pray to God for the gift of forgiveness. He said to ask for a loving and forgiving heart. A possible prayer would be: "Lord, I am a sinner, but I love You. Please forgive me."

Father Bill said that sometimes people are afraid to go to Confession because they think the priest will think less of them for what they did, but that it is actually quite the opposite. Priests have respect for a person who humbles himself like this and in fact, it often "makes their day," especially if it has been a long time between confessions.

The fact that the Lord will go to any length to bring someone to Confession is illustrated by the following story (The name of the priest involved has been changed for privacy):

Fr. Tom said that he was in Walmart on the feast of the Sacred Heart of Jesus, and a lady he did not know approached him. She said that her husband was very ill and she was worried because he had not been to Confession in 30-40 years, although he went to Mass every Sunday. She said he NEEDED to go to Confession and that they always argued about this. On the way there, they had passed a house that had a big picture of the Immaculate Heart of Mary in the picture window. The lady remembered that Saturday was the feast of the Immaculate Heart of Mary and that day was the feast of the Sacred Heart of Jesus. So she prayed to Them that her husband would go to Confession. As they argued in the car about his going to Confession, her husband blurted, "If Walmart is having confessions today, then I will go." So when she saw Father Tom dressed in his clerics, she approached him and asked him to hear her husband's confession!

Father was a little reluctant to do this, but looked at his watch and saw that it was a few minutes before 3:00, the Hour of Mercy, and being that it was the feast of the Sacred Heart, a favorite devotion of his, he agreed. He went out to the car where the man had been waiting for his wife and knocked on the window and told the man what his wife had said about Wal-Mart having confessions. How could the man resist?

Father said he shared this story to show the great love of the Sacred Heart for us, and also to impress upon us to never give up praying for our loved ones to come back to Confession. You never know when that moment of grace will come. Like "Candid Camera" – when you least expect it!

When I spoke with Fr. Tom about this story I mentioned that it was good that he was wearing his clerics. Otherwise the woman would not have known he was a priest. He said he had just come from mowing his mother's lawn and just stopped into Wal-Mart to get one thing and normally would not have been wearing his clerics after mowing the lawn. Who but God could orchestrate this scenario? What lengths He goes to for one lost sheep!

"I am happy because you have begun to prepare for monthly observance of the Sacrament of Reconciliation. That will be good for the whole world" (Our Lady, 10/1/82).

Sr. Emmanuel, holding a copy of
"The Spirit of Medjugorje" newsletter

(12/08)
The Angelus at Stake!

By Sr. Emmanuel

An Italian friend shared with me a precious testimony about the Holy Virgin of Nazareth: One day she was driving from Citluk back to Medjugorje, and Vicka was with her in the car. When noon came, both friends started to recite the prayer of the Angelus. As the prayer was over, Vicka spontaneously turned to my friend, and, her face radiant with joy, told her, "You know, the Blessed Mother likes this prayer very much! All Her being thrills with joy when She hears it because it reminds Her of the moment of the Annunciation."

Saint Louis de Montfort, also, wrote that every time we recite the Angelus, Mary feels the same joy as the one She felt when She received the visit of the Archangel Gabriel in Nazareth.

Many Catholics still do not know this prayer by heart. Then why not memorize it and say it at least once a day at noon? Or better: three times a day? It would be a beautiful present to the Blessed Mother during this Lent [Advent], in thanksgiving for Her graces!

Prayer of the Angelus:

V. The Angel of the Lord declared unto Mary.
R. And She conceived of the Holy Spirit.
Hail Mary, full of grace . . .

V. Behold the handmaid of the Lord.
R. Be it done unto me according to Thy word.
Hail Mary . . .

V. And the Word was made Flesh.
R. And dwelt among us.
Hail Mary . . .

V. Pray for us, O holy Mother of God.
R. That we may be made worthy of the promises of Christ.

LET US PRAY! Pour forth, we beseech Thee, O Lord, Thy grace into our hearts, that we to whom the Incarnation of Christ Thy Son was made known by the message of an angel, may by His Passion and Cross be brought to the glory of His Resurrection. Through the same Christ Our Lord. Amen.

Children of Medjugorje,www.childrenofmedjugorje.com (2/15/08)

(3/07)
Healing

By June Klins

Since my return from Medjugorje last June, few days have gone by without someone requesting one of our Medjugorje prayer cloths.

So many people are in need of healing, and questions sometimes arise: Why are some people healed and some not? God alone can answer that, but perhaps we can gain a little bit of insight by looking at the Scriptures. My pastor, Fr. Larry Richards, says, "The best way to know the mind of God is to read the Word of God."

In reading the gospel stories about Jesus' healings we see that Jesus did not heal everyone in His time either. According to Mk 1:34 and Mk 3:10, "He cured *many*" (not all). There seemed to be some diversity in His healings too. Sometimes the healing was immediate, as in the cleansing of a leper in Mt 8:3, and sometimes it was gradual, as with the blind man in Mk 8:23-25. In some instances Jesus told the people He healed not to tell anyone, such as the deaf man in Mk 7:36. But there were also times when Jesus directed those He healed to proclaim His glory. In Mk 5:19, Jesus tells the man who was healed, "Go home to your family and announce to them all that the Lord in his pity has done for you." After Jesus healed Peter's mother-in-law, she fed them (Lk 4:39), but after Jesus healed the girl in Mk 5:43, He directed others to feed her.

However, there is one consistent theme throughout the stories of Jesus' healings, and that is the word "faith." It was either the faith of the person who was healed or the faith of others, for example the mother's faith in Mk 7:29, the centurion's faith in Lk 7:9, or the faith of the four friends in Mt 9:2. In contrast, it was because of a lack of faith that Jesus could not work many miracles in his hometown (Mt 13:58), and that the apostles could not perform a healing in Mt 17:20.

As any good mother, Our Lady wants us to be healed, so it is no coincidence that one of Her main messages in Medjugorje is "faith." In a recent interview Vicka said, "Everyone of us must witness his faith and pray for the gift of faith." Vicka frequently says that what Our Lady wants the most is for us to have a **firm faith.**

Fr. Michael Scanlon, president of the Franciscan University of Steubenville, has a healing ministry, and devoted a chapter in his book, *Let the Fire Fall,* to the subject of healing. Father wrote: "A key element in healing is faith. Healing is almost always associated with someone's faith – the faith of the sick person, the faith of the minister, the faith of the assembly . . . before you pray for healing, pray for faith." He said we should pray with perseverance. He said that the watchword is "**pray**." This, too, is another of Our Lady's main messages.

Fr. Scanlon alluded to the fact that one thing that can block healing is unrepentant sin. I recall one time I went to a healing service of a priest who has the gift of reading souls, and there was a crippled man there who wanted to be healed. The priest told him that he would be healed after he forgave his brother. The man was adamant that he would never forgive, and he went home in a worse state than when he came because now he was angry. I remember how sad I felt, both because of his physical condition, but also his hardened heart. **Reconciliation** is another of Our Lady's messages.

So we see that faith, prayer and reconciliation are associated with healing. Is there anything else? There was an occasion in the gospel when the apostles could not heal a boy who had been possessed by demons. After healing the boy, Jesus said to them," This kind can only come out through prayer and **fasting**." (The word "fasting" is sometimes omitted from modern texts of Mk 9:29). Fasting is another of Our Lady's main messages.

Why did Jesus tell some of those He healed not to tell anyone? By "God-incidence," as I was writing this article someone sent me a reflection about healing. It said that the reason Jesus told them not to tell was that "Jesus had another deeper concern, which was based upon his unparalleled insight into human nature. He knew that the temptation would be to focus on the 'magic' and to get caught up in the 'bread and circuses' and to miss entirely the *inner* dimension, which was the root and core of the healing."

Fr. Scanlon wrote regarding physical healing: "We should seek it when we are ill, and pray for it whenever we get a chance, yet we should never seek healing for itself." The Lord tells us, "You ask but do not receive, because you ask wrongly, to spend it on your passions" (James 4:3). Fr. Scanlon continued, "And never forget that healing is a sign of the Lord's desire to repair our sin – the greatest wound." Jesus said to the healed paralytic in Mt 9:2, "Your sins are forgiven," and to the man who had been ill for 38 years, "Do not sin anymore" (Jn 5:14). And He rebuked the towns that did *not* repent after witnessing His mighty deeds (Mt 11:20).

According to Webster's Dictionary the word healing comes from the Old English word "hal," meaning "more at whole." Fr. Scanlon continued that the rightful perspective for healing is the perspective of eternity. "Until Jesus comes in glory, there will be death, disappointment, frustration, confusion and failure even when we pray . . . until the Lord comes again there will be much we do not understand . . . We know that anything *can* be healed, but not everything *will* be healed. We know that the experience of enduring illness can build character. We know that suffering has a redemptive quality to it. We don't know why some people are healed and some are not, but we do know that all will be made whole when we are with the Lord. It is better to die young and spend eternity with the Lord, than it is to live a full and healthy life on earth and lose eternal life."

Somewhere in Heaven is a young man shaking his head, saying "You've got that right, Father." The day after I typed the words, "It is better to die young . . ." I heard a corroborating testimony. A young man in Florida had been in a motorcycle accident and was near death. A lady who had been given one of our prayer cloths prayed over him with it. As she was praying, she was inspired to ask if he had ever been baptized. He was conscious enough to say he had not been baptized, but would like to be. He died immediately after he was baptized. Did he receive a healing? The world would say no. However, we know that he got the best healing possible – a spiritual healing – a free ticket to Heaven!!! He hit the jackpot – this is what it is all about!!!

When Father Scanlon published his book in 1998, he felt that the outpouring of healing graces seemed to be unprecedented in the history of the Church. Our Lady confirmed this last October: "Today the Lord permitted me to tell you again that you live in a time of grace." Fr. Scanlon wrote, "I believe that the healing we see all over the world signifies a new urgency in the Lord's work in the world . . . He is announcing His presence unmistakably. Those who see it will be saved; those who avert their eyes from the Savior's work will be lost."

Editor's note: Because of space limitations we cannot share all the blessings we have heard, but we would like to share two astounding testimonies about the prayer cloths. A man in Texas who was in danger of losing his leg because of a gaping infected wound that would not heal baffled doctors when it completely healed after the cloth was laid on the wound and people prayed. And a woman in the Philippines was completely healed of endometriosis and a tumor after praying with the cloth on her stomach. Praise God! You can visit our website, www.spiritofmedjugorje.org to learn more about the prayer cloths and read more testimonies.

(6/05)
Life in the "Fast" Lane

By Elizabeth Ficocelli

There is a running joke in the Ficocelli family about how much food I can pack away in a single sitting. I hold the award for out-eating even my father-in-law, which is no small endeavor. So, with my indiscriminate love for foods of all kinds, it is understandable that one of the more difficult concepts for me to embrace when I entered the Catholic Church was fasting.

My first attempts to restrict my repeated trips to the refrigerator began, naturally, on Ash Wednesday and the Fridays of Lent. The meatless part of the sacrifice didn't bother me much, since I can savor a seafood dinner as much as I can a strip steak or a bowl of pasta. But the notion of modest meals – and no snacks in between – was downright painful. For a long time, I would rationalize my low-blood sugar as a reason that I was never meant to live in the "fast" lane. If I went too long without food, I would suffer from headaches, dizziness and nausea, not to mention extreme grumpiness. Surely God would understand my limitations – after all, He created me this way. But as I began to learn more about fasting and its effectiveness as a means of prayer, I realized that if I were going to advance in my spirituality and grow closer to God, I had to put my soul before my stomach.

In the Bible, fasting was commonplace. The prophets fasted, and so did Jesus and His apostles and disciples. Fasting could change the course of events, like saving Nineveh after Jonah warned them that their future was in jeopardy. Certainly, this was a powerful form of prayer. I read that the early Christians traditionally fasted on Wednesdays and Fridays, and so my husband and I decided to incorporate a bread-and-water fast on Wednesdays, as Fridays were far more difficult for us to schedule.

Admittedly, this was not an easy endeavor for me. Bread has never been one of my all-time favorite culinary delights, and I would find myself so grouchy and hungry by nighttime that I had to eat dinner with the children. I would also dread the following Wednesday, sorrowfully counting the days that I had left until I would be denied food again. Eventually, I was able to make it to midnight without giving in, but

I still felt irritated and sorry for myself. How, I wondered, was this improving my relationship with God?

Through prayer, God showed me that I could pray for the gift of fasting and, more importantly, that I needed to fast with love. My attitude, He taught me, was all wrong. Once I changed my mindset and fasted with love, the difference was amazing. My headaches began to subside and I no longer dreaded Wednesdays. More importantly, I began to experience the spiritual benefits of fasting. I find that fasting increases my desire for God. It makes me more humble and more willing to do His will – even at times helping me to discover what that Will is in a given situation. Fasting equips me to be stronger with my trials, temptations, and bad habits. Most beneficial to my family, it seems to be helping me become more peaceful, more patient, and more even-tempered.

When I say "no" to my body and "yes" to my spirit, I become less self-centered and a more usable instrument for God. It seems I am able to listen to God better and live His word more. My husband and I offer up our weekly fasts for those who are truly hungry, for peace in the world, and for sinners (especially ourselves). I really believe that these weekly fasts are helping in some small way to make the world a better place.

We've discovered that fasting is to the soul what jogging is to the body. The more we fast, the better spiritual shape we are in, and the easier it is to do. We've even been able to do two nine-day bread-and-water fasts, and discovered to our surprise that it wasn't that difficult at all. Of course, I know it is only through the grace of God that I am able to fast in the first place. I have learned that fasting is a gift, not that we are giving God, but that God gives us in order to draw us closer to Him. My hope is that this powerful form of prayer will keep me on the right path to one day earn a seat at the Heavenly Banquet. And that will be a feast well worth the wait.

*Editor's note: Elizabeth has written many books, among them **The Fruits of Medjugorje**. You can visit her website at www.elizabethficocelli.com.*

(9/07)
The Best Kept Secret of the Church

By June Klins

As Catholics, we are so blessed to have Our Lady, the saints, the Rosary, the sacraments, especially the Eucharist – but there is another source of holiness that is often overlooked. It is the best kept secret of the Church.

One night in July, the young Redemptorist priest leading our annual St. Ann Novena, talked about the concept of redemptive suffering. Father Matthew lamented, "The words 'Offer it up' are rarely heard any more."

Father Matthew, who is wise beyond his years, started out by asking what makes a "saint" different from other good people, other followers of Jesus, who seem to do all the right things. What sets them apart? Father said that through his readings of the writings of the saints, he has come to the conclusion that the one thing that sets them apart is how they react to suffering. He called it "the secret of the saints." The saints embraced their suffering. He gave the example from the Acts of the Apostles where Peter and John were scourged and left "REJOICING that they had been found worthy to suffer dishonor for the sake of the name" (Acts 5:41).

Father said that suffering can become a great victory. When we embrace our suffering and unite our suffering with Jesus, we can be a source of grace and apply it to others and situations in the world. As we offer up our suffering, the suffering loses its power over us because now our suffering has a purpose. Father told a story about a conversation he had as a seminarian with a woman in a nursing home. This woman, who was not Catholic, complained to him that although she prays and prays and prays, her condition was getting worse instead of better. Father went out on a limb and explained to her the Catholic perspective on suffering and suggested that she offer up her suffering for her family. She smiled widely and said, "That is beautiful! You mean my suffering does not have to be in vain?"

After that her whole countenance changed. A few days later the head chaplain of the nursing home, who was not Catholic, asked Father what he had said to that woman because all the nurses had remarked about her attitude change. After Father explained to the chaplain about redemptive suffering, the chaplain asked if the Church had any documentation on that. Father told him to read Pope John Paul's Encyclical on the Christian Meaning of Human Suffering. After the chaplain read it, he remarked that it was the best piece he had ever read on suffering. From then on, the head chaplain made this encyclical mandatory reading for all those training to be chaplains.

Father Matthew said that we all have suffering, either great suffering or many little trials, and that we waste the benefits of suffering when we complain and want people to feel sorry for us. He said that St. Catherine of Siena appeared after her death and said that the only regret she had about her life was that she did not suffer for Christ more. St. Padre Pio once said, "The angels envy us for one thing only, that we can suffer as Christ did, and they cannot."

Father said that when we rejoice in our suffering, the devil has NO POWER over us. The devil always tries to frustrate us and disturb our peace, but when we offer it up for God's glory, the devil's plan BACKFIRES! The saints say that the devil comes around less because we thwart his plans by transforming the suffering into God's glory, just the opposite effect that he wants. Suffering can actually be a powerful weapon of spiritual warfare!

Father ended his talk by saying that God allows suffering so we can become sources of grace to benefit ourselves and others, as the saints did. Father admitted that it is easier said than done, and suggested that we pray for the grace to be able to see Jesus in our suffering.

One person who has definitely been able to do this is 53 year-old Andy Meier, who was paralyzed in the bus accident of Medjugorje pilgrims we reported on last month. The "Milwaukee Catholic Herald" quoted Andy: "All I have left is Christ. I'm a lot closer to God now, no doubt about it . . . Out of the suffering any of us may have gone through, our number one hope is that if anything, this will motivate people to turn back to God. If vocations can come out of this suffering, that's the greatest gift." He added, "Spiritually, I don't think I've ever been stronger."

"Dear children! For these days while you are joyfully celebrating the cross, I desire that your cross also would be a joy for you. Especially, dear children, pray that you may be able to accept sickness and suffering with love the way Jesus accepted them. Only that way shall I be able with joy to give out to you the graces and healings which Jesus is permitting me. Thank you for having responded to my call" (Our Lady, September 11, 1986).

Crucifix in Medjugorje

(10/05)
Confessions on a Milk Stool

By Msgr. James Peterson

Years ago, on my first trip to Medjugorje, I had heard many different reports of healings and miracles. What really attracted me was the conviction of several people I talked to that Mary, God's mother, was appearing there. I left with the firm conviction that the apparitions were real and that they were important for the whole world.

But what brought me to that conviction were the confessions I heard sitting on a milk stool outside St. James Church. They involved marvels of conversion. There were tourists who came out of curiosity, who went past all the side-show possibilities to an interior repentance. From an honest admission of sin, they went to a surrender-to-God for the first time in their lives.

There were burnt-out men and women, priests, sisters, religious who were made new, because Mary brought them to Christ, Who makes all things new.

In the later trips that I made, it was the same sharing in sacramental reconciliation that made my faith – and my joy – firmer than ever.

What concerns me in this country now is the unimportant role that is given to Reconciliation in our society. Bishop Sheen often said that if we don't live the way we believe, we try to believe the way we live.

Many Catholics today go for weeks without Confession, for years without Confession. In that frame of mind, it is difficult to respond to Mary's pattern of prayer and sacrifice for peace in the world.

The world is in spiritual chaos that is beyond the chaos of Katrina. If we look at New Orleans and weep over it, we need to share with Mary Her yearning to bring the shattered world to Christ. A song of praise from hearts that are reformed is the melody that brings peace to the tired world. Let us pray.

(3/08)
Examination of Conscience

By Father Bill Kiel

I. **You shall love the Lord your God with all your heart, and with all your soul, and with all your mind**.
    *   Am I faithful to my daily prayers? What is my attitude toward God that allows me to neglect prayer?
    *   Do I participate in the prayers of the Mass? Do I pray the prayers from my heart?
    *   Do I put trust in God's loving care for me?
    *   Do I read Scripture, so that I may know and hear Jesus and His Father?
    *   Am I angry with God? Am I afraid of God?
    *   Do I accept that God loves me? If not, why? Am I seeking to know God's will in my life?
    *   Am I unwilling or afraid to say "yes" to God? If so, why?

II. You shall love your neighbor as yourself.

* Do I take my life seriously and live up to my responsibilities?
* Do I use the gifts God has given me for God's greater glory?
* Am I a prisoner of fear, anxiety, worry, guilt, or hatred of myself, showing a lack of trust in God?
* Do I allow my past to trouble me?
* Do I prudently plan for the future things that are within my choice and control and hand the rest to God?
* Do I thank God for all the blessings He has given to me? Do I take the credit for achieving what I have?
* Am I greedy?
* Do I employ behavior patterns that are destructive to my body, i.e. gluttony, cutting, purging?
* Do I use alcohol, drugs, food, sex for relieving my frustrations and anxieties?
* Do I have lustful thoughts that I dwell on?
* Do I use other individuals to satisfy my selfish pleasures?
* Do I plagiarize or cheat in my daily activities, i.e. academics, sports, games, relationships?

III. In my relationships with others

* When someone has needed me, have I refused to help? If so, why?
* Have I shared what I have with those less fortunate?
* Have I failed to respect any family member, parents, friends or strangers?
* Have I failed to respect other's possessions?
* Do I try to bring peace into my family life, social life, work life?
* Have I been patient with another's differences from me?
* Have I been tolerant with another's shortcomings?
* Have I talked in a negative way about others, and hurt them or their reputation?
* Do I hurt others for the intention of making me look good?
* Do I get angry with others and hurt them by what I say or do to them?
* Do I criticize and find fault with others?

* Am I nursing a grudge, have I not forgiven a person I know I should forgive?

* Have I not asked forgiveness from one I have hurt?

Editor's note: Father Kiel is pastor of St. Bernard of Clairvaux Parish in Indiana, PA. His story is in Chapter 3. Father used the above Examination of Conscience at a healing Mass he celebrated at my parish and I asked his permission to publish it. Father told me that he sometimes makes changes to this as the Holy Spirit prompts him.

(3/05)
Coming Out of the Spiritual Closet

By June Klins

A few months ago a woman I have never met confided to me over the phone that she was having "evil thoughts" during prayer, and that I was the only person with whom she ever shared this. I knew right then that her call had been a "Divine set-up," since my internet Medjugorje prayer group had just discussed this very topic. I was able to share with her that she was not alone, since I had never seen so many people respond to a discussion like this before. It was as if everyone felt relieved to know that they were not alone with this problem. One person said, "It has been a comfort to read other stories of attacks during prayer. I was starting to wonder if I was crazy." Another said, "I also thought I was alone in experiencing evil thoughts in prayer. I really felt terrible about it, even though I was told in confession that it was the devil trying to discourage me." One person admitted to being so disturbed by this problem and felt tormented and in mortal sin. But in confession, the priest said, "Oh, you would not believe how many people this happens to! It especially happens coming up to receive Communion!" In 1Peter, we read, "Stay sober and alert. Your opponent the devil is prowling like a roaring lion looking for someone to devour. Resist him, solid in your faith, realizing that the brotherhood of believers is undergoing the same suffering throughout the world" (1Peter 5:8-9). Indeed, Our Lady warned about this too: "Be on your guard. This period is dangerous for you. The devil is trying to lead you astray from the way. Those who give themselves to God will be the object of attacks" (7/26/83).

Why should we be so surprised that this would happen anyway? Wasn't Jesus Himself besieged by the devil in prayer? And His temptations in the desert were not His only temptations. Luke tells us, "He (the devil) departed from Him *for a time*" (Lk 4:13). Remember the opening scene from "The Passion of the Christ?"

One member of the prayer group shared that when she first confessed this to a priest, he said, "You are close to God and you are trying to do His work. The devil is trying to discourage you, so when this happens, keep saying, 'Jesus I love You; You are my salvation.'" Others suggested similar ejaculations: Jesus, I trust in you; Jesus, help me; Mary, conceived without sin, pray for us who have recourse to You, etc.

One person shared that she invites Mary and her guardian angel as she begins to pray, and another said she asks Jesus to purify her prayers. Still another person shared that she found it very effective to say, "I command you to leave me alone in Jesus' name." One member said that her attacks stopped after spending an hour with the Lord in Adoration. Another suggestion was to open the Bible and read from Isaiah, Sirach or the Psalms.

One person shared a prayer from the Holy Rosary book: **O Immaculate One of the Holy Spirit, through the power the Eternal Father has bestowed upon You over the Angels and the Archangels, send us a host of Angels headed by Michael the Archangel to free us from Satan and to heal us.**

Fr. Slavko wrote in his book *Give Me Your Wounded Heart*, " . . . when praying (some) have experienced intense thoughts of cursing or a desire to insult. Whenever this happens, the person tempted should quietly continue praying and blessing God."

Some of the saints wrote about this problem too. St. Padre Pio wrote, "Don't dwell voluntarily on what the enemy presents to you . . . at the first sign stop thinking of it and turn to God saying 'Have mercy on me.'" St. Faustina wrote in her diary, "Every time I entered the chapel for some spiritual exercise, I experienced even worse torments and temptations. More than once, all through Holy Mass, I had to struggle against blasphemous thoughts which were forcing themselves to my lips."

St. Catherine of Siena was horribly taunted by evil spirits. No matter what she did, she couldn't make them stop. Then one day the Lord told her that if she wanted to overcome the enemy's power, she should take the cross as her "refreshment." After this, a hideous demon told her that if she did not give in to him and his cronies, they would persecute her all the days of her life. Catherine answered, "I do not avoid pains, for I have chosen pains for my refreshment." With that, the spirit disappeared and Jesus appeared to her. She asked Jesus where He was when her heart was so disturbed by all the temptations. Jesus replied, **"I was beside thee. For I move not, and never leave My creature, unless the creature leave Me through mortal sin."** Confused by this, Catherine asked Him how she could possibly believe that He was in her heart when it was full of ugly creatures. Jesus answered, "Dost thou wish Me to show thee, daughter mine, how in those conflicts thou didst not fall into mortal sin, and how I was beside thee? Tell me, what is it that makes sin mortal? Only the will." Jesus went on to say that since these thoughts brought her sorrow and displeasure, that it was because He was there, hidden at the center of her heart, and that if He had not been there, they would have entered her heart and she would have felt pleasure in them. It was His presence there that caused them to displease her.

How awesome to know that God is with us even when we do not feel His presence.

Editor's note: The quotes in the last paragraph were taken from the writings of St. Catherine of Siena.

(4/08)
Stand Fast and Keep Your Feet Moving

By Father Neil Buchlein

I encourage my parishioners to "go the distance" as they "run the race." There are going to be plenty of obstacles and they should be seen as an opportunity to grow stronger, not to complain or feel as if God has abandoned them. I think many Catholics think that if they pray the Rosary, go to Mass during the week, volunteer their time, fast, etc.

that nothing bad will ever happen to them. WRONG! Yes, the book by Rabbi Harold Kushner that became a bestseller and translated into many languages, *When Bad Things Happen to Good People,* encouraged its readers to make the choice to do the alternative.

A lot of talk recently regarding "being attacked" has been weighing heavily on my mind and heart. What I have found troubling is the surprise of "being attacked." Yes, we are under attack. WHY? Because you and I have pledged our faithful love, even though we often fall, to grow closer to Our Lord through the messages and intercession of our Mother Mary. Don't you think that is going to get Satan a little miffed?! The last thing that he wants is for us to grow deeper in love and move away from him. Take a look at yourself and ask yourself, "Am I praying, fasting, reading the Bible, looking forward to Eucharist and Reconciliation?" Well, if you answered "YES" or "Well . . . I'm trying but at times I fall short," welcome to the "brotherhood and sisterhood of believers."

Take a look at 1Peter 1:6-7 which says, "In this you rejoice, even if now for a little while you have had to suffer various trials, so that the genuineness of your faith, being more precious than gold, though perishable, is tested by fire, may be found to result in praise and glory and honor when Jesus Christ is revealed." Peter goes on to say in 5:8-11, "Discipline yourselves, keep alert. Like a roaring lion your adversary the devil prowls around, looking for someone to devour. Resist him, steadfast in your faith, for you know that your brothers and sisters in all the world are undergoing the same kinds of suffering. And after you have suffered for a little while, the God of all grace, who has called you to His eternal glory in Christ, will Himself restore, support, strengthen, and establish you." You see, we will go through trials and temptations. Remember the First Sunday of Lent where we read that Jesus was tempted?

It is so easy to think that we are in this alone. No. Look at those around you and in your families, we are all suffering or being tempted. God is looking to "refine us" like that of gold in the fire. At times we are tested so that we will grow. God has not put us in a bubble where we are sheltered from everything negative. Jesus let Himself be tempted so He, too, would know what we would also be going through. I don't know about you, but I could not have lasted 40 days in the desert with those three mighty temptations. I would have "sold out" somewhere along the way. After 40 days were over, Matthew then says, "and He was hungry." HELLO! Yes, indeed hungry. My hunger right now is staying focused on what Jesus is calling me to do and not what Satan is asking me to do.

St. Teresa of Avila had Satan appear to her one night when she was sleeping. She felt a strange presence in the room as if someone were watching her. She rolled over and saw Satan standing there. She responded, "Oh, it's only you." She rolled back over and went to sleep. You and I have the power to do the same when it comes to being tempted. What about all the messages from Our Lady? Go to www.Medjugorje.org and look up Satan in the Concordance and see how many times Our Lady is intervening and encouraging us. What about "The Five Stones"? Have we forgotten them?

Rather than acting out of fear and doubting, we should be focusing on the blessings instead. How do you look at your glass of blessings or faith? Is it half full or half empty? Share what you have been doing that has made a positive difference in your life and perhaps someone else's. Too much talk about being "under attack" only gives Satan more power and control over our fragile lives. Don't give him the time of day. Rather, practice saying, "Oh, it's only you." Grace be with all of you.

Editor's note: Fr. Neil is the pastor of Ascension Catholic Church in Hurricane, WV. You can visit his website, www.blessedmotherschildren.com.

(11/08)
Do Not Fear or Worry

By June Klins

Last week one day as I was walking into Mass, the lady who parked behind me said, "I like your bumper sticker." My bumper "magnet" says, "Prayer, not despair." The lady continued with worry in her voice, "Boy, we really need that right now with the economy the way it is." I told her that this is why Our Lady of Medjugorje has been telling us all these years that we should read Matthew 6:24-34 every Thursday. I went on that I call it the "Don't Worry Gospel" and that maybe we

every day now. The lady took note of the scripture verses
nto the chapel.

week, a lady called me to request a prayer cloth, and
in our conversation, she told me that she was told by someone at the
Divine Mercy shrine to read Psalm 91 every day. I knew that Psalm 91
is the Psalm that the song "On Eagle's Wings" is based on, but after we
hung up I went and read it. I might dub this the "Don't Fear" Psalm.
I have been reading it every day since. I recall someone once telling
me that we are supposed to have our Bibles open to that Psalm in our
homes as protection.

So between these two readings, we are told by Almighty God
Himself not to fear and not to worry. What comforting words in these
times of turmoil. Jesus, I trust in Thee!

CHAPTER FIVE

Other Bits and "Peaces"

"Now I invite you to continue in humility and with an open heart speak to all who are coming" (6/28/85).

(12/09)
The Pope Prayed for Our Lady to Come to Earth . . .

By Judy Pellatt

In a recent question-and-answer session with English-speaking pilgrims at Medjugorje (October 3), the visionary Mirjana revealed that the late Pope John Paul II had prayed to the Blessed Virgin, asking Her to come on earth once more to assist him against the threat of Communism. Two months later, She appeared in Medjugorje!

This was revealed in a response given by the visionary Mirjana to a question, asking if she, or any of the other visionaries, had ever met with the Holy Father.

"I was in St. Peter's Basilica in the Vatican with all the other pilgrims. I was with an Italian priest. The Pope (John Paul II) was walking by, and he was blessing. He blessed me and just passed by. The priest with me said, 'Holy Father, this is Mirjana from Medjugorje,' and he came back and blessed me again. Then he left. And I said to priest, 'Most likely he thought I just need a double blessing!'

"In the afternoon, we received a note to go to Castle Gondolfo, close to Rome, the next day. And myself and the Pope were alone together, and among other things, he said to me, 'I know everything, I have been following everything. Ask pilgrims to pray for my intentions. Take care of Medjugorje, because Medjugorje is the hope for the entire world.'

"A priest told me that, from the very beginning, the Pope was very fond of Medjugorje, because two months before the apparitions in Medjugorje started, he was praying to Our Lady to come again on earth. He said, 'I cannot do it all alone because Yugoslavia, Czechoslovakia, Poland, etc., are all Communist. I cannot do it on my own. I need You.' And later he heard that in Yugoslavia, a Communist country, in a little village (Medjugorje), Our Lady appeared and he said, 'That is the response to my prayers.' "

The Medjugorje Message, UK

Fr. Petar Ljubicic, ofm

(7/07)
Fr. Petar Ljubicic Speaks About the Secrets

The following questions were asked at the Panel Discussion at the Notre Dame Medjugorje Conference on 5/27/07:

Question: *Do you have any thoughts about when the secrets will be revealed?*

Fr. Petar: We are in the process of patiently waiting for when that's going to take place. From the very beginning Our Lady was preparing Mirjana how she would reveal those secrets. I was present several times on such discussions Our Lady had with Mirjana. I saw she was crying sometimes, and my question was, "Why are you crying?" She said, "I am crying because [of]what She's announcing that would take place – it's no good, it's very serious."

As I look into the situation in which the world is today, I have the feeling that this should take place very soon. The world cannot go on as it is, under the present condition. Something has to take place. Some intervention from Heaven has to take place. It appears as though everything is going towards perdition, but we know that for those that love, God works for good in all events, because God can even write in crooked lines the right way.

What I would like to emphasize is what is most important – that we should not look for the time when it would take place, but put emphasis on: Are we ready to face it when it does take place? He who lives the Gospel in accordance to expectations of the Gospel and Christ has nothing to fear. When Jesus comes, such a person will be ready.

We will know 10 days before it takes place what will take place. There will be like a parchment that I will receive from Mirjana. It will be about this size (showing), 8 by 10. All the secrets are written there – where it will take place, where, when and how will be written there. Then for the next seven days it will be time to fast and pray [both Mirjana and Fr. Petar]. Three days before, it will be revealed to the world what will take place. We must say that the first two secrets are involved with Medjugorje. They will be a warning of that which is to take place, because Our Lady did appear first in Medjugorje. And the parishioners of that parish of St. James are called to live those messages and to spread them as well. Many will be surprised because they weren't really taking into account what will take place. And the third secret will be on the Mount of Apparitions. There will be a visible sign. That sign will be a great joy for those who were in Medjugorje and who accepted these messages and have been living them.

Question: *In your opinion, would you consider situations such as 911, Katrina, tsunami, the hurricanes, disasters, the present status of the war, that it is so widespread – would you link these directly to what Our Lady has been saying in Medjugorje with respect to the chastisements?*

Fr. Petar: Yes, no matter what is taking place in nature and in the world there would be different opinions about it. But we Catholics have a different kind of opinion. We have learned and know that God is our loving Father, that He loves us, as Our Lady would say. But then take an earthly father for example. He does whatever he can do so his children will be fulfilled and happy. But, you see, the children refuse, the children want to live their own lives. They don't listen to the wish of the father. For tsunami maybe we can say this: "This for me is God's call to conversion because we were saved just a few seconds from total destruction of the area where we were. Instead of celebrating with Holy Mass the birth of Jesus, we decided to go there and enjoy life. I did not go there to sin as many others did go there to sin. All during these future holy days I shall never go anywhere, but be home. I will pray for those who do not know that, to be converted, but I will stay here."

I see some of these events as a warning of God that we would convert and that we would turn to God. I desire not to say that this is God's punishment. I would say it is a caution, a warning by God to us. God is saying, "Man, be ready." Make it well with God because tonight might be too late. That's what's important for us. Many are now prophesying that many disasters will take place in the world, but let's not speculate about that. What's important is that we know where we are coming from, what we need to do, and where we are geared to go. We come from God, for God and our neighbor we live, and then we go to God. So in that manner it is important when we will encounter our Maker, but how happy we will be when He comes to meet us and takes us to be with Him for all eternity. But it's important to emphasize to our children: "You see, dear children, there are many who are losing their lives on the road. Tsunami comes, Katrina comes, and you're gone. Therefore, make your life right in alignment with God **NOW**. Your mom and your dad desire to be in Heaven with you someday and that's not a fairy tale. That's the truth and a fact."

Therefore, during your Mass, consecrate your children and your family to God. As the priest is consecrating bread, at that moment say, "I believe, God, You are here. Now I am dedicating my life, my children, my future, my family, my troubles, my sickness to You for Your glory." And therefore, I dare to say, you are helping Jesus so that He and His grace may save you and your family.

One family had a son who was a drunkard. They were in Lourdes and Fatima. When they came to Medjugorje finally this is what they told me: the son had encountered a car accident because he was under the influence of alcohol. He came to Medjugorje. He was converted. He had a call to become a priest, and he became a priest. Two years ago he was ordained, and now he's in Romania as a missionary. This family said, "In a special way we were praying at the moment of Consecration and lifting him up and consecrating him to Jesus so that Jesus could make him holy. Because of alcohol he was already shaken. You see what God can do!"

Pray! God is ready to act!

(11/08-5/09)
Is Medjugorje Real?

The following is a transcription of a talk given my Dr. Mark Miravalle at the Medjugorje Conference at Notre Dame University in May, 2008:

For almost 27 years there have been reports of apparitions of the Mother of God in Medjugorje. Almost 27 years have also brought a multitude of questions, and in some cases, objections. The ultimate question is – "Is Medjugorje real?" Is it supernaturally authentic? Is the Mother of God really appearing there? And I think to properly respond to that question amidst a sea of questions and objections which remain, we have to take a very serious look at the objections directly, objectively, theologically so that we can arrive at the truth.

So what I would like to do is to take the five most frequently asked questions or objections to the authenticity of Medjugorje and examine them directly and straight-forwardly. But before we do that, we need to use the criteria that the Church herself uses when the Church examines any reported apparition, and as Fr. Laurentin so well summarized, the criteria of the Church. We find three fundamental elements the Church looks at when there is a reported apparition.

Number one – Is the message contents in conformity with the faith and moral teachings of the Catholic Church's magisterium? Is the message sound? Is the message one with the voice of the Holy Father, because the Holy Spirit will never contradict Himself, and the Holy Spirit speaks through the Holy Father in the Body of the Church, and therefore the Holy Spirit would never contradict the Church through a reported apparition. So the first criteria is the message – is it sound, doctrinally orthodox?

Number two – Do the phenomena that are reported conform with the Church's mystical tradition? In other words, anything that is not explainable by nature that is reported at an event – ecstasy, potential solar miracles, other elements of potential healing – do they follow in conformity with the mystical tradition of the Church?

Number three – The spiritual fruits – are there lasting, perduring, spiritual fruits that come forward? Because even from a false apparition there can be some initial positive fruits (someone could go back to Confession or to Mass or pray the Rosary on a weekend trip to some reported place), but, in fact, it doesn't necessarily indicate that the apparitions are authentic. It can be the sacraments and the impetus to go there, even for false reasons. So the issue is – are there lasting, perduring, universal spiritual fruits from the apparitions?

So, with those three general criteria in mind, I want to address five questions or objections, the most commonly raised questions or objections raised regarding the Medjugorje messages, and respond to them with theology, with the Church's criteria, and with hard facts because as John Paul II said when he went to the University in Switzerland, "The Church never fears the truth, because in the truth you find Christ who is the Truth." So we can boldly and honestly examine questions from a perspective of truth. If it's truth, it reflects Jesus, and if it's truth it will reflect the Mother of Jesus.

The first question: *What is the official position of the Church regarding Medjugorje? Would it be an act of disobedience to pilgrimage to Medjugorje before the Church has given the apparitions final and definitive approval?*

Let's go to the facts. On April 10, 1991, the Yugoslavian Episcopal Conference made a declaration regarding Medjugorje. It is known as the "Declaration of the ex-Yugoslavian Bishops' Conference," in Zadar. In the statement of 1991, the bishops say the following: They do not approve Medjugorje as supernaturally authentic; they do not prohibit Medjugorje as a fraudulent apparition. They rather conclude, without saying a positive statement of Medjugorje, that the pilgrims can come, and they are to be pastorally tended to. Now, theologically this is what we call the middle category of "non constat supernaturalitate." Now once again, bear with me on these distinctions because they're important for clarity and understanding what is the official position of the Church on Medjugorje. An approved apparition receives what is called "constat de supernaturalitate." which means it consists of a supernatural origin. The third category is the prohibition category, that is, "constat de non – supernaturalitate." That is where the local bishop says officially these are not approved, and you cannot come, and there can be no sacraments celebrated at this site. Well, there's a middle position, and it's "non constat supernaturalitate," which means the Church, and here the Zadar statement, does not approve the apparitions, it does not discredit the apparitions, and people are, indeed, free to go.

So the 1991 Zadar statement makes clear that personal pilgrimages to Medjugorje are done, can be satisfied within proper biddings to the Church. Now, on May 26, 1998, the Vatican Congregation to the Doctrine of the Faith made a statement on Medjugorje in response to a letter from a French bishop, Bishop Aubrey, and at that time the secretary to Cardinal Ratzinger, Archbishop Bertone, who is now the Secretary of State. Cardinal Bertone made a very important confirmation from the Vatican of the 1991 Zadar statement. Archbsihop Bertone, in this statement in 1998, said the following: Number one – that the Zadar statement, without approving and without condemning – is the position of the Church on Medjugorje at the present position. Number two – the statement of Archbishop Bertone stated that the personal opposition of the local bishop is his own personal position. It is not the official position of the Catholic Church, and I quote from the letter, "that the position of Msgr. Peric is and remains his personal opinion." Thirdly, the statement of 1998 states once again that pilgrims can pilgrimage to Medjugorje on a private, personal, that means non-diocesan organized basis.

My friends, this is extremely important if we're after the facts. **This is Rome; this is the Holy See; this is the Vatican Congregation for the Doctrine of the Faith saying that the position of the local bishop, which is a negative position, is not the official Catholic position at this time.** And we know from our Catechism, and we know from our teaching that you always go with Rome. You go with the Holy See. You go with the voice of the Congregation of the Doctrine of the Faith. So, in answer to question one, is it an act of disobedience to pilgrimage to Medjugorje, it absolutely is not an act of disobedience. It is permitted in the 1991 Zadar statement, from the bishops of ex-Yugoslavia. It is confirmed by the Congregation for the Doctrine of the Faith in the letter of Archbishop Bertone, May 26, 1998.

Question number two: *This is regarding the issue of potential disobedience. I have heard that there may be acts of disobedience by the Franciscan priests at St. James parish in Medjugorje against their local bishop. Is this true? And if so, how could Our Lady ever bless acts of disobedience by appearing there?*

We begin with an important distinction as we just mentioned. The Church at present provides people not only personal belief in Medjugorje, but the right to pilgrimage to Medjugorje. Now that's a universal right for anyone who is Catholic. That must include the personal rights of the Franciscan priests at Medjugorje. In other words, in virtue of being Catholic, they too have the freedom on a personal level to exercise the right that the Church gives them to personally say, "Yes, I believe Medjugorje is authentic and I will continue to believe so as the investigation continues." Therefore, any accusations of disobedience by the Franciscan priests at Medjugorje, because they believe in Medjugorje, is intrinsically an invalid accusation.

It's also important to note that there are no reported cases of disobedience by the priests in Medjugorje in violating any canonically licid directive of the bishop. Now, because we've got to face this straight forwardly and honestly – technically, if there had been, let's say, a Franciscan did an act of disobedience, and what I just got finished saying was that there's no such case recorded in terms of anything canonically appropriate for the bishop to ask them to do – technically, if you're on a board of investigation and you found a priest at Medjugorje who acted disobediently, that, technically, does not stand as a ground of disvalidating or invalidating the apparitions unless it was something, for example, of the spiritual director and somehow had a proximity to the visionaries.

And let me give you an example of why this has to be made clear. Let's use our own situation in the Church in our own country. Imagine if an individual pastor, a pastor loyal to the Church, loyal to the Holy Father, loyal to his bishop, had a brother priest in the diocese or had a brother religious who is also a priest within a three hour radius of his parish do something that was scandalous or was disobedient, and as a result of that other priest's actions some three hours away, the good pastor was indicted for being disobedient. But we would all quickly ascend to the idea that this is not acceptable, this is not fair. This is guilt by association. Well, indeed, historically there have been tensions between the bishop and the Franciscans which have lasted approximately 100 years and they began with the Muslim-Turk invasions when many of the Franciscans stayed with the people and in that situation some of the diocesan priests decided to leave.

But the issue is – if you're investigating authenticity from a Church position, the issue is – is there any act of disobedience immediate, proximate to the visionaries or the spiritual directors of the visionaries? Therefore, theologically it's not valid to say there was a case of disobedience three hours away from Medjugorje between the bishop and the Franciscans. There may have been, but it is illogical to apply that to Medjugorje. So, I say once again, in terms of the charge of disobedience, there's simply not a single case of recorded disobedience from a priest, from a Franciscan at St. James, in relation to the bishop, in anything that the bishop would canonically ask for.

Question number three: *This concerns the objections that the apparitions are simply too long. The messages of Medjugorje have been going on for 26 years now. Isn't that too long for authentic supernatural messages to take place? Can these apparitions really be true when they've been reportedly happening for so long?*

If again, we start with the criteria the Church uses, then we say from the get-go the Church has no criteria of length when it investigates reported revelations. In other words, it is a non-issue. Having said that, looking at the precedence of the Church regarding apparitions, the Medjugorje apparitions are of no sense the longest apparitions or mystical experiences. And let me give you a few cases from the mystical tradition of the Church. For example, we have the apparitions and visions of St. Bridget of Sweden in the 14th century, which lasted well over 25 years. In the same 14th century there were the visions and apparitions of St. Gertrude, which lasted over 30 years. We have the 12th century visions and mystical experiences of St. Hildegard which lasted over 65 years! It will be known more publicly that Sr. Lucia of Fatima continued to have supernatural communications very close to the year she died, in the first part of the 21st century. And if you've been following the news, you've heard of a newly approved apparition in France, Our Lady of Laus, where the visionary had apparitions for over 50 years!

My friends, I would consider that if we return to what the purpose of authentic private revelation is, I would consider a new examination of length. Why does Heaven send the Mother of God to humanity? It's not for curiosity; it's not for the sake of a new phenomenon. The purpose of authentic revelation is always to return us to the Gospel, and quite frankly, my friends, to the tough part – to the generous prayer, to the fasting which can be difficult, to the real acts of charity, which call for humility, to conversion, and ultimately to spiritual peace. If that's the purpose of authentic private revelation, and the Church says it is, then the fact that the Blessed Mother may be coming over 25 years should say something to you and to me and to humanity. How much encouragement do we need right now to get back to the Gospel? Sounds like we need a little more than a quarter of a century of encouragement, just from these apparitions, if indeed it is from God, through Our Lady.

And I would encourage instead of an argument of length against the apparitions, I would encourage an attitude of gratitude. Thank God that Heaven does not grow impatient with our own stiff-necked people. Thank God that Heaven continues to come.

The fourth question or objection: *This concerns potential false ecumenical teaching. The question: Do the messages reported by the visionaries contain false teachings regarding ecumenism which contradicts the official teachings of the Catholic Church's magisterium? I've heard that one reported message calls for a type of religious indifferentism, where one religion is as good as another.*

As we mentioned, the first criteria the Church looks at in terms of any reported apparitions, "Is the message doctrinely in conformity with the faith and moral teachings of the Church?" The message of Medjugorje has been examined thoroughly by a great number of recognized scholars. In fact, well over 20 years ago there was a doctoral dissertation on the subject of the message of Medjugorje, the thesis of which was simply to say, "The message of Medjugorje as reported is in conformity with Scripture, the Fathers of the Church, the Second Vatican Council, and the messages of Lourdes and Fatima, on the basis of private revelation." And that thesis was accepted as a legitimate thesis at the Pontifical University in Rome. Since that time, there has been a great score of theologians and bishops and priests and religious who have examined the message and have not found a single doctrinal error.

But let's get right to the point. The posed objection is the issue of ecumenism, so let's be as fair as we can to the objection. There have been two messages reportedly from the Mother of God in Medjugorje on the issue of ecumenism, and I want to read both of them to you.

The first one, somewhere in between 1981 and 1983, goes as follows: "In God's eyes there are no divisions and there are no religions. You in the world have made the divisions. The one Mediator is Jesus Christ. Which religion you belong to cannot be a matter of indifference. The presence of the Holy Spirit is not the same in every church."

The second message was relayed by Mirjana in approximately the same time period. Mirjana summarizes or reports the message of Our Lady: "The Madonna deplores the lack of religious unity, especially in the villages. She said that everybody's religion should be respected and of course, one's own." So what does the message reportedly say? Number one, man has made the divisions. Number two, all religions do not have equal presence of the Holy Spirit, and number three, the dimension of respecting religions, even if it's not your particular religion.

Let me read you the words of the Second Vatican Council regarding religious respect and the relationship between the Catholic Church and other religions. And I quote from the document: "The Catholic Church rejects nothing of what is true and holy in other religions. She has a high regard for their manner of life and conduct, precepts and doctrine, which although different in many from her own teachings, nevertheless often reflect a ray of that truth which enlightens all men. Yet, she is in duty, bound to proclaim without fail Christ, Who is the Way, the Truth and the Life. In Him, in Whom God reconciled all things to Himself, men find the fullness of their religious life."

The documents of the Second Vatican Council, the Catechism of the Catholic Church, and the Pontifical Magisterium tell us that there is only one true Church. It is one, holy, Catholic and apostolic in its fullness. And yet elements of truth can be found in certain degrees in other religions. But ultimately we're also called to respect the religions of other individuals, even if there's a disagreement about the truth that's being posed or the theological position that's being posed.

My friends, the Medjugorje message as it's relayed is a complete capsule of the teachings of the Second Vatican Council and the Catholic Catechism. Fullness of Catholic truth, respect for other religions, and that is indeed the Medjugorje message regarding ecumenism. I would also add that not only does the Medjugorje message reflect the traditional concept of the one true Church, in terms of Catholic Church, but it as well reflects the newer emphasis of the Second Vatican Council, with at least an accentuation to a deeper dialogue in respect with other religions. So I'm saying that the messages not only reflect Catholic teaching, but contemporary authentic post-conciliar Catholic teaching.

Question number five: *This concerns the possibility of false visionaries. "I've heard that the visionaries were not particularly devout before the apparitions began. How do we know they have not simply falsified these apparitions for reasons of their own personal gain?"*

We once again go back to the Church's criteria. The Church does not require great holiness for the reception of a supernatural visit from Heaven. What the Church does require is a fundamental moral integrity. Why does the Church not require it? Because in the history of the Church, God Himself does not require exceptional holiness. In fact, in history, there are cases of individuals that from external sights could have been out of grace when Jesus or Mary or one of the saints chose to appear to them. And we have to be consistent, because if we're looking at the authenticity of Jesus Christ in the gospels, what would we do with a situation of having a tax collector, let alone a prostitute, be among His closest apostles and disciples? And yet indeed we have St. Matthew and by the love of God, we have St. Mary Magdalene. So to look back in the history of an individual before a supernatural intervention, the Church considers in terms of commission evaluation irrelevant, invalid. The issue is: number one – is there a moral integrity from the time the apparitions began? Therefore, once again it doesn't require a good track record before the apparitions began. And again, this is Catholic Church precedence.

Having said that, I want to say a word about the visionaries of Medjugorje. Now, they have been under the public microscope for over a quarter of a century. They have been interviewed by hundreds of bishops and priests and theologians and laity and journalists. The overall consensus of a quarter century of interviews can be summarized as follows: 1. That the visionaries conduct a very positive model of Christian faith and life. 2. The visionaries are straightforward and down to earth. As one theologian said, "What you see is what you get with the visionaries." There is no pretense. 3. That their lives overall reflect not of self gain, but of sacrifice, as one person was commenting, "It would be fun to be a visionary for about two weeks." You get attention, you get notoriety, but then you'd be ready to go back to a real life where you wouldn't have sacrifice every private moment of existence. There's great crosses that come with receiving heavenly messages.

Of the six visionaries, I think of particular mention – deserves pointing out, highlighting – the visionary Vicka. Vicka, I would say, from an objective perspective, does manifest indications of exceptional holiness. I do not say this in discouragement of the other visionaries. I'm simply trying to examine objectively, saying there's indication of exceptional holiness with Vicka. Why do I say so? For two fundamental reasons. Number one – She has had a great degree of victim suffering, things like an inoperable brain cyst, extreme spinal pain and other penances, which she has received, and she continues to offer all with a remarkable charitable smile. So I think Vicka has some grounds for being beyond moral integrity and beyond just very positive Christian faith and life. I think there are grounds for holiness in an objective examination of her life. And again, I don't say that in detriment to the other visionaries, but I think there's something documentable in the case of Vicka.

I also want to note two medical teams that have investigated the visionaries in terms of Medjugorje. After examining the visionaries, their conclusion was: "These children are communicating with someone outside their own time/space reality." They could not say it was the Blessed Virgin, because science can't predicate that, but they could say (a) that there is no collective hallucination, and (b) they are, in fact, communicating with a person. The second team was from Milan, a medical scientific team. They came to exactly the same conclusion: no hallucinations, no deception – indications of authentic communication with someone outside of our time/space reality.

In terms of what the Church's criteria look for – message, phenomena, fruits, I would make the following conclusions: That the message is without error, that the phenomena, ecstasies, solar miracles, healing are completely in the heart of the tradition of the mystical Church, that the spiritual fruits that have been testified by over 33 million pilgrims who have been to Medjugorje are ubiquitous.

Now, I do want to draw attention to three particular testimonies, the first two of great significance. The first testimony of authenticity to Medjugorje I want to refer to is from Blessed Teresa of Calcutta. On August 14, 1993, I had the unmerited privilege of going down and spending a couple of days with Mother Teresa. She had asked for presentations to her Sisters of Charity on the proposed Fifth Marian Dogma of Co-Redemptrix, Mediatrix and Advocate, and in the few days down there, I gave six presentations on the Fifth Marian Dogma, two of which Mother herself sat in. And no, I wasn't nervous at all!

It was particularly difficult when she went for the second one and I said, "Mother, I'm not coming up with new material here." During that time I went and sat with Mother outside her office in Calcutta, and above her desk area was a picture, a calendar, actually of Our Lady of Medjugorje. And I said to her, point blank, "Mother, do you believe in Medjugorje?" and she gestured to me as follows, putting her finger over her lips as if to be discrete. But she said to me, and I quote: "I asked Our Lady of Medjugorje to come to the first home for the dying in Calcutta and She did." Now I unfortunately did not have the guts to ask her, "How did She come, Mother?" But she left it with that, with a great big smile on her face.

The second testimony, a testimony that is getting more and more well known, is the testimony of John Paul II. Now let's be clear and factual. John Paul II made no official statement on Medjugorje, but indeed, in many dialogues, I have personally spoken to three American bishops who heard from the lips of the Holy Father, Pope John Paul II, when asking is Medjugorje authentic, the Holy Father said, "Go and pray for me in Medjugorje." But I want to quote something even more objective. This is the statement of the late Cardinal Tomasek, the Eastern cardinal close to the Holy Father who said that John Paul told him, "If I were not the Pope, I would like to go to Medjugorje to help at the work with the pilgrims."

We also have received eight documented letters of personal letters written by Pope John Paul II to the Skwarnicki family. This would be a family he knew in Poland, to Marek and Sophia, in which on several occasions he talks about Medjugorje. I am going to read you two quotes from the letters of Pope John Paul II. The first, December 8, 1992, and I quote the words of John Paul II: "I thank Sophia for everything concerning Medjugorje. I, too, go there every day as a pilgrim in my prayers: I unite in my prayers with all those who pray there or receive a calling for prayer from there."

The second quote of John Paul II comes February 25, 1994. Once again I quote: "I guess Medjugorje is better understood these days. This kind of 'insisting' of our Mother is better understood today when we see with our very eyes the enormousness of the danger. At the same time, the response in the way of special prayer – and that coming from people all around the world – fills us with hope that here, too, the good will prevail."

John Paul II, Mother Teresa of Calcutta, not a bad pair of discerning saintly individuals in our time about the authenticity.

The third testimony is least important. In fact, it's the least important thing I'll share with you today, but, nonetheless, I feel called to also convey this to you. This is my own personal testimony.

As a doctoral student in Rome in December of 1983, I happened into a Roman bookstore and there was a very thin book by Fr. Robert Faricy on Medjugorje. It was one of the first two books on it. Being an impoverished Roman theological student, I did not buy the book, but I went into the corner of the bookstore and read it in about 90 minutes. As I was reading the book, I had a certain inflaming of my heart and I decided that there was enough in this to investigate. So I went to my beloved wife Beth, and we had one child at that time, and I said, "Beth, I'm going to go over to this place. Let's just fast for the four days I'm gone, we'll fast for the holiness of our kids. If it is not the Blessed Mother, there's no loss because we'll be offering the fast." My wife kindly agreed. So I went over.

On December 7, I arrived at Medjugorje. And in December of 1983, of course there were no hotels, and there were no restaurants, and there were no stores. And so that first night I got there I spent the night in the church with nine other pilgrims from the area of Croatia. We all slept on the pews, and the next morning we were delivered to various homes. On December 8, in one of these homes, five little kids came down with their mother and they started doing the "Sevens" [a nickname given to the prayer of the Creed and seven Our Father's, Hail Mary's, and Glory Be's, as explained in Chapter 2]. I decided it would be the time to take the walk to Krizevac.

At that time, I had a doctrinal topic approved at the Angelicum in Rome entitled "Holiness for the lay person, according to the writings of

St. Catherine of Sienna, St. Alphonsus Liguori, St. Francis de Sales, and the Doctors of the Church," and as I was praying the Rosary, walking up the hill of Krizevac, it occurred to me the remarkable presumption that I had in thinking that I could summarize how to become holy as a lay person better than the Mother of God and the Mediatrix of all graces. So I went back to the Angelicum and changed my topic. The first time I offered my topic on the message of Medjugorje to the doctoral board of the Pontifical University of St. Thomas Aquinas in Rome, the Angelicum, it was rejected, and the second time a Father suggested, "Why don't you add Lourdes and Fatima so you can examine the message in continuity with them?" It was then accepted.

Apart from my own experience, I just want to pass on, that for us, a young family, I prayed, my wife prayed, but we didn't pray as a family. Our spiritualities were separate. The gift of Medjugorje for our family was twofold. First of all, we prayed as a family. We prayed the Rosary and other prayers as a family. Secondly, we fasted as a family. We thought it remarkable how quickly the children accustomed to fasting. If anything, they became the "fasting police," not us. "Dad, are you supposed to have that cup of coffee?" "Mom, are you sure you want to have that roll?" because they became habituated to saying, of Wednesdays and Fridays, "Yes, we give up something for Jesus, and we give up something for souls."

So in conclusion, to answer the question we started with, "Is Medjugorje real?" – the most objective, theological answer I can give you in light of the Church's teachings and precedence is, "Oh, yes, it is real" and more than that, She is real! And if you still doubt, I invite you, in fact, I challenge you – go and investigate. Go to this land yourself. Go with an open heart, but if you don't have an open heart, go anyway because the Mother is waiting for you. Be open and be grateful for the gift of the Queen of Peace. Thanks be to God for Her!

Picture of Bl. Pope John Paul II in St. James Church
in Medjugorje

(5/05)
News from Medjugorje

By Sister Emmanuel

As the whole world is focused on the extraordinary life and death of the Holy Father John Paul II, I want to join with the millions of people who praise this most admirable man, this reflection of Jesus' love and light on earth!

Some news has been released these days in connection with Medjugorje and it might need some clarification. Here is how things took place: The Pope departed this earth in Rome at 9:37 P.M., Saturday, April 2, during the Vigil of the Feast of the Divine Mercy, the feast he himself instituted in April, 2000. That morning, as on each second day of the month, Mirjana Soldo received her apparition in the new building of Cenacolo and prayed with Our Lady for unbelievers. The atmosphere was charged with emotion knowing that Pope John Paul II was hanging between life and death. So we prayed with an intense fervor to Our Lady at the time of the apparition entrusting him into Her hands. After Mirjana emerged from her ecstasy, she said: "The Gospa has blessed all of us with Her Motherly Blessing. She said that the greatest blessing we could receive on earth is that of a priest. She also blessed the religious articles that we have brought. Then the Gospa said, '**In this time, I ask you to renew the Church.**' Then I (Mirjana) said to Her, 'This is a big request! Am I able to do it? Are we able to do it?' And Our Lady said, '**But my dear children, I will be always with you! My apostles, I will always be with you and I will help you! Renew yourselves first and your families, and then everything will be easier.**'" Mirjana also reported that she had asked Our Lady about the Pope, but Our Lady did not reply. Instead they prayed together for the Pope.

Ivan Dragicevic, (one of the six visionaries), was on a mission in the United States on April 2nd. The next day April 3rd, Divine Mercy Sunday, he went to Bangor, Maine, to give a talk and he found that everyone there was deeply affected by the death of the Holy Father. Ivan told the audience in Maine that the day before, Saturday, April 2nd, he was in a parish in New Hampshire. Because of the time difference with Europe, he received his apparition just a few hours after the death of the Pope. He explained that when the Blessed Mother appeared to him, She was alone as usual. But then the Holy Father himself appeared at the left side of Our Lady. He was dressed in a long white robe and a cape of gold! Ivan said that he looked very young and both the Holy Father and Our Lady had great joy. Our Lady said to Ivan: "He is my son, he is with me!" Ivan reported to the group that after that apparition he was so overwhelmed he could hardly sleep! Those present during the apparition reported that they had never seen Ivan so happy.

Because of her great love for the John Paul II, Vicka went to Rome to attend the Holy Father's funeral (leaving her two children at home with Mario). She had met him several times in the past bringing sick and crippled pilgrims from her country for his blessing. The Holy Father also blessed her when she went to Rome as a newlywed with her husband, Mario, just after they were married in Medjugorje.

I want to point out something beautiful: Just before he passed from this earth, on Saturday evening, the Holy Father suddenly turned toward

St. Peter's Square and blessed the crowd gathered there. And when he had said "Amen," he breathed his last. This "Amen" was actually his last word! How wonderful! And this blessing is the gift he left to each one of us. We'll always be supported by the intercession of Jesus' powerful vicar, John Paul the Great!

Last night (April 8), the whole parish of Medjugorje celebrated evening Mass especially for the Holy Father. All other Masses were cancelled so that the village could watch this historical and unique funeral live on TV. This profound event reverberated with the Glorious Mysteries rather than to the Sorrowful Mysteries.

Of course, many of us feel orphaned by his absence. But what gives us deep joy, besides knowing he is so happy in Heaven, is that at last we can relate to him directly through prayer, as we do with anyone in the Heavenly Court! At last, everybody can have an audience with him. At last he has time to listen to each word we have to tell him! And as we have done for Fr. Slavko, we are not going to leave him jobless!

As he stated several times, (publicly on April 6, 1995), the Holy Father would have come to Medjugorje, if he had been invited into the diocese. Let us not feel sorry that he never made it, because now is his time to come! The vision that Ivan reported is just a little glimpse of what could be his ministry in Medjugorje. Wait and see! I will never forget the day I saw a handwritten letter from the Pope to Sofija, a friend of his who lives in Krakow. In reply to the testimony she had sent him about the fruit of Medjugorje in her life, he wrote to her saying that every day *he too was making a pilgrimage to Medjugorje in his heart so that he could join his prayers with the prayers of the pilgrims flocking there*. He is our hero! From Heaven, he'll be a powerful intercessor and he'll help the plans of the Queen of Peace.

It was very beautiful to see at the funeral in St. Peter's Square all the banners saying "Santo subito" (Saint immediately). According to the Vatican rules, a Pope is given the right to canonize a holy person right after his/her death, without going through the normal process for canonization. This rule is not known by most of the faithful. If this rule does not apply in the Holy Father's case, then for whom would it ever apply!?

Children of Medjugorje, www.childrenofmedjugorje.com

(1/09)
1981 – Precursor to the "New Springtime"

By Dawn Curazzato

When my granddaughter was born with multiple handicaps, I went in search of the Divine Healer. I found Him at the bedside of another child, who laid in a coma in Worcester, Massachusetts, Little Audrey Santo, whose cause for canonization is underway. I went with a child-like faith and a strong conviction in the truth of the healing stories in the Bible. I witnessed a Eucharistic Miracle which changed my life immediately and forever! I believed in miracles and perhaps that is part of the reason why our Katelin experienced a complete healing as outlined in the book, *Memoir of a Miracle*.

I met many nuns and priests during our trials and I never forgot the words of one of the priests when I asked about signs from God. He said, "Did you know God often speaks to us through nature and dates?" I guess I had never really thought about it. It was AFTER he said that to me that I began seeing the Lord speak to me in such a way. We went to Audrey Santo's between Easter and Divine Mercy Sunday, two holy times on the church calendar. Divine Mercy Sunday was my daughter's birthday that year. The Host I saw bleed, bled on June 5th, my mother's birthday and that made me wonder if Katelin's birthday had any Church significance. She was born February 11, the Feast Day of Our Lady of Lourdes – Lourdes, a place of healing! My hands shook as I held the religious calendar and looked at her birth date, and it was then I knew Katelin would be healed. They were not coincidences, they were "God-incidences!" There was personal and religious meaning to those dates which awakened something in me and made my heart leap with great joy.

In the Old Testament God speaks to His servants over 20,000 times and they responded, "Speak, Lord, your servant is listening!" Today people complain that God does not speak to His people any more, that He doesn't answer prayers, but that is not true! There is so much noise around us and so many distractions that today people say, "Listen, Lord, your servant is speaking!" How can we hear the Lord if we are doing all the talking? I find Adoration to be a wonderful place to hear the Lord, but if we find a quiet place and pray openly and fervently we will hear that inner voice and we will recognize it as His! It was in Adoration that I got a prompting, a date and I wasn't quite sure what it meant. I had begun a second book, but I was getting a great deal of "interference" which continues, but I thought I might share some highlights of one of the chapters simply called "1981."

In 1981 the first portable computer came out. Computers can be wonderful tools of information but they are, unfortunately, also harbingers of misinformation and confusion as well. They are one of the biggest sources of "distraction" in the world today. Distraction and confusion are tools of the devil, so is pornography. Thanks to the computer, pornography, which means "the devil's pictures," is the biggest addiction in the world.

In 1981 AIDS was first identified as a disease. Though we know there are innocent victims of AIDS, it is primarily spread through sexual contact and intravenous drugs. Immorality is also a rampant "disease" and tool of the devil.

In 1981 the first test tube baby was born. Here we have man playing God!

In 1981, on the Fatima date, May 13th, Pope John Paul II was shot and almost killed. He would later visit his would-be assassin and forgive him. He took the bullet that entered his body and had it put in the Statue of Our Lady of Fatima. At a later date he would declare Jacinta and Francesco beatified. It is widely believed that the outcome of the Third Secret of Fatima, in which the Pope appeared to be killed in the vision the children were shown, was mitigated due to the prayers and reparation of the Fatima children.

In 1981 a crippled, cloistered nun, with no financial means, began the largest Catholic Communications system in the world and EWTN was born, making Mother Angelica a household name!

In November of 1981 the Apparitions in Kebeho, Africa began. The Blessed Mother gave important messages to seven visionaries. She called for prayer and repentance and She called the people to turn away from their immorality. She told them if they did not have a change of heart the rivers would run red with blood and swollen bodies. Her warning went unheeded and the terrible genocide in Rwanda resulted with reporters describing the carnage in almost the exact words Our Lady used!

And in 1981, a little more than a month after Pope John Paul II was shot, on June 25th the Blessed Mother reportedly began appearing to six children in a town called Medjugorje in the former Yugoslavia! The children will each be given 10 secrets which will be divulged to the world in their life time. Three of the children already have 10 secrets the other three have nine. Our Lady also leaves a message for the world on the 25th of each month. She calls for Mass, fasting, monthly Confession, reading the Bible and receiving Communion. No one knows when the secrets will unfold, but several will be worldwide events and are ominous! Our Lady has promised to leave a permanent sign on Apparition Hill at the spot where She first appeared. She has told the visionaries these are Her LAST apparitions in this way.

1981 was an important year! God is speaking to us, through His mother and through dates and events. Are we getting the message? It seems not, as the world capitulates deeper and deeper into sin. Abortion is the greatest genocide of our times killing almost 50 million babies of all races. Unless we hear the cries of the unborn and speak out against this great evil we will never be delivered from genocide. I believe the culmination of the above events will usher in, what Pope John Paul II called "The New Spring Time" because they will take us on a journey from the head to the heart. Greatness is born of suffering and oppression. We may witness an event never before seen in our history. We are being called to "greatness," and greatness is not defined by a title, or by what we own, or by how many friends we have or even by how many people love us; it is defined by *how we love others*! If we truly love as God has called us to love in the two great commandments, there would be no genocide, no AIDS, no abortion, no sin! Will this time of great evil, of rampant sin and intense hatred give rise to The New Spring Time by awakening in us heroic love that will see evil for what it really is? I think it will. I think we will see a great Spiritual Revival but unfortunately we have a ways to go. God is speaking to us. He is showing us the way. He IS the WAY the TRUTH and the LIFE! Awake, O Sleeper!

Editor's note: Dawn is from Williamsville, NY. A condensed version of her granddaughter's miracle is in **The Best of "The Spirit of Medjugorje," Volume II.**

(9/05)
Two Popes and Medjugorje

As I began working on Volume II of *The Best of "The Spirit of Medjugorje"* I read something interesting in the Dec. 3, 1997 Press Bulletin from the Information Center in Medjugorje. This excerpt is from an interview with a bishop from Brazil.

Press Bulletin: As a bishop, pastor of the Church you know that our local bishop is not favorable to these events. Does that bother you?

Bishop Martin: No, because there are also other bishops who think otherwise. I would like to recall the archbishop of Pescara who is my great friend and every year we go to the spiritual exercises in San Marino together with Fr. Gobbi. Every year spiritual exercises are organized for priests and bishops and that way also the archbishop of Pescara often comes. One time he told me that he asked the Holy Father about these events. "Holy Father what should I do when the faithful from my diocese of Pescara want often to go on pilgrimage to Medjugorje?" "What are they doing?" asked the Holy Father. "They pray and go to holy Confession." "Well, isn't that good?" answered the Holy Father.

I worked for ten years with the Holy Father and with Cardinal Ratzinger. Cardinal Ratzinger is a wonderful man, full of spirituality and very pleasant. Sometimes I hear it said about him that he is very strict and serious, but I think he is a man with a big heart. Once I asked him what he thinks about this movement. He answered me that the tree is recognized by the fruits, because good fruits are a sign of God's presence.

Press Bulletin: Cardinal Ratzinger told you that?

Bishop Martin: Yes.

Press Bulletin: About Medjugorje?

Bishop Martin: Yes, about Medjugorje

Information Centre "Mir" Medjugorje, www.medjugorje.hr

(9/07)
Reagan, Gorbachev and Medjugorje

Just prior to signing the Peace Accord in 1987, President Reagan was given (by Alfred Kingon, at the time, America's Ambassador to Europe) a letter from Marija Pavlovic, one of the visionaries in Medjugorje. According to Kingon, President Reagan, visibly moved, phoned his thanks to Marija in Medjugorje, and then proceeded to his meeting with Gorbachev after first exclaiming, "Now I'm going to this meeting with a new spirit!" Marija would later write Gorbachev, "at the request of Ambassador Kingon," informing him, as she had the American President, of Our Lady's message of peace from Medjugorje. Kingon testifies that it was translated into Russian and put into the hands of Gorbachev at the Kremlin.

Also some time later, Reagan wrote Fr. John Villanova, chaplain of the Sanctuary of Fatima, Portugal, thanking him for having sent the Pilgrim Statue of Our Lady of Fatima. It was "upstairs in Nancy's and my bedroom" at the White House when he and Gorbachev "were meeting downstairs."

A non-Catholic, Ambassador Kingon, secretary to President Reagan's cabinet before being named Ambassador to Europe, gave the testimony – and also his own, after his pilgrimage to Medjugorje – at the 1992 National Conference on Medjugorje at the University of Notre Dame: "Our Lady is now coming for all Her children on earth, in preparation for a major turning point in the affairs of men!"

Used with permission **Medjugorje and the Church** *by Denis Nolan* © *2007*
Note: The text of Marija's letter to President Reagan can be read in **The Best of "The Spirit of Medjugorje," Volume I.**

(5/05)
Pope John Paul II and Medjugorje

Holy Father has never officially recognized the apparitions of Medjugorje, but he believed in them, and he told this to many. During his pontificate, he was putting into practice what Our Lady was inviting us to.

Pope John Paul II about Medjugorje

These statements are not confirmed by the Pope's seal and signature, but are brought by trustworthy persons.

– In a private conversation with the visionary Mirjana Soldo the Pope said: "If I were not Pope I would already be in Medjugorje confessing" (1987).

– Msg. Maurillo Kreiger, former bishop of Florianopolis (Brazil), visited Medjugorje four times. He writes as follows: "In 1988, after a private Mass with the Pope, before leaving Rome, he said, without having been asked anything, 'Pray for me in Medjugorje.' On another occasion, I told the Pope, 'I am going to Medjugorje for the fourth time.' He concentrated his thoughts and said, 'Medjugorje, Medjugorje, it is the spiritual heart of the world.' On the same day I spoke with other Brazilian bishops and the Pope at lunchtime and I asked him: 'Your holiness, can I tell the visionaries that you send your blessing?' He answered: 'Yes yes,' and embraced me."

– To a group of doctors, who work for the defense and protection of the life of the unborn, the Pope said on the 1st of 1989, "Yes, today the world has lost the sense of the supernatural. In Medjugorje, many seek and re-find this sense in prayer, fasting and confession."

On November 11, 1990, the Korean national weekly newspaper ("Catholic News") published an article by Msg. Angelo Kim, President of the Korean Bishops' Conference: "Prior to the conclusion of the last Bishops' Synod in Rome, the Korean bishops were invited to a lunch with the Holy Father. On this occasion, Msg. Kim addressed the Holy Father directly and said, 'Father, thanks to you, Poland was able to liberate itself from Communism.' To this, the Holy Father responded, 'No, this is not my merit. This is the work of the Blessed Virgin Mary, as She had predicted in Fatima and in Medjugorje.'"

– The Pope said to Fr. Jozo Zovko on the 20th July, 1992: "Busy yourself with Medjugorje, look after Medjugorje, don't tire. Persevere, be strong, I am with you. Watch over, follow Medjugorje."

– The Archbishop of Paraguay, Msg. Felipe Santiago Bentez, in November of 1994, asked of the Holy Father, the Pope, if he was right to give approval to the faithful gathering in the spirit of Medjugorje, especially with the priests of Medjugorje. The Holy Father answered: "Approve all that is related to Medjugorje."

– In the unofficial part of the meeting of Pope John Paul II with the Croatian delegation of Church and State held in Rome on the 7th of April, 1995, the Holy Father amongst other things said that there was some possibility of renewing his visit to Croatia. Together with this he mentioned the possibility of arriving in Split, and from there on to the shrine of "Marija Bistrica" and Medjugorje. ("Slobodna Dalmacija," 8th of April, 1995, page 3.)

– On March 15, 1997, the Croatian President, Dr. Franjo Tudjman, said: "Again I repeat that on the occasion of my last conversation with him Pope John Paul II said that, on the occasion of his visit to Bosnia-Herzegovina, he would like also to visit Medjugorje."

Our Lady about Pope John Paul II

– According to the testimony of the visionaries, May 13, 1982, on the occasion of the assassination attempt on the Pope, Our Lady said, "His enemies tried to kill him, but I have protected him."

– Through the visionaries on June 26, 1982, Our Lady sends Her message to the Pope, "Let him be considered as the father of all people and not just of Christians; let him tirelessly and courageously announce the message of Peace and Love among men."

– Through Jelena Vasilj who had an internal locution September 16, 1982, Our Lady pronounced about the Pope, "God has given him permission to defeat Satan." She requests of all and especially of the Pope "to spread the message that I have received from my Son. I desire to entrust to the Pope the word with which I have come here to Medjugorje: Peace; he should spread it to all parts of the world . . . he should unite Christians by his word and his preaching. Let him mainly among youth spread the messages that he has received from the Father in prayer. God inspires him then."

– Taking into consideration the difficulties of the parish regarding the bishop and the commission for investigation of the events in the parish of Medjugorje, Our Lady said, "Church authority should be followed. However, before it pronounces its judgment it is necessary to progress spiritually. It will not pronounce its judgment hastily. It takes place as with a birth that is followed by baptism and confirmation. The Church will confirm that which is born of God. We should go and progress in the spiritual life, impelled by these messages."

– On the occasion of the Pope's visit in Croatia Our Lady said, "Dear children! Today I am united with you in a special way, praying for the gift of the presence of my beloved son in your homeland. Pray, little children, for the health of my dearest son, who is suffering, and whom I have chosen for these times. I pray and intercede before my Son, Jesus, so that the dream that your fathers had may be fulfilled. Pray, little children, in a special way, because Satan is strong and wants to destroy hope in your heart. I bless you. Thank you for having responded to my call" (8-25-94).

© *Information Centre "Mir" Medjugorje, www.medjugorje.hr*

(6/09)
Why is Our Lady Appearing so Long?

By June Klins

A few months ago, the International Internet Prayer Group (IIPG), had a discussion on why Our Lady is appearing for so long. Although there was much lively discussion on this topic, I felt inspired to share two particular testimonies. I am grateful to both people for granting me permission to share their stories.

Tom Hubbard of Louisville, KY, wrote: "I'd like to
of a message being repeated for an extended period th
a young age wondering what 'Grace' and 'Hail Mary'
I did not grow up Catholic. I'm from a Protestant backg
particular devotion to Our Lady was present in our home. L   ..cn day,
my mom usually had the radio on a local station she listened to regularly.
Every afternoon this station would broadcast the Rosary. No one paid
a lot of attention to the broadcast in our home, with the exception of
our parakeet, Corkey. Corkey managed to memorize 'Hail Mary full
of Grace, Hail Mary full of Grace.' Over and over I heard Corkey say
this one line. Each day he would repeat his Hail Mary and finally one
day this simple message clicked in my mind. The words were simple
but eternal, given by an angel to Our Lady. How many days, weeks, did
Corkey remind me, how many times did I hear this simple message and
not realize what I was hearing? The number of days isn't important,
only the fact that I eventually came to understand what I was hearing.
I think this is what Our Lady desires by Her continued coming to visit,
that we eventually hear and understand what She is saying. We have no
idea how much longer the Blessed Mother will be visiting with us, but
it's important to remember what She said a few years back, 'but soon a
time will come when you will lament for these messages.'"

Suzanne de Friesse, of New Milford, CT, wrote, "I will never forget
the testimony of an Irish Priest during his homily at St. James a few
years ago. He was on his first pilgrimage many years ago and was very
impressed with much of what he saw, but was troubled by the fact that it
was going on for so long. He questioned why, and allowed this to put a
pall on his view of the Shrine. As he was preparing to leave Medjugorje,
he decided to climb Apparition Hill one more time before leaving. As
he sat up on the hill, he again pondered the length of the time Our
Lady was appearing. It was then that he quite plainly heard a voice say,
'If I can come to you every day in a little round piece of bread, what
makes you think that I cannot send my Mother every day for 20 years?'
Needless to say, this Priest is a great supporter of Medjugorje . . . and a
wonderful homilist!"

*Editor's note: If you are interested in joining the internet prayer group,
which is an extension of Ivan's prayer group in Medjugorje, go to
www.iipg.org.*

"If you knew how much I love you you'd cry for joy"

Medugorje

(6/05)
Sweet Lady in Gray

Tribute to Our Lady of Medjugorje
By Carolyn Morris

Sweet Blessed Lady, dressed in gray,
You've come from very far away,
You've come from Heaven up above,
To show us God's almighty love.

It's a little village that You chose,
To open hearts that once were closed.
You've come over twenty years now,
To touch and wipe our sweaty brow.

At times you bring Your Son with you
And ask for lives to be renewed.
You teach us how to clearly know
Our love for Jesus needs to grow.

You tell us each to pray, pray, pray
Because that is the only way,
To climb the mountain, to reach the mound,
That takes us to our Heavenly crown.

We must open our hearts, make the room,
Because Our Lord is coming soon.
On You, Our Mother, we must depend
If we want our hearts to truly mend.

I want to be with You again,
In this holy place where You descend.
So Lovely Lady, if it's your wish,
Please bring me back into that bliss.

But Mother, if this be not your desire,
Lovely Lady set my heart on fire;
So until it beats for the very last time
I will always call You and Jesus mine.

Editor's note: Carolyn was the Coordinator of Outreach Ministries for The Marian Center of Louisville, Kentucky. She passed away shortly after we published her poem.

Appendix: The Messages
January 2005 – December 2009

Message of January 25, 2005
"Dear children! In this time of grace again I call you to prayer. Pray, little children, for unity of Christians, that all may be one heart. Unity will really be among you inasmuch as you will pray and forgive. Do not forget: love will conquer only if you pray, and your heart will open. Thank you for having responded to my call."

Message of February 25, 2005
"Dear children! Today I call you to be my extended hands in this world that puts God in the last place. You, little children, put God in the first place in your life. God will bless you and give you strength to bear witness to Him, the God of love and peace. I am with you and intercede for all of you. Little children, do not forget that I love you with a tender love. Thank you for having responded to my call."

Annual Apparition to Mirjana on March 18, 2005
"Dear children! I come to you as the mother who, above all, loves her children. My children, I desire to teach you to love also. I pray for this. I pray that you will recognize my Son in each of your neighbors. The way to my Son, who is true peace and love, passes through the love for all neighbors. My children, pray and fast for your heart to be open for this my intention."

Message of March 25, 2005
"Dear children! Today I call you to love. Little children, love each other with God's love. At every moment, in joy and in sorrow, may love prevail and, in this way, love will begin to reign in your hearts. The Risen Jesus will be with you and you will be His witnesses. I will rejoice with you and protect you with my motherly mantle. Especially,

little children, I will watch your daily conversion with love. Thank you for having responded to my call."

Message of April 25, 2005
"Dear children! Also today, I call you to renew prayer in your families. By prayer and the reading of Sacred Scripture, may the Holy Spirit, who will renew you, enter into your families. In this way, you will become teachers of the faith in your family. By prayer and your love, the world will set out on a better way and love will begin to rule in the world. Thank you for having responded to my call."

Message of May 25, 2005
"Dear children! Anew I call you to live my messages in humility. Especially witness them now when we are approaching the anniversary of my apparitions. Little children, be a sign to those who are far from God and His love. I am with you and bless you all with my motherly blessing. Thank you for having responded to my call."

Message of June 25, 2005
"Dear children! Today I thank you for every sacrifice that you have offered for my intentions. I call you, little children, to be my apostles of peace and love in your families and in the world. Pray that the Holy Spirit may enlighten and lead you on the way of holiness. I am with you and bless you all with my motherly blessing. Thank you for having responded to my call."

Annual Apparition to Ivanka on June 25, 2005
"Dear children, love each other with the love of my Son. Peace, peace, peace."

Message of July 25, 2005
"Dear children! Also today, I call you to fill your day with short and ardent prayers. When you pray, your heart is open and God loves you with a special love and gives you special graces. Therefore, make good use of this time of grace and devote it to God more than ever up to now. Do novenas of fasting and renunciation so that Satan be far from you and grace be around you. I am near you and intercede before God for each of you. Thank you for having responded to my call."

Message of August 25, 2005

"Dear children! Also today I call you to live my messages. God gave you a gift of this time as a time of grace. Therefore, little children, make good use of every moment and pray, pray, pray. I bless you all and intercede before the Most High for each of you. Thank you for having responded to my call."

Message of September 25, 2005

"Dear children! In love I call you: convert, even though you are far from my heart. Do not forget, I am your mother and I feel pain for each one who is far from my heart; but I do not leave you alone. I believe you can leave the way of sin and decide for holiness. Thank you for having responded to my call."

Message of October 25, 2005

"Little children, believe, pray and love, and God will be near you. He will give you the gift of all the graces you seek from Him. I am a gift to you, because, from day to day, God permits me to be with you and to love each of you with immeasurable love. Therefore, little children, in prayer and humility, open your hearts and be witnesses of my presence. Thank you for having responded to my call."

Message of November 25, 2005

"Dear children! Also today I call you to pray, pray, pray until prayer becomes life for you. Little children, at this time, in a special way, I pray before God to give you the gift of faith. Only in faith will you discover the joy of the gift of life that God has given you. Your heart will be joyful thinking of eternity. I am with you and love you with a tender love. Thank you for having responded to my call."

Message of December 25, 2005

"Dear children! Also today, in my arms I bring you little Jesus, the King of Peace, to bless you with His peace. Little children, in a special way today I call you to be my carriers of peace in this peaceless world. God will bless you. Little children, do not forget that I am your mother. I bless you all with a special blessing, with little Jesus in my arms. Thank you for having responded to my call."

Annual Apparition to Jakov on December 25, 2005

"Dear children! Today, with Jesus in my arms, in a special way I call you to conversion. Children, through all this time which God permitted me to be with you, I continuously called you to conversion. Many of your hearts remained closed. Little children, Jesus is peace, love and joy; therefore now decide for Jesus. Start to pray. Pray to Him for the gift of conversion. Little children, only with Jesus can you have peace, joy and a heart filled with love. Little children, I love you. I am your mother and give you my motherly blessing."

Message of January 25, 2006

"Dear children! Also today I call you to be carriers of the Gospel in your families. Do not forget, little children, to read Sacred Scripture. Put it in a visible place and witness with your life that you believe and live the Word of God. I am close to you with my love and intercede before my Son for each of you. Thank you for having responded to my call."

Message of February 25, 2006

"Dear children! In this Lenten time of grace, I call you to open your hearts to the gifts that God desires to give you. Do not be closed, but with prayer and renunciation say 'yes' to God and He will give to you in abundance. As in springtime the earth opens to the seed and yields a hundredfold, so also your heavenly Father will give to you in abundance. I am with you and love you, little children, with a tender love. Thank you for having responded to my call."

Annual Apparition to Mirjana on March 18, 2006

"Dear children! In this Lenten time, I call you to interior renunciation. The way to this leads you through love, fasting, prayer and good works. Only with total interior renunciation will you recognize God's love and the signs of the time in which you live. You will be witnesses of these signs and will begin to speak about them. I desire to bring you to this. Thank you for having responded to me."

Message of March 25, 2006

"Courage Little Children! I decided to lead you on the way of holiness. Renounce sin and set out on the way of salvation, the way which my

Son has chosen. Through each of your tribulations and sufferings God will find the way of joy for you. Therefore, little children, pray. We are close to you with our love. Thank you for having responded to my call."

Message of April 25, 2006
"Dear children! Also today I call you to have more trust in me and my Son. He has conquered by His death and resurrection and, through me, calls you to be a part of
His joy. You do not see God, little children, but if you pray you will feel His nearness. I am with you and intercede before God for each of you. Thank you for having responded to my call."

Message of May 25, 2006
"Dear children! Also today I call you to put into practice and to live my messages that I am giving you. Decide for holiness, little children, and think of Heaven. Only in this way, will you have peace in your heart that no one will be able to destroy. Peace is a gift, which God gives you in prayer. Little children, seek and work with all your strength for peace to win in your hearts and in the world. Thank you for having responded to my call."

Message of June 25, 2006
"Dear children! With great joy in my heart I thank you for all the prayers that, in these days, you offered for my intentions. Know, little children, that you will not regret it, neither you nor your children. God will reward you with great graces and you will merit eternal life. I am near you and thank all those who, through these years, have accepted my messages, have poured them into their life and decided for holiness and peace. Thank you for having responded to my call."

Annual Apparition to Ivanka on June 25, 2006
"Dear children, thank you for having responded to my call. Pray, pray, pray."

Message of July 25, 2006
"Dear children! At this time, do not only think of rest for your body but, little children, seek time also for the soul. In silence may the Holy Spirit

speak to you and permit Him to convert and change you. I am with you and before God I intercede for each of you. Thank you for having responded to my call."

Message of August 25, 2006
"Dear children! Also today I call you to pray, pray, pray. Only in prayer will you be near to me and my Son and you will see how short this life is. In your heart a desire for Heaven will be born. Joy will begin to rule in your heart and prayer will begin to flow like a river. In your words there will only be thanksgiving to God for having created you and the desire for holiness will become a reality for you. Thank you for having responded to my call."

Message of September 25, 2006
"Dear children! Also today I am with you and call all of you to complete conversion. Decide for God, little children, and you will find in God the peace your heart seeks. Imitate the lives of saints and may they be an example for you; and I will inspire you as long as the Almighty permits me to be with you. Thank you for having responded to my call."

Message of October 25, 2006
"Dear children! Today the Lord permitted me to tell you again that you live in a time of grace. You are not conscious, little children, that God is giving you a great opportunity to convert and to live in peace and love. You are so blind and attached to earthly things and think of earthly life. God sent me to lead you toward eternal life. I, little children, am not tired, although I see that your hearts are heavy and tired for everything that is a grace and a gift. Thank you for having responded to my call."

Message of November 25, 2006
"Dear children! Also today I call you to pray, pray, pray. Little children, when you pray you are close to God and He gives you the desire for eternity. This is a time when you can speak more about God and do more for God. Therefore, little children, do not resist but permit Him to lead you, to change you and to enter into your life. Do not forget that you are travelers on the way toward eternity. Therefore, little children, permit God to lead you as a shepherd leads his flock. Thank you for having responded to my call."

Message of December 25, 2006
"Dear children! Also today I bring you the newborn Jesus in my arms. He who is the King of Heaven and earth, He is your peace. Little children, no one can give you peace as He who is the King of Peace. Therefore, adore Him in your hearts, choose Him and you will have joy in Him. He will bless you with His blessing of peace. Thank you for having responded to my call."

Annual Apparition to Jakov on December 25, 2006
"Today is a great day of joy and peace. Rejoice with me. Little children, in a special way, I call you to holiness in your families. I desire, little children, that each of your families be holy and that God's joy and peace, which God sends you today in a special way, may come to rule and dwell in your families. Little children, open your hearts today on this day of grace, decide for God and put Him in the first place in your family. I am your Mother. I love you and give you my Motherly Blessing."

Message of January 25, 2007
"Dear children! Put Sacred Scripture in a visible place in your family and read it. In this way, you will come to know prayer with the heart and your thoughts will be on God. Do not forget that you are passing like a flower in a field, which is visible from afar but disappears in a moment. Little children, leave a sign of goodness and love wherever you pass and God will bless you with an abundance of His blessing. Thank you for having responded to my call."

Message of February 25, 2007
"Dear children! Open your heart to God's mercy in this Lenten time. The heavenly Father desires to deliver each of you from the slavery of sin. Therefore, little children, make good use of this time and through meeting with God in Confession, leave sin and decide for holiness. Do this out of love for Jesus, who redeemed you all with His blood, that you may be happy and in peace. Do not forget, little children: your freedom is your weakness, therefore follow my messages with seriousness. Thank you for having responded to my call."

Annual Apparition to Mirjana on March 18, 2007
"Dear children! I come to you as a Mother with gifts. I come with love and mercy. Dear children, mine is a big heart. In it, I desire all of your hearts, purified by fasting and prayer. I desire that, through love, our hearts may triumph together. I desire that through that triumph you may see the real Truth, the real Way and the real Life. I desire that you may see my Son. Thank you."

Message of March 25, 2007
"Dear children! I desire to thank you from my heart for your Lenten renunciations. I desire to inspire you to continue to live fasting with an open heart. By fasting and renunciation, little children, you will be stronger in faith. In God you will find true peace through daily prayer. I am with you and I am not tired. I desire to take you all with me to Heaven, therefore, decide daily for holiness. Thank you for having responded to my call."

Message of April 25, 2007
"Dear children! Also today I again call you to conversion. Open your hearts. This is a time of grace while I am with you, make good use of it. Say: 'This is the time for my soul.' I am with you and love you with immeasurable love. Thank you for having responded to my call."

Message of May 25, 2007
"Dear children! Pray with me to the Holy Spirit for Him to lead you in the search of God's will on the way of your holiness. And you, who are far from prayer, convert and, in the silence of your heart, seek salvation for your soul and nurture it with prayer. I bless you all individually with my motherly blessing. Thank you for having responded to my call."

Message of June 25, 2007
"Dear children! Also today, with great joy in my heart, I call you to conversion. Little children, do not forget that you are all important in this great plan, which God leads through Medjugorje. God desires to convert the entire world and to call it to salvation and to the way towards Himself, who is the beginning and the end of every being. In a special way, little children, from the depth of my heart, I call you all to open yourselves to this great grace that God gives you through my presence

here. I desire to thank each of you for the sacrifices and prayers. I am with you and I bless you all. Thank you for having responded to my call."

Annual Apparition to Ivanka on June 25, 2007
"Dear children, receive my motherly blessing."

Message of July 25, 2007
"Dear children! Today, on the day of the Patron of your Parish, I call you to imitate the lives of the saints. May they be, for you, an example and encouragement to a life of holiness. May prayer for you be like the air you breathe in and not a burden. Little children, God will reveal His love to you and you will experience the joy that you are my beloved. God will bless you and give you an abundance of grace. Thank you for having responded to my call."

Message of August 25, 2007
"Dear children! Also today I call you to conversion. May your life, little children, be a reflection of God's goodness and not of hatred and unfaithfulness. Pray, little children, that prayer may become life for you. In this way, in your life you will discover the peace and joy which God gives to those who have an open heart to His love. And you who are far from God's mercy, convert so that God may not become deaf to your prayers and that it may not be too late for you. Therefore, in this time of grace, convert and put God in the first places in your life. Thank you for having responded to my call."

Message of September 25, 2007
"Dear children! Also today I call all of you for your hearts to blaze with more ardent love for the Crucified, and do not forget that, out of love for you, He gave His life so that you may be saved. Little children, meditate and pray that your heart may be open to God's love. Thank you for having responded to my call."

Message of October 25, 2007
"Dear children! God sent me among you out of love that I may lead you towards the way of salvation. Many of you opened your hearts and accepted my messages, but many have become lost on this way and

have never come to know the God of love with the fullness of heart. Therefore, I call you to be love and light where there is darkness and sin. I am with you and bless you all. Thank you for having responded to my call."

Message of November 25, 2007
"Dear children! Today, when you celebrate Christ, the King of all that is created, I desire for Him to be the King of your lives. Only through giving, little children, can you comprehend the gift of Jesus´ sacrifice on the Cross for each of you. Little children, give time to God that He may transform you and fill you with His grace, so that you may be a grace for others. For you, little children, I am a gift of grace and love, which comes from God for this peaceless world. Thank you for having responded to my call."

Message of December 25, 2007
"Dear children! With great joy I bring you the King of Peace for Him to bless you with His blessing. Adore Him and give time to the Creator for whom your heart yearns. Do not forget that you are passers-by on this earth and that things can give you small joys, while through my Son, eternal life is given to you. That is why I am with you, to lead you towards what your heart yearns for. Thank you for having responded to my call."

Annual Apparition to Jakov on December 25, 2007
"Dear children! Today, in a special way I call you to become open to God and for each of your hearts today to become a place of Jesus' birth. Little children, through all this time that God permits me to be with you, I desire to lead you to the joy of your life. Little children, the only true joy of your life is God. Therefore, dear children, do not seek joy in things of this earth but open your hearts and accept God. Little children, everything passes, only God remains in your heart. Thank you for having responded to my call."

Message of January 25, 2008
"Dear children! With the time of Lent, you are approaching a time of grace. Your heart is like ploughed soil and it is ready to receive the fruit which will grow into what is good. You, little children, are free to

choose good or evil. Therefore, I call you to pray and fast. Plant joy and the fruit of joy will grow in your hearts for your good, and others will see it and receive it through your life. Renounce sin and choose eternal life. I am with you and intercede for you before my Son. Thank you for having responded to my call."

Message of February 25, 2008
"Dear children! In this time of grace, I call you anew to prayer and renunciation. May your day be interwoven with little ardent prayers for all those who have not come to know God's love. Thank you for having responded to my call."

Annual Apparition to Mirjana on March 18, 2008
"Dear children, today I extend my hands towards you. Do not be afraid to accept them. They desire to give you love and peace and to help you in salvation. Therefore, my children, receive them. Fill my heart with joy and I will lead you towards holiness. The way on which I lead you is difficult and full of temptations and falls. I will be with you and my hands will hold you. Be persevering so that, at the end of the way, we can all together, in joy and love, hold the hands of my Son. Come with me; fear not. Thank you."

Message of March 25, 2008
"Dear children! I call you to work on your personal conversion. You are still far from meeting with God in your heart. Therefore, spend all the more time in prayer and
Adoration of Jesus in the Most Blessed Sacrament of the Altar, for Him to change you and to put into your hearts a living faith and a desire for eternal life. Everything is passing, little children, only God is not passing. I am with you and I encourage you with love. Thank you for having responded to my call."

Message of April 25, 2008
"Dear children! Also today, I call all of you to grow in God's love as a flower which feels the warm rays of spring. In this way, also you, little children, grow in God's love and carry it to all those who are far from God. Seek God's will and do good to those whom God has put on your way, and be light and joy. Thank you for having responded to my call."

Message of May 25, 2008
"Dear children! In this time of grace, when God has permitted me to be with you, little children, I call you anew to conversion. Work on the salvation of the world in a special way while I am with you. God is merciful and gives special graces, therefore, seek them through prayer. I am with you and do not leave you alone. Thank you for having responded to my call."

Message of June 25, 2008
"Dear children! Also today, with great joy in my heart, I call you to follow me and to listen to my messages. Be joyful carriers of peace and love in this peaceless world. I am with you and I bless you all with my Son Jesus, the King of Peace. Thank you for having responded to my call."

Annual Apparition to Ivanka on June 25, 2008
No message, Ivanka said, "Our Lady spoke to me about the ninth secret. She gave us Her motherly blessing."

Message of July 25, 2008
"Dear children! At this time when you are thinking of physical rest, I call you to conversion. Pray and work so that your heart yearns for God the Creator who is the true rest of your soul and your body. May He reveal His face to you and may He give you His peace. I am with you and intercede before God for each of you. Thank you for having responded to my call."

Message of August 25, 2008
"Dear children! Also today I call you to personal conversion. You be those who will convert and, with your life, will witness, love, forgive and bring the joy of the Risen One into this world, where my Son died and where people do not feel a need to seek Him and to discover Him in their lives. You adore Him, and may your hope be hope to those hearts who do not have Jesus. Thank you for having responded to my call."

Message of September 25, 2008
"Dear children! May your life, anew, be a decision for peace. Be joyful carriers of peace and do not forget that you live in a time of grace, in

AMM

Association of the Miraculous Medal
1811 West Saint Joseph Street • Perryville, Missouri 63775-1598

1-800-264-MARY (6279) • 573-547-2508

www.amm.org • ammfather@amm.org

ZH98

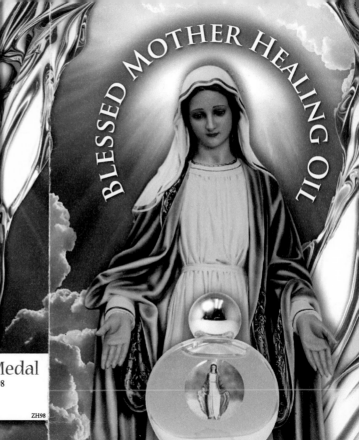

BLESSED MOTHER HEALING OIL

How to Use the Oil

Oil has long been associated with healing, and this blessed oil is a beautiful way to seek the healing that Jesus wants to give. You may use the oil on yourself or others by anointing any injury or ache, asking Mary's intercession by praying, "O Mary conceived without sin, pray for us who have recourse to thee." A similar anointing can ask Jesus' protection from harm for ourselves or others. Anoint yourself or others on the forehead in the form of a cross, again praying, "O Mary conceived without sin..."

Prayer to Our Lady for Healing

Mary Immaculate, you have given yourself to us as our Lady of the Miraculous Medal. You have asked us to pray with confidence, and we will receive great graces. We know your compassion, because you saw your Son suffer and die for us. In your union with his suffering you became the mother of us all. Mary, my mother, teach me to understand my suffering as you do and to endure it in union with the suffering of Jesus. In your motherly love, calm my fears and increase my trust in God's loving care. According to God's plan, obtain for me the healing I need. Intercede with your Son that I may have the strength I need to work for God's glory and the salvation of the world. **Amen.**

Mary, health of the sick, pray for me.

which God gives you great graces through my presence. Do not close yourselves, little children, but make good use of this time and seek the gift of peace and love for your life so that you may become witnesses to others. I bless you with my motherly blessing. Thank you for having responded to my call."

Message of October 25, 2008
"Dear children! In a special way I call you all to pray for my intentions so that, through your prayers, you may stop Satan's plan over this world, which is further from God every day, and which puts itself in the place of God and is destroying everything that is beautiful and good in the souls of each of you. Therefore, little children, arm yourselves with prayer and fasting so that you may be conscious of how much God loves you and may carry out God's will. Thank you for having responded to my call."

Message of November 25, 2008
"Dear children! Also today I call you, in this time of grace, to pray for little Jesus to be born in your heart. May He, who is peace itself, give peace to the entire world through you. Therefore, little children, pray without ceasing for this turbulent world without hope, so that you may become witnesses of peace for all. May hope begin to flow through your hearts as a river of grace. Thank you for having responded to my call."

Message of December 25, 2008
"Dear children! You are running, working, gathering – but without blessing. You are not praying! Today I call you to stop in front of the manger and to meditate on Jesus, Whom I give to you today also, to bless you and to help you to comprehend that, without Him, you have no future. Therefore, little children, surrender your lives into the hands of Jesus, for Him to lead you and protect you from every evil. Thank you for having responded to my call."

Annual Apparition to Jakov on December 25, 2008
"Dear children! Today, in a special way, I call you to pray for peace. Without God you cannot have peace or live in peace. Therefore, little children, today on this day of grace open your hearts to the King of

peace, for Him to be born in you and to grant you His peace – and you be carriers of peace in this peaceless world. Thank you for having responded to my call."

Message of January 25, 2009
"Dear children! Also today I call you to prayer. May prayer be for you like the seed that you will put in my heart, which I will give over to my Son Jesus for you, for the salvation of your souls. I desire, little children, for each of you to fall in love with eternal life which is your future, and for all worldly things to be a help for you to draw you closer to God the Creator. I am with you for this long because you are on the wrong path. Only with my help, little children, you will open your eyes. There are many of those who, by living my messages, comprehend that they are on the way of holiness towards eternity. Thank you for having responded to my call."

Message of February 25, 2009
"Dear children! In this time of renunciation, prayer and penance, I call you anew: go and confess your sins so that grace may open your hearts, and permit it to change you. Convert little children, open yourselves to God and to His plan for each of you. Thank you for having responded to my call."

Annual Apparition to Mirjana on March 18, 2009
"Dear children! Today I call you to look into your hearts sincerely and for a long time. What will you see in them? Where is my Son in them and where is the desire to follow me to Him? My children, may this time of renunciation be a time when you will ask yourself: 'What does my God desire of me personally? What am I to do?' Pray, fast and have a heart full of mercy. Do not forget your shepherds. Pray that they may not get lost, that they may remain in my Son so as to be good shepherds to their flock."
Our Lady looked at all those present and added: "Again I say to you, if you knew how much I love you, you would cry with happiness. Thank you."

Message of March 25, 2009
"Dear children! In this time of spring, when everything is awakening from the winter sleep, you also awaken your souls with prayer so that they may be ready to receive the light of the risen Jesus. Little children, may He draw you closer to His Heart so that you may become open to eternal life. I pray for you and intercede before the Most High for your sincere conversion. Thank you for having responded to my call."

Message of April 25, 2009
"Dear children! Today I call you all to pray for peace and to witness it in your families so that peace may become the highest treasure on this peaceless earth. I am your Queen of Peace and your mother. I desire to lead you on the way of peace, which comes only from God. Therefore, pray, pray, pray. Thank you for having responded to my call."

Message of May 25, 2009
"Dear children! In this time, I call you all to pray for the coming of the Holy Spirit upon every baptized creature, so that the Holy Spirit may renew you all and lead you on the way of witnessing your faith – you and all those who are far from God and His love. I am with you and intercede for you before the Most High. Thank you for having responded to my call."

Message of June 25, 2009
"Dear children! Rejoice with me, convert in joy and give thanks to God for the gift of my presence among you. Pray that, in your hearts, God may be in the center of your life and with your life witness, little children, so that every creature may feel God's love. Be my extended hands for every creature, so that it may draw closer to the God of love. I bless you with my motherly blessing. Thank you for having responded to my call."

Annual Apparition to Ivanka on June 25, 2009
"Dear children, I call you to be apostles of peace. Peace, peace, peace."

Message of July 25, 2009
"Dear children! May this time be a time of prayer for you. Thank you for having responded to my call."

Message of August 25, 2009
"Dear children! Today I call you anew to conversion. Little children, you are not holy enough and you do not radiate holiness to others, therefore pray, pray, pray and work on your personal conversion, so that you may be a sign of God's love to others. I am with you and am leading you towards eternity, for which every heart must yearn. Thank you for having responded to my call."

Message of September 25, 2009
"Dear children, with joy, persistently work on your conversion. Offer all your joys and sorrows to my Immaculate Heart that I may lead you all to my most beloved Son, so that you may find joy in His Heart. I am with you to instruct you and to lead you towards eternity. Thank you for having responded to my call."

Message of October 25, 2009
"Dear children! Also today I bring you my blessing, I bless you all and I call you to grow on this way, which God has begun through me for your salvation. Pray, fast and joyfully witness your faith, little children, and may your heart always be filled with prayer. Thank you for having responded to my call."

Message of November 25, 2009
"Dear children! In this time of grace I call you all to renew prayer in your families. Prepare yourselves with joy for the coming of Jesus. Little children, may your hearts be pure and pleasing, so that love and warmth may flow through you into every heart that is far from His love. Little children, be my extended hands, hands of love for all those who have become lost, who have no more faith and hope. Thank you for having responded to my call."

Message of December 25, 2009
"Dear children! On this joyful day, I bring all of you before my Son, the King of Peace, that He may give you His peace and blessing. Little children, in love share that peace and blessing with others. Thank you for having responded to my call."

Annual Apparition to Jakov on December 25, 2009
"Dear children! All of this time in which God in a special way permits me to be with you, I desire to lead you on the way that leads to Jesus and to your salvation. My little children, you can find salvation only in God and therefore, especially on this day of grace with little Jesus in my arms, I call you to permit Jesus to be born in your hearts. Only with Jesus in your heart can you set out on the way of salvation and eternal life. Thank you for having responded to my call."

For Further Information . . .

To be "fed" monthly by Our Lady's messages to the world, you can subscribe to the monthly newsletter "The Spirit of Medjugorje" by sending a free will offering along with your name and address to P.O. Box 6614, Erie, PA 16512.

Hopefully this publication has given you an introduction to Our Lady of Medjugorje and Her messages. For further information, we suggest you consult the hundreds of books and websites on Medjugorje. Two books we particularly recommend are Volume I and Volume II of *The Best of "The Spirit of Medjugorje."* They are an extension of what you have just read here. Catholic author Elizabeth Ficocelli calls Volume I, ". . . a compelling presentation of articles that help the reader to understand what Medjugorje is all about – the messages, the visionaries, the testimonies of changed hearts and lives. It is both an excellent introduction to and an important recap of the most important apparitions of our times. Focused on the early years of the apparitions, it leaves the reader yearning for the next edition."

We present to you here other books deemed as favorites by an informal survey taken several years ago with the members of the International Internet Medjugorje Prayer Group, which has ties to Ivan's prayer group in Medjugorje. The members determined the following to be their favorite books on Medjugorje in this order:

1. Visions of the Children – Janice Connell
2. Medjugorje the Message – Wayne Weible
3. Final Harvest – Wayne Weible
4. Medjugorje the Mission – Wayne Weible
5. Queen of the Cosmos – Janice Connell
6. Pilgrimage – Fr. Svetozar Kraljevic
7. Pray with the Heart – Fr. Slavko Barbaric
8. Medjugorje in the 90's – Sr. Emmanuel

9. Letters from Medjugorje – Wayne Weible
10. Medjugorje Day by Day – Fr. Richard Beyer

Suggested Medjugorje websites:
http://www.medjugorje.hr (The official Medjugorje website)
http://www.medjugorje.org (One of the most popular Medjugorje websites, has links to other sites too)
http://www.medjugorjeusa.org (This site was designed with the "doubting Thomas" in mind.)
http://www.childrenofmedjugorje.com (Has excellent audio tapes and books by Sr. Emmanuel)
http://crownofstars.blogspot.com (Awesome photos and inspirational testimonies)
http://www.iipg.org (International Internet Prayer Group, Queen of Peace)

Caution should be used in purchasing credible resources since there are some books and videos on the market that are "New Age" material. When in doubt seek advice from proper sources at the above websites.